THE BRAHMIN AND HIS BIBLE

THE BRAHMIN AND HIS BIBLE

Rammohun Roy's Precepts of Jesus 200 Years On

R. S. Sugirtharajah

LONDON • NEW YORK • OXFORD • NEW DELHI • SYDNEY

T&T CLARK
Bloomsbury Publishing Plc
50 Bedford Square, London, WC1B 3DP, UK
1385 Broadway, New York, NY 10018, USA
29 Earlsfort Terrace, Dublin 2, Ireland

BLOOMSBURY, T&T CLARK and the T&T Clark logo are
trademarks of Bloomsbury Publishing Plc

First published in Great Britain in 2019
Paperback edition first published 2021

Copyright © R.S. Sugirtharajah, 2019

R.S. Sugirtharajah has asserted his right under the Copyright,
Designs and Patents Act, 1988, to be identified as Author of this work.

For legal purposes the Acknowledgements on p. vii constitute
an extension of this copyright page.

Cover design: Terry Woodley
Cover image: Statue of Ram Mohan Roy, 1772-1833, in College Green,
Bristol, England. Stu's Images/Wikimedia Commons.

All rights reserved. No part of this publication may be reproduced or
transmitted in any form or by any means, electronic or mechanical,
including photocopying, recording, or any information storage or retrieval
system, without prior permission in writing from the publishers.

Bloomsbury Publishing Plc does not have any control over, or responsibility for,
any third-party websites referred to or in this book. All internet addresses given
in this book were correct at the time of going to press. The author and publisher
regret any inconvenience caused if addresses have changed or sites have
ceased to exist, but can accept no responsibility for any such changes.

A catalogue record for this book is available from the British Library.

A catalog record for this book is available from the Library of Congress.

ISBN: HB: 978-0-5676-8568-1
PB: 978-0-5677-0199-2
ePDF: 978-0-5676-8569-8
eBook: 978-0-5676-8571-1

Typeset by Integra Software Services Pvt. Ltd.

To find out more about our authors and books visit
www.bloomsbury.com and sign up for our newsletters.

CONTENTS

Acknowledgements	vii
Publisher's note	viii
INTRODUCTION	1
Chapter 1 TRIMMING THE TEXT, MUTILATING THE MESSAGE	5
Chapter 2 THE REFORMER AND HIS REASONS FOR COMPILING *THE PRECEPTS*	9
Chapter 3 THE RAJAH AND HIS REDUCED VERSION	13
Chapter 4 PUBLISH AND BE PILLORIED	21
Chapter 5 THE BENGALI AND HIS BIBLICAL ENGAGEMENTS	27
Chapter 6 VEDAS AND THE VETHAGAMAS	35
Chapter 7 GOSPEL HARMONIES, BIBLE VERSIONS AND TRANSLATIONS	39
Chapter 8 HEATHENISH AND IRRATIONAL DOCTRINES	45
Chapter 9 MODEST PROPOSALS, UNEXPLAINED PROPOSITIONS	53
Chapter 10 TO CONVERT OR NOT TO CONVERT	57
Chapter 11 THE MLECCHA AND HIS MORAL CODES	61

Chapter 12
THE INDIAN REFORMER, THE AMERICAN PRESIDENT
AND THEIR DESIGNER GOSPELS   69

Chapter 13
HERMENEUTICAL ACHIEVEMENTS: STRENGTHS AND
SHORTCOMINGS   81

Chapter 14
READING RAMMOHUN ROY TODAY   89

THE PRECEPTS OF JESUS   97

Bibliography   143
General Index   146
Scriptural References   148

ACKNOWLEDGEMENTS

Most author acknowledgements start with a routine cliché 'I couldn't have written this book without ….' Like all clichés there is a considerable amount of truth in it. Without the help of the people I mention below this book wouldn't have been possible:

Dominic Mattos, Editorial Director, Bloomsbury T&T Clark, who responded to my email within a few seconds of sending the proposal and who has since then shown tremendous interest in the project and continued confidence in my work;

Sarah Blake, the editorial assistant at Bloomsbury for dealing with my questions with care and sensitivity and skilfully guiding the manuscript through various stages of production;

Ralph Broadbent for his perceptive reading of the manuscript and for his smart suggestions;

Pat Budgen, Sian Wyre, Helen Morten, Lorraine Fletcher, Susan Wiyzell and Stephanie Rose all of the Orchard Learning Resources Centre at the University of Birmingham for their expert knowledge, especially in retrieving books that seemed to have gone missing, and the cordial manner in which they handled my requests;

Dan O'Connor for more than two decades of stimulating conversation about and superb guidance in all my research projects; and

finally, my wife Sharada for her intellectual support and sharing her wisdom in all the writings I do. Her value is beyond words.

R. S. Sugirtharajah
Bournville
24 July 2019

PUBLISHER'S NOTE

It is somewhat unusual to publish a note of this sort at the start of a volume. But serendipity being what it is I hope I may be permitted a few lines for the sake of record, and I am grateful for Professor Sugirtharajah's indulgence in this regard.

In 1821, the publishing house of T&T Clark was founded in Edinburgh, and Rammohun Roy's *The Precepts of Jesus* were just starting to make an impact, although not of course as a T&T Clark title at that time. It is somehow fitting, as T&T Clark looks forward to its bicentenary, to be republishing, and making available and alive again, a work of roughly the same age as ourselves.

In 200 years a lot can change, and through time and acquisition T&T Clark has come to be part of Bloomsbury Publishing Plc and is now based in London. Roy's own life is the subject of some comment in this book. But he too spent some time in London, before moving to Bristol, where he died in 1833. Neither Messrs T&T Clark nor Rammohun Roy could have known that their labours 200 years ago would still be bearing fruit today, much less that those labours would unite in a joint publishing endeavour. Moreover, they would also not have known that the work on that joint endeavour would be taking place in offices located at 49 Bedford Square, which just so happened to be where Rammohun Roy lived during his time in London, as I found out – some months after having signed this volume up – when I paused on the steps to read the blue plaque on the outside of the building in which I work in every day.

Dominic Mattos
Editorial Director
T&T Clark

INTRODUCTION

In 1820 a pithy booklet of nearly ninety pages rolled off the Baptist Missionary Press on Circular Road in Calcutta. The press was renowned for publishing Bibles in vernacular languages, dictionaries and grammars with the singular purpose of converting Indians. The superintendent of the press, W. H. Pearce, would have anticipated that his new release would further enhance the cause of the press, which was regarded as an 'influential force in the work for Christ and His Kingdom' in colonial India, and that it would form part of the long list of suitable material for India's evangelization. To the chagrin of the Calcutta missionaries the text proved to be textually toxic: challenging the version of Christianity they cherished and contesting its cardinal doctrines, and effectively making Jesus a mere human being preaching morality. The author was Rammohun Roy (1772–1833), a formidable and erudite Brahmin and a good friend of the Baptist missionaries William Carey, Joshua Marshman and William Ward, with whom he collaborated in the translation of the Bible into Bengali and also whom he personally funded for their educational work. The title of this tiny text was *The Precepts of Jesus.*

The Precepts was the result of and a response to the prevailing religious, political and social context of the time. What Roy did was take control of the sacred text of another religious tradition, empty it of its fundamental tenets and dogmas, reframe and reduce its essential teachings to a simple moral truth of love of God and love of one's neighbour. It was a compilation of the moral teachings of Jesus, chiefly extracted from the first three Gospels minus genealogies, miracles, historical and doctrinal references and allusions. In effect, *The Precepts* did away with the powerful pillars of evangelical Christianity – the belief in atonement, the doctrine of the Trinity, the divinity of Jesus and the self-sufficiency of the Scriptures. Roy was severely contemptuous of Christian creeds, which he called 'heathen notions', and believed that anyone rational enough to reject Hindu mythologies would find them unhelpful. His object was to present the essence of the Gospels, which, he believed, lay not in the doctrines, as the missionaries insisted, but in the moral teachings of Jesus. Roy was attracted to the ethical wisdom of Jesus but repelled by the dogmatic garb in which it was wrapped up and presented.

The Precepts was principally pitched at his fellow Hindus and Christians, but the ensuing controversy indicated that Roy wanted Muslims also to benefit from the social comfort of the ethical teachings of Jesus.

Roy's claim that the moral teaching of Jesus was a sufficient guide to life without having to pay much attention to the doctrines was hermeneutically unpalatable to the missionaries. They put up an energetic and at times acrimonious resistance led by Joshua Marshman. This textual toing and froing went on for three years. Roy published three *Appeals to the Christian Public,* the last one running to more than two hundred pages. This controversy was covered widely both in the UK and America where the Unitarians took a special interest in Roy's anti-Trinitarian and rationally based hermeneutics. This notoriety or popularity propelled Roy into the position of the first global Indian.

What this volume does is place *The Precepts* in its context and discuss the hermeneutical issues it raises. The chapters here address the following: the social, cultural and political context of *The Precepts*; the exegetical clash between Roy and the missionaries over the interpretation and the authority of the Bible; their often differing hermeneutical presuppositions and strategies; their contradictory construals of Jesus; and disputes about translations. Besides these, the other issues discussed include: the place of *The Precepts* among earlier Gospel Harmonies, Roy's use of the Improved Version, a highly disputed Unitarian Bible, his translations of both the Christian Bible and his own Vedas. An additional feature is a chapter which explores the convergences and divergences between Roy's *Precepts* and Thomas Jefferson's (the third president of the United States of America) *The Life and Morals of Jesus of Nazareth*, which appeared in the same year and had a similar interpretative ambition. The volume ends with a chapter on the significance of Roy's work today.

What these chapters reveal is that the radical motive and momentum Roy showed in his *Precepts* was not later reproduced by him with the same vigour and intensity in his disputes with missionaries. Roy's perceived anti-doctrinal and pro-rationalistic stance is not robust and absolute but complicated. The Jesus he portrayed in *The Precepts* was not a meek and mild dispenser of moral precepts but someone who brings division and disunity. Roy did not shake the foundations of Christian doctrines, as it is popularly believed, but reframed and made them meaningful and in the process strengthened them for Christians. His initial strident rationalistic streak, too, gave way to emotions and intuition.

Roy's *Precepts* received a considerable amount of attention when it was first published but has been consigned to unjustifiable obscurity in our time. It was neglected both by Western and Indian scholars. The West which always assumes that the 'other' is at its disposal for diagnosis and prescription has surprisingly overlooked and ignored the importance of *The Precepts*. In India, where current hermeneutics are regretfully marked by identity politics (read caste), Roy is further peripheralized as another meddling brahmin. What is at work is the hermeneutic of untouchability. There is a tendency among Western biblical scholars to dismiss the hermeneutical efforts of Roy – or, for that matter, expositions of anyone outside Western academic circles – as subjective, situational and nativist impressions rather than anything of critical or intellectual merit. At home, Roy is dismissed as a representative of the upper caste – a caste which was perceived to have caused a caste-conscious hierarchal system. The bicentenary of the publication of *The Precepts of Jesus* provides an opportunity to redress this omission.

The secondary literature on Roy is enormous and most of it does not deal with the central concern of this volume. Written by Roy's devotees or his detractors, their assessments obscure rather than illuminate. My interaction with them is very minimal unless they have anything relevant to the current work. A health warning. In these gender sensitive days, the masculine tone of Roy and his contemporaries could be irksome to many. Cleansing this loathsome language would mean erasing the history of our cultural and intellectual thought process. One thing is certain. If Roy was writing today as the champion of women's causes, he would certainly be sensitive about his language.

When *The Precepts* emerged, it was put on a pedestal and at the same time pilloried. This compendious compilation embodied the preoccupations and prejudices of its time. This embattled colonial text now looks profoundly inoffensive and tame, but its significance lies in its daring undermining of the missionaries' version of Christianity. At a time when the imperialists were engaged in controlling, measuring, regulating and recovering texts, histories and natural resources of the subjugated people, Roy's *Precepts* reversed this imperially ambitious project. It subjected the invader's text – the Bible – to a similar exercise. Just as the Western Orientalists did to Indian texts, Roy inverted the process and tried to redeem and reform the iconic text of the invader. *The Precepts* has another merit. It is a meticulous illustration of cultural appropriation. Roy took over a text of a foreign religion, cleansed what he perceived as spurious elements, used its monotheistical ideals to strengthen his claims of a Supreme Being in his own tradition and found resources in the ethical tenets of that religion to uplift his own people from moral decay and apathy. There is another value, too. It is an example of a Hindu reader of the Bible, setting the tone for the later demythologization project which had a great impact on twentieth-century biblical scholarship, and provided markers, impetus and confidence for future theologians to extend and amplify these themes. His calling of Jesus an Asiatic, now a tiresome cliché, was an audacious hermeneutical move in colonial India. Credit should be given to Roy for believing that he was better at presenting the Christian religion than the Baptist missionaries of Bengal themselves who were intransigently preoccupied with their particular brand of evangelical, austere, humourless theology.

This volume is a bicentennial return to Rammohun Roy's *Precepts of Jesus*. It also includes the text which caused so much concern and anxiety, especially to the Baptist missionaries labouring in colonial Bengal. My hope is that this reissuing of *The Precepts* will earn again the attention that the text once deservedly enjoyed.

Chapter 1

TRIMMING THE TEXT, MUTILATING THE MESSAGE

Today with a clever combination of media manipulation and swooning adulation of his sycophantic admirers, Narendra Modi, the prime minister of India, is hailed as a global rock star. Before him, the first truly global Indian was Rammohun Roy (1772–1833), the principal focus of this volume. The activities of Roy, his social reforms, his espousal of Hindu theism and his controversial writings on Christianity were extensively covered in the print medium of America, Britain and France between 1818 and 1840 by high-ranking journals of the time. *The Christian Register*, a Unitarian weekly which had a massive circulation in America, has over one hundred references to his work.[1] His tracts and books were also published both in Britain and in the United States. Adrienne Moore, who catalogued all references to Roy's works in Western publications, has also listed the leading libraries which stocked his writings.

Roy's momentous life story has been recounted eloquently elsewhere based on a succinct biographical note that he himself had left behind and on the recollections of those who knew him. His long bold struggle for religious and social reforms, especially his involvement in the abolition of sati, his plea for the right to property for Hindu women, his tireless attempts at restructuring educational matters, his agitation for journalistic freedom, his vernacular publishing in the form of Bengali and Persian weeklies, and his translation and interpretation of Sanskritic texts have drawn in equal measure much celebration and censure. The books on Rammohun Roy are too numerous to mention here.[2]

The purpose of this volume is to look at a work that caused much controversy during his life time but was drowned out by his other achievements and, very regrettably, after his death went unnoticed. The work in question is a slim but incendiary text he published in 1820 called *The Precepts of Jesus*. Its full title *The Precepts of Jesus: The Guide to Peace and Happiness; extracted from the books of the New Testament, ascribed to the four evangelists with translations into Sungscrit and Bengalee*.[3] *The Precepts* was one of the rare books that managed to be both slim in size and hermeneutically huge at the same time. This thin tract, contrary to popular impression, was not primarily aimed at fellow Hindus. Roy had in his mind Muslims as well. He desired that the 'common comforts of life'[4] that the moral teachings of Jesus would bring should be extended to and enjoyed by Muslims, too. A number of times, he advised missionaries that without any 'preparatory instruction' the Musalmans (Roy's phrase), who were strangers to the Christian world, would not benefit from the peculiar doctrines of Christianity.

Looking at *The Precepts* two hundred years after its publication, especially with the benefit of the tumultuous changes that have happened in biblical scholarship, it appears as a reasonably inoffensive text, but for the missionary propagators of the time this ostensibly anodyne text concealed materials which unsettled their cherished beliefs and doctrines. In a Christian propaganda-charged colonial Bengal when the missionaries were seriously engaged in proclaiming the uniqueness of the Christian Gospel and were involved in the business of rescuing the natives from their moral depravity, *The Precepts* proved to be textually toxic. It was a compilation of the moral sayings of Jesus, largely drawn from the first three Gospels, without the Jewish ancestry of Jesus; the critical events in his life such as birth, death and crucifixion; narratives related to the Roman imperial history; miraculous and supernatural events; and doctrinal allusions. It was a kind of Christian apocryphal Gospel, produced by a Hindu, as an alternative to the missionary version of Christianity. *The Precepts* was a continuation of the practice of the early Christians in creating gospels to meet new Christian pieties and, in Roy's case, to address the non-Semitic and complex multicultural situation of India.

There is a vast and rich literature on the life and work of Roy but nothing of significant value on this small booklet. This volume will explore Roy's use of the Bible mainly through this volume and the fierce exegetical exchanges that ensued between him and the Christian missionaries. Ironically, *The Precepts* was published by the Baptist Mission Press in Calcutta – the very denomination which hoped for his conversion and later turned against him.

The Precepts was primarily a personal premier and not composed with the noble notions of academic facticity and objectivity. But it had the wider public as the target. *The Precepts* simultaneously stripped Christianity of its strict stern image and challenged its doctrinal aspects which smacked of irrationalism, sectarianism and triumphalism. Roy was convinced that 'no other religion can produce anything that [might] stand in competition with the precepts of Jesus'.[5] He wrote that as the result of his 'long and uninterrupted researches into religious truth' he had realized that the 'doctrines of Christ [were] more conducive to moral principles, and better adapted for the use of rational beings, than any others which had come to his knowledge.[6] Roy wanted Indians to benefit morally, socially and politically from the ethical teachings of Jesus as well as European education, literature and science, but never envisaged nor encouraged conversion to Christianity.

Notes

1. A. Moore, *Rammohun Roy and America* (Calcutta: Satis Chandra Chakravti, 1942), 3.
2. The books on Rammohun Roy are too numerous to mention here. For a judicious evaluation of his life and work, see A.P. Sen, *Rammohun Roy: A Critical Biography* (New Delhi: Viking, 2012); V.C. Joshi, ed., *Rammohun Roy and the Process of Modernization in India* (Delhi: Vikas Publishing House, 1975); for a critical study of *The Precepts*, see R.S. Sugirtharajah, *Asian Biblical Hermeneutics and Postcolonialism*

(Sheffield: Sheffield Academic Press, 1988), 29–53 and *The Bible and Empire: Postcolonial Explorations* (Cambridge: Cambridge University Press, 2005), 9–59.
3 The promised Bengali version appeared after Roy's death. It was translated in 1859 by the Brahmo leader Rakhal Das Halder. It was called *Jishupranita Hitopadesha*, see Sen, *Rammohun Roy*, 187. There was no evidence of the Sanskrit version that had Roy promised.
4 Rammohun Roy, *The English Works of Raja Rammohun Roy*, ed. J.C. Ghose (New Delhi: Cosmo Print, 1906), 557.
5 Ibid., 615.
6 'Review: Hindoo Unitarianism', *The Monthly Repository* 14, no. 165 (1819): 562.

Chapter 2

THE REFORMER AND HIS REASONS FOR COMPILING *THE PRECEPTS*

To everything there is a season, says the Preacher. To this one could add, to everything there are reasons. Briefly, then, the historical, political and theological factors that promoted Roy to come out with *The Precepts of Jesus*. Firstly, the political context: Roy's collection of the moral sayings of Jesus appeared at a time when India was going through a remarkable period of political changes and upheavals. Moghul rule and Muslim dominance were on the wane. There was the menacing presence of the mercantile traders in the form of the East India Company, and the British were yet to become the rulers of India. Roy, who was troubled by the long subjugation of the Hindus at the hands of Muslims and disturbed by the 'cruelty allowed by Musalmanism against Non-musalmans',[1] knew that the new invaders once they entrenched themselves would be in India for the long haul. The inadequacy of his ancestral faith to meet the challenges of the new situation soon dawned on Roy. Faced with such an impending change, Roy was earnestly seeking a sustainable religious tenet which was both moral and rational, and one that would sustain and benefit his fellow Indians during those trying times. He thought he had found one in the moral precepts of Jesus.

Secondly, the religious context of the nineteenth-century colonial Bengal. The prevailing state of two competing faiths – Hinduism and Christianity – was another compelling reason for Roy to assemble the moral sayings of Jesus. The Hinduism that was practised then seemed to be full of superstitious customs and, more lamentably, most Hindus were ignorant of their own faith and were not in the mood to receive a foreign religion. Christianity, propagated at that juncture, was another factor. Roy found it to be arrogant, austere, dogmatic and unappealing.

Roy was genuinely concerned that the popular Vaishanvism, the prominent sect in Bengal, had 'sunk to a very low level of superstition, extravagance and immorality'.[2] He dejectedly noted that the social conditions of his people were deplorable. The Hindus, in his opinion, 'were in general more superstitious and miserable, both in performance of their religious rites, and in their domestic concerns, than the rest of the known nations on earth'.[3] He found that the widespread Hindu subspiritual practices such as the rigid caste system, immolation of widows, and infanticide; the pitiable treatment of women; and the illiterate and exploitative priests were part of the 'puerile and unsociable system' of Hindu phenomena. Added to these were the useless dietary habits; rules regarding pollution, purity and auspicious times; and idolatrous worship, which made Hinduism not only 'vain and useless' but also pushed it into a 'very low ebb'. This despicable state of affairs prompted Roy to realize that this ancient faith had not only no means within itself to promote 'political interest' or 'patriotic feeling' but also no intellectually and theologically astute Hindu leaders to explain and interpret Hindu faith. While he himself detested these Hindu customs, he felt sympathy for his fellow Hindus whose idolatrous, polytheistic, pantheistic practices pushed them back into history and believed, as such, they needed to be rescued.

Roy bemoaned that 'there was darkness all over the land, and no man knew when it would be dispelled'.[4] He realized that in order to lift his fellow Bengalis from this religious morass, they needed a different set of morals, both to rejuvenate them and to face the modern India which was in the throes of unparalleled changes. Roy recognized that the Hindus needed a coterminous set of moral teachings that would lift them up from their ethical misery. It was possibly against this background that Roy's *Precepts* emerged. He was persuaded that Hindus needed changes 'at least for the sake of their political advantage and social comfort'.[5] Ironically, he found these moral changes in the teachings of Jesus – the very teachings which came with the invaders. He envisaged that these imported morals might promote harmony and coexistence among Hindus. A few years before his death, he confirmed to a friend what he had thought all along: 'there is nothing so sublime as the precepts taught by Christ, and there is nothing equal to the simple doctrines he inculcated'.[6] He was convinced that the ethical teachings of Jesus were 'calculated to elevate men's ideas to high and liberal notions of God' and he was 'desirous of giving more full publicity in this country to them'.[7] He reassured his fellow Hindu Bengalese that following the precepts of Jesus did not mean becoming Christians but continuing to remain as Hindus but adopting the teachings of Jesus for the sake of peace and harmony and for gaining political advantage.

The doctrinally driven and 'be saved or damned' type of Christianity proclaimed by missionaries could have been another reason which caused Roy to bring out his compilation.

The missionaries' version of Christianity was ridiculously replete with guilt-inducing and bewildering doctrines and a terrifying end-time message that unrepentant sinners would be cast into the hottest part of hell. All this could have been another reason for the compilation of *The Precepts*. Roy's concern – abetted by his extensive knowledge of the Christian Scriptures – made him realize that the illogical doctrines and ferocious preaching of the missionaries went against the fundamental tenets of the teacher of that religion. Just as Roy cared for his benighted fellow Hindus, he showed a similar commitment towards Christians. He earnestly felt that Christians also had to be rescued from the type of evangelical Christianity that was unleashed by the missionaries which was as equally heathenish and superstitious as the Hinduism that missionaries vilified.

Roy was genuinely mortified that a religion like Christianity with such sublime teachings and pure morality was being 'reduced almost to a level with Hindoo theology, merely by human creeds and prejudices'.[8] He was equally mortified when one of the representational corner stones of Christianity – the Trinity – came under ridicule from both Hindus and Muslims. He cited the case of two Muslim

2. The Reformer and His Reasons for Compiling Precepts

converts – Sabat and Ena et Ahmud – who speedily returned to their faith and turned violently against Christianity saying that they were unable to reconcile themselves to the dogmas imparted to them. He was also worried that these heathenish and irrational doctrines were 'very much calculated to lower the reputation of Britons both as a learned and as a religious people'.[9] He blamed the missionaries by quoting from the very Bible that the missionaries were trying to weaponize against Hindus: 'You blind guides, who strain out a gnat and swallow a camel!' He was indirectly telling them that they were obsessed with tiny and useless details while neglecting the weightier matters of the Gospel such as showing love and being obedient to God, demonstrated in benevolence towards fellow human beings.

Under these circumstances, Roy envisaged his task as reintroducing 'the simple code of religion and morality' of the Gospels woefully neglected by the Christians. *The Precepts* was his attempt to rescue, redeem and defend the Christian message that would truly reflect the mind of its founder. Roy cast himself as a fellow labourer 'in the promulgation of Christianity'[10] and decided to publish only the moral teachings of Jesus. He also respectfully counselled missionaries not to hold on to those doctrines, which were unscriptural, unconvincing, unintelligible, unreliable and unhistorical, and that they should keep these materials 'entirely out of view' of Indians.

He explained his action solemnly as if it were a moral mission on behalf of his people: 'A sense of the duty which one man owes to another, compels me to exert my utmost endeavours to rescue them from imposition and servitude, and promote their comfort and happiness.'[11]

To sum up: it was against this mixture of both political and religious backgrounds that Roy took the trouble to produce *The Precepts*. This Gospel compilation was aimed at addressing the hermeneutical demands of the intimidating presence of two empires, one on the decline and the other on the rise. In addition, it was compiled to meet the needs of two different constituencies. One, his own fellow, largely upper-class orthodox Hindus. The other, Christians both at home and abroad. To both these constituencies – Hindus and Christians, to which one could add Muslims – he wanted to introduce properly the sufficiency of the precepts of Jesus that would lead them to happiness, peace and social comfort without taking refuge in the cross or adhering to polytheistic or heathenish notions. In essence, Roy's *Precepts* functioned at two levels: a panacea for social happiness and well-being for Hindus, and as a subversive tract for Christians to rethink their unattractive version of Christianity.

Roy rarely imagined that his selection of the Gospel materials would be destructive and hurt the feelings of Christians. Roy all along maintained fervently that *The Precepts* was 'entirely founded on and supported by the express authorities of Jesus of Nazareth',[12] and based on the 'constant example of the gracious author of this religion'.[13] He assumed and expected that these tenets would have universal appeal and would be 'intelligible to all, conveying conviction with them, and best inculcated to lead mankind to universal love and harmony'.[14] He very much looked forward to a day 'when everyone [would] regard the Precepts of Jesus as the sole Guide to Peace and Happiness'.[15]

He felt fully vindicated in publishing this pamphlet. He envisioned the publication of the *The Precepts* as a patriotic act and a 'discharge of his duty towards his countrymen'.[16] He ended the Second Appeal with these words stating that his conscience was clear and he intended no malice towards any one: 'I therefore enjoy the approbation of my conscience in publishing the Precepts of this religion as the sources of Peace and Happiness.'[17]

Notes

1. Roy, *The English Works of Raja Rammohun Roy*, 580.
2. K.M. Panikkar, *Asia and Western Dominance: A Survey of the Vasco Da Gama Epoch of Asian History 1498–1945* (London: George Allen and Unwin Ltd., 1959), 241.
3. 'Review: Hindoo Unitarianism', 562.
4. J. Murdoch, compiler, *The Brahmo Samaj and Other Modern Eclectic Systems of Religion in India: Religious Reform Part IV* (Madras: The Christian Literature Society, 1893), 5.
5. S.D. Collet, *The Life and Letters of Raja Rammohun Roy*, ed. D.K. Biswas and P.C. Ganguli (Calcutta: Sadharan Brahmo Samaj, 1900), 213.
6. Ibid.
7. Roy, *The English Works of Raja Rammohun Roy*, 551.
8. Ibid., 666.
9. Ibid., 193.
10. Ibid., 568.
11. Ibid., 116.
12. Ibid., 550.
13. Ibid., 597.
14. Ibid., *558*
15. Ibid., 671
16. Ibid., 636.
17. Ibid., 675.

Chapter 3

THE RAJAH AND HIS REDUCED VERSION

Some general observations about *The Precepts*: in keeping with the style of the Hindu Vedas, the text runs through without chapter and verse division indicating the narrative possibility of the Gospels. It was issued without comments or notes but had chapter details of the Gospels at the bottom of the page. One relies purely on the text to get informed, enlightened and in the case of the Calcutta missionaries, enraged. The absence of any marginal notes could be attributed to Roy's reliance on the Authorized Version which was published without any comments after the theological and political furore caused by the Geneva Bible with its incendiary marginal comments. There is no notification of parallel passages nor any discussion of the literary relationships between the Gospels. The literary dependency of the Gospels, known as the Synoptic Problem, emerged in the West only three decades after Roy's death. Unlike other gospel harmonies, more of which later in the volume, Roy was not keen on removing repetition. For instance, his compilation retains both Matthew's and Mark's versions of the Parable of the Sower and Mark's and Luke's versions of the Widow's mites.

The Precepts follows the canonical sequence of the Gospels. It begins with Matthew's version of the Sermon on the Mount, which Roy found as 'indispensable and all-sufficient to those who desire to inherit eternal life' and which contained 'every duty of man, and all that is necessary to salvation'. More significantly, for his liking, the Sermon on the Mount expressly excluded 'any of the mysterious or historical' accounts.[1] The fact that the Sermon on the Mount did not refer to the lineage of Jesus, or to his divine status, was a perfect fit with Roy's perception of Jesus as a one-off moral teacher. He did not reproduce the entire Sermon. He left out vv. 33-43 of ch. 5, which deals with oath taking and resistance to evil, thus omitting one of Jesus's often-quoted sayings which inspired many non-violent movements: 'That ye resist not evil: but whosoever shall smite thee on thy right cheek, turn to him the other also' (Mt. 5.39).

Another celebrated saying of Jesus, which was used as a recruitment text for missionary workers in India, was understandably removed by Roy: 'The harvest truly is plenteous, but the labourers are few.' He retained Jesus sending his disciples to the lost house of Israel in Matthew ch. 10 but removed it from Mark and Luke. The inclusion of the mission of the twelve could have been motivated by three factors. One, the instruction to the disciples was to proclaim the kingdom rather than the proclaimer, Jesus; two, the mission was confined to Israel and with specific instructions to avoid the Gentiles and the Samaritans (proselytization, as we will see later, was an irksome issue for Roy); and three, the references to the hardship faced by the disciples would have readily resonated with Roy's own situation. He, too, like the disciples went to his own community with a view to redeeming them from their idolatrous practices and polytheistic beliefs, and like the disciples Roy faced persecution and antagonism from his fellow Brahmins.

Moving on to Matthew ch. 11, he skipped the questions John's disciples asked about Jesus's identity, Jesus's own testimony about John and the curses of Jesus on the cities. But Roy retained the revelation of Jesus's identity as God's commissioned agent to the children, the marginalized and not to the elite. This retention of the revelation of Jesus further reinforces Roy's claim that Jesus was God's agent chosen to disclose God's purpose and rule. He selected two passages in ch. 12. One is the healing of the man with the withered hand. Though Roy was sceptical about miracles, he kept this episode in his Mark and Luke selection as well, presumably as he saw it as integral to the teaching of Jesus. The other is Jesus's response to the identity of his family. The inclusion could have been prompted by the new definition of the family as dependent on doing the will of God. Obviously, ch. 13 finds its way in simply because it contains the major teachings of Jesus. Roy would have been fascinated not so much by the Kingdom which features predominantly in this major discourse of Jesus and provided the support for these parables but by how God controls people's destiny and exercises sovereignty over the world. Interestingly, of the seven parables mentioned here, Roy selected four, and inexplicably left out three (vv. 44-58).

Roy skipped ch. 14 of Matthew which contains healings and feeding miracles – both were blatantly irrational in his view. He then chose a passage from ch. 15 which emphasizes the inner moral aspect rather than external rituals – the very issue he had been engaged in with his own brahmin priests. Then he included a rare historical event: the Caesarea Philippi incident. This narrative is left out in his selection of Mark's (8.27-33) and Luke's (9.18-22) version. What would have interested him about the narrative was not so much the confession of Peter of Jesus as the expected Messiah but Jesus's rebuke of Peter which fitted in with Roy's claim that Jesus never thought of or aspired to the role of the Messiah. This was further reiterated by the fact that he left out the rest of the passages which describe the eschatological role of Jesus.

Then Roy jumped to ch. 18, which deals with the teachings of Jesus about sustaining communal relationships, not causing each other to stumble, and taking care of and forgiving one another as God takes care of and forgives everyone. Then he reproduces ch. 19 minus the first two verses, which deal with healing, which were of little interest to Roy. The attractive part of the narrative for him was the ideal discipleship described here. He selected two narratives from ch. 20 – the parable about the householder hiring labourers and the request of the mother of the sons of Zebedee. Roy only included twenty-one out of forty-six verses from ch. 21, because they describe Jesus's confrontation with the religious leaders, which paralleled that of, and was akin to, Roy's endless disputes with his own Brahmin pundits. Roy reproduced three passages from ch. 22 which resonate with his hermeneutical agenda – the scepticism about the resurrection, loving God and your neighbour, and Jesus's refutation of being identified as the son of David. He retained ch. 23 in its entirety, including the scathing attack on the Scribes and the Pharisees – an attack which equally befitted his own Brahmin pundits – and the lament over Jerusalem. His selection from ch. 24 begins with v. 42. He omitted what is known as the little apocalypse discourse and three parables of the End Time because they were theologically unappealing, but he included the fourth parable about the faithful and unfaithful servants. His choice from Matthew ends with ch. 25, which contains three great parables: the Ten Maidens, the Talents, and the Sheep and the Goats. Roy would not have been enamoured by the judgemental and apocalyptic tone of these parables, but by the idea of the tasks committed to people and taking care of the needy. Roy included the parables of the Kingdom but not with the intention of explaining its nature or its eschatological potency but to describe the type of people who were eligible to enter it.

The rest of the selections from the Synoptic Gospels follow a similar pattern of retaining the moral teachings of Jesus, discarding all historical, supernatural and healing events, and including Jesus's dismissal of ritual practices. Roy's choice from Mark starts not with Jesus announcing the Kingdom of God but the announcement of a new teaching and new practices which will shatter traditional teaching and observances. This is followed by ch. 3, where Jesus defines the new family as those who do God's will. From ch. 4 Roy selected the major teachings of Jesus, the reasons for teaching in parables and some of Jesus's enigmatic sayings. The rest of his selection from Mark includes Jesus's anti-ritual and anti-legal teachings that place an emphasis on morality rather than outward rituals, service to others, the cost of discipleship and instructions on wealth and prayer. It includes the three controversial issues raised by the Pharisees, Sadducees and the Scribes – paying taxes to secular authorities, the meaning of resurrection, and love of God and neighbour as the core of the faith. His Markan extraction ends with the Widow's offering at the temple. Roy simply redacted out the last four chapters of Mark.

Roy's selection from Luke was limited to eighteen chapters; he omitted the first three and the last three chapters. He begins with what is now known as the Nazareth Manifesto, and he ends it – just as he did with Mark – with the Widow's small contribution to the temple. Only seven verses are taken from ch. 5 (vv. 32-39). They speak about new wine and new garments, thus effectively disassociating the teachings of Jesus from the Mosaic Covenant, the legalistic religion of Judaism. Roy incorporated Luke's Sermon on the Plain and the episode about the woman who anointed Jesus, an incident he left out of his extractions from Matthew and Mark. The woman's repentance and acceptance without any atoning or sacrificial death would have prompted Roy to include her in his text. Her reconciliation exemplified one of Roy's major sore points in his argument with the missionaries, namely that remission or forgiveness is possible without someone shedding blood or paying a ransom. Roy included Luke's version of the Lord's prayer from ch. 11 – which he praised for its brevity, simplicity and for satisfying the needs of humankind – as well as the passage which excoriates the Pharisees for their outward rituals – a practice which plagued his own Hindu tradition – and the saying of Jesus about the blessed status of those who hear the words of Jesus and obey them. Roy reproduced the entirety of ch. 12, which is full of exhortations and warnings. Out of Luke's forty-five special materials, Roy included the narrative related to Martha and Mary, parables of the Good Samaritan, Friend at Midnight, Severe and Light beatings, Guests and Hosts, Counting the Cost, the Prodigal Son, the Shrewd Manager, the Richman and Lazarus, the Widow and the Judge, the Rich Fool, the Pharisee, and the Tax-Collector. The inclusion of these materials had been motivated by Roy's pet hermeneutical theme – one's behaviour towards fellow human beings.

Roy's choice from John's Gospel is limited to six passages, roughly fifty-six verses, but he was not reluctant to use materials from the fourth gospel in his controversy with Marshman, one of the trio of the famous Baptists missionaries. A closer reading of these passages reveals that he might have chosen them because they reiterated his theological interests: the unity of God, the redundancy of rituals and purity of worship (3.1-21; 4.23), the stance against conversion (6.27), redemption without sacrificial and juridical process (8.3-11; 9.39) and loving fellow human beings and doing the truth (15.1-17).

What was most interesting to general readers and at the same time disturbing to the Calcutta Baptist missionaries was not the selection of his materials but what he discarded: the divine status of Jesus; historical events in Jesus's life; supernatural events that sanctioned Jesus's role in salvation history; supernatural interventions that sanctioned Jesus's designated role; Jesus's sacrificial death; the doctrine of the Trinity; miracles and healings; and the references to the power of the Holy Spirit.

Any references to the divinity of Jesus, or proclamation that he was God's son were promptly edited out. For instance, the striking opening line of Mark's Gospel – 'The beginning of the gospel of Jesus Christ, the Son of God.' – which boldly announced that he was the Son of God, was erased. Similarly, any endorsement of Jesus as God's son was excised. The exclusion of the Baptism of Jesus is illustrative of this. Both narratives have words of endorsement of Jesus as God's Son by mysterious voices. At his baptism a mysterious voice called out 'This is my beloved Son, with whom I am well pleased' (Mt. 3.17), and at his transfiguration another voice uttered: 'This is my Son, whom I love; with Him I am well pleased.' By erasing these narratives Roy neutered the traditional understanding of baptism and the transfiguration as the preparation for the future role of Jesus as the Messiah. The Davidic lineage of Jesus was also omitted, especially that he was the son of David: 'The book of the generation of Jesus Christ, the son of David, the son of Abraham.' Matthew 1.1 (Mt. 11.22; Mk 10.47), or even any references to David as the son of god, were excluded. On the rare occasion when Roy refers to David he is seen as a famished man breaking the priestly rituals rather than as an eschatological hero with messianic credentials (Lk. 6.3). Jesus's messianic role was also underplayed. His answer to the disciples of John as to whether he was the expected Messiah was redacted. Any questions about his identity, especially the sayings recorded in John – 'I and the Father are one' – were all eliminated. The seven triumphalistic 'I am' sayings of Jesus which defined Jesus's relation to God the Father were all promptly discarded.

3. The Rajah and His Reduced Version 17

Any textual references to Jesus coming to establish the Kingdom were scrupulously scissored out. Roy removed the sayings about the imminent arrival of the external Kingdom or the internal realization of it – 'Kingdom of God is within you' (Lk. 17.20-21). This text of Luke comes close to the advaitic notion of the human soul being absorbed into the Godhead. Roy's omission of this saying could be that the Vedantis, whom he called the 'Hindu metaphysicians', would be 'comfortable' with such a union, but Christians would find it 'inconsistent' with their faith.[2]

The Gospels record Jesus fulfilling numerous foreshadowings and types found in the Old Testament. There are a number of historical events as foretold in the Hebrew Scriptures which were glibly employed by the Gospel writers to strengthen his role in the salvation history of Israel which were missing in Roy's *Precepts*. These included the Wise men searching for him ['Nations shall come to your light, and kings, shall bring gold and frankincense', (Isa. 60:2-6)], his flight to and return from Egypt ['When Israel *was* a child, then I loved him, and called my son out of Egypt', (Hos. 11.1)], and his riding on the donkey ['Lo, your king comes to you; triumphant and victorious is he, humble and riding on an ass, on a colt the foal of an ass', (Zach. 9.9)]. Out went also Matthew's 'fulfilment citations' which portrayed Jesus as the realized expectations of the Hebrew prophets. Also any attempt to situate Jesus in the line of great eschatological prophets prefigured in Elijah had been discarded.

Roy's aversion to aggressive conversion prompted him to leave out the important ministerial functions of Jesus, such as the calling and the naming of the twelve disciples, commissioning them to preach to the nations, the missionary commands (Mt. 28.18-20; Luke 24.46-49; Jn. 20.21) and the final words of Jesus to his disciples directing them to make disciples of all nations. He did include Matthew's sending out of the twelve to the lost house of Israel, which he would have interpreted as an exercise in the inner renewal of Israel and therefore more to his liking, as it prohibited the disciples entering the gentile territories. In *The Precepts*, Roy's Jesus does not enter Gentile territory, the implication being that Roy expected Jesus to remain spatially located in his own territory rather than crossing over to alien territories. But Roy was astute enough to cut out the most important aspect of the sending, namely to preach that the Kingdom of Heaven is at hand; all the references to the authority over unclean spirits; and the power to heal and forgive. These omissions were largely due to his intense dislike of aggressive evangelical and conversion practices of the Christians that he himself witnessed personally in Calcutta.

Ironically, the person who fought for the rights of women, left out women who shared the ministry of Jesus such as Joanna, Susanna and Mary Magdalene, and erased those women who were prominent in the resurrection narrative. A notable omission is the Syrophoenician woman whose addressing of Jesus as the son of David might have encouraged Roy to leave out the narrative.

Roy's selection is not always uniform. He discarded the cursing of the fig tree but retained the seven woes against the Pharisees displaying the darker side of Jesus. He left out the story of Zacchaeus, a perfect example of the salvation of a person without the efficacy of sacrificial death – an idea which resonated with Roy's theological predisposition.

In *The Precepts*, Roy effectively removed any scriptural semblances to the cherished doctrines of Christianity. To use Trumpian language, Roy wanted to drain Christianity of its dogmatical swamp. One such doctrine which came under his merciless criticism was the integral tenet of Baptist theology – the Trinity to which I will return later in this volume. Although the term, the Trinity, as such does not occur in the Gospels, or for that matter in the rest of the New Testament, there are vague references to the concept of one God consisting of three persons – Father, Son and the Holy Spirit. There is a thinly disguised allusion at the baptism of Jesus (Mt. 3.16-17; Mk 1.10-11; Lk. 3.21-22; and Jn 1.32) and in John's account of the Last Supper that the Paraclete is intimately related to Father and Son (Jn 14.16-17). The exception being Matthew 28.19, where there is a direct hint. Roy was ruthless in dropping these references claiming that he found 'no scriptural authority' for the idea of a triune God.

Another doctrine that gets a clean cut is any reference to the Holy Spirit. Roy did not envisage the Holy Spirit as a deity, or as possessing a distinct personality, or as a person of the Godhead. He omitted the role the Holy Spirit played in Mary conceiving the child Jesus. This for him was not 'consistent with the perfect nature of the righteous God'.[3] Blasphemy against the Holy Spirit also was removed.

What really exasperated the Baptist missionaries was his ruthless rejection of the doctrine of the atonement and the resurrection. Roy was careful to leave out any references to Jesus's imminent death, his death as a ransom for many as predicted at the Last Supper, the death of Christ signified in such sayings as the falling of the grain of wheat into the ground, his awareness of the betrayal by one of his disciples, his foreknowledge of his crucifixion, the trial, the carrying of the cross, his agonizing cry, his death and burial. Roy found the sacrificial work of Jesus 'unscriptural' and offered a non-expiatory and non-vicarious alternative such as 'prayers and obedience' as a perfect 'means of pardon'.[4]

Along with Jesus's death, Roy also left out one of the foundations of the Christian faith – the resurrection of Jesus. Any references alluding to the resurrection such as Jonah, the Son of man, being in the heart of the earth for three days and three nights, and any stories about bringing people back to life such as the raising of Lazarus, the raising of the widow's son at Nain, and the risen Jesus appearing to Mary and other disciples followed by his ascension were all savagely cut. Roy also omitted John as witness to Jesus raising the dead: 'the dead are raised up' (Lk. 7.22). The sceptical question of Sadducees regarding the resurrection finds Roy's approval presumably because it resonated with his doubtful view of the resurrection.[5] This did not prevent him, later in his life, from professing belief in the Resurrection,[6] which is not clearly evident in *The Precepts*.

The miracles in the Gospels which the missionaries claimed as 'manifested forth' God's glory,[7] Roy found to be 'less wonderful' compared to the teachings of Jesus. He was dismissive of them on a number of grounds. One, Roy reminded the missionaries that Jesus reproached those who asked for miracles and blessed those who having no recourse to the proof of miracle, professed belief in his teachings.

Two, had the teachings of Jesus made their due impression on the hearers, there would not have been the necessity for the people to depend on these miraculous performances. Three, miracles would not appeal to the Hindus who were accustomed to 'infinitely more wonderful' and 'superior' wonders and marvels performed by their Gods and saints. Four, he even argued that the creator had no power to violate laws and 'create impossible things'. For him, the most pertinent reason to omit them was that he was first attracted by the 'sublimity of the Precepts of Jesus'[8] and feared that these supernatural incidents might weaken the ethical message of Jesus.

The Precepts did not dispense with all the miracles, as is often presumed given Roy's predisposition towards weeding out irrational elements. He neither questioned their authenticity nor dismissed them as insignificant but doubted whether they would have any serious impact on Indians. He regarded them as events essentially performed by Jesus to persons who doubted his Messiahship, or required some external signal to firm up their faith in his mission. Roy included some of the miracle narratives when they were inextricably interwoven with the teachings of Jesus. The healing of the man with the withered hand is a perfect example. The healing of the woman with infirmity was cut out, but the theological reason behind the healing was retained. Apparently, he did not have any qualms about the Virgin Birth. What he did was to neuter the role of the Holy Spirit impregnating Mary, reframing the conception as the 'miraculous influence of God'.[9] Roy is an equal opportunity discarder of miracles. He dismissed the eyewitness accounts of miracles performed by the prophet Mohammed, such as dividing the moon into two parts and working in sunshine without casting shadow, as having 'little weight' with Hindus.

In effect, The Precepts did away with the powerful pillars of evangelical Christianity – the belief in atonement, the doctrine of the Trinity, the divinity of Jesus and the self-sufficiency of the Scriptures. Roy rigorously iterated that the doctrines were an invention by church authorities. The Precepts also undermined the unique message of Christianity by asserting that these moral principles existed universally. While he declared that the morality he advocated was 'no other than that of the gospel',[10] he simultaneously weakened the distinctiveness the missionaries claimed for it by declaring that 'this simple code of religion and morality is so admirably calculated to elevate men's ideas to high and liberal notions of God', had been equally experienced by all living creatures, 'without distinction of caste, rank or wealth'.[11] It was a reminder to the missionaries that what they professed to be as unique was found in other religious traditions as well.

The Precepts advocated a non-doctrinal Christianity based purely on the moral teachings of Jesus which Roy found 'beyond the reach of metaphysical perversion, and intelligible alike to the learned and to the unlearned'.[12] Nowhere in The Precepts did Roy provide a rational for his compilation. For him, the moral ingredient of the Gospels and the humane personhood of Jesus were of lasting value and superseded any theological testaments. Roy, in effect, personalized the text, humanized Jesus and purged the narrative of what he considered as illogical and scripturally unjustifiable doctrine through pre-ordained readings. The Precepts was placid, preachy and grandstanding. It was essentially, a text for his times and for his hermeneutical purposes and motives.

Notes

1. Roy, *The English Works of Raja Rammohun Roy*, 555.
2. Ibid., 578.
3. Ibid., 618.
4. Ibid., 704.
5. Ibid., 484.
6. M. Carpenter, *The Last Days in England of the Raja Rammohun Roy* (London: Trübner and Co., 1866), 137.
7. *A Defence of Some Important Scripture Doctrines* (Calcutta: The Baptist Missionary Press, 1822), 10. This volume which contains twelve essays was brought out by the Baptists in Calcutta during the height of the controversy in order to reassert the Christian orthodox position. The first five were written by Rev. T. Scott and the rest by William Yates. See, J. Hoby, *Memoir of William Yates, D.D., of Calcutta* (London: Houlston & Stoneman, 1847), 168.
8. Roy, *The English Works of Raja Rammohun Roy*, 614.
9. Ibid., 619.
10. *A Defence of Some Important Scripture Doctrines*, 2.
11. Roy, *The English Works of Raja Rammohun Roy*, 485.
12. Ibid., 484.

Chapter 4

PUBLISH AND BE PILLORIED

The publication of *The Precepts*, to use today's parlance, went viral. The reaction of the missionaries in Calcutta (now Kolkata) was predictable. The Baptist missionaries treated *The Precepts* not as an innocent text produced by an amiable Brahmin friend but an incendiary text, a 'deadly weapon aimed at the very vitals of Christianity […] calculated to produce universal unbelief in the Bible'.[1] Joseph Ivimey, a Baptist ministering in England, instead of hearing what a Hindu had to say about the teachings of Jesus, attacked the messenger. He found Roy 'still a Pagan'[2] and accused of him being an 'idolater of eminence'.[3] Ivimey derisively dismissed Roy for not worshipping Jehovah, the God of Israel, the creator and the governor of the world but an abstract and undefined being called the soul of the universe. The Anglican response came from Thomas Middleton, the first Bishop of Calcutta, who respected Roy yet criticized him in his unfinished reply to *The Precepts* for his excessive use of Gospel materials which made the Acts and the epistles 'wholly useless for the proof of either precepts or doctrines'.[4] W.H. Mill, the principal of Bishop's College, Calcutta, argued that *The Precepts* 'set the *morality* of the Gospels against its *mysteries*' diligently overlooking the fact that these two were intimately connected,[5] but he also grudgingly accepted that if *The Precepts* was to be divested of its 'insidious' preface it was 'calculated to do good'.[6] A more light-weight and less-significant Anglican retort to Roy was offered by Frank Lillingston, an assistant curate of Heavitree, Exeter, who called Roy's *Precepts* an 'extravagant censorship'.[7] On the other hand, the Unitarians were measurably euphoric. Robert Aspland, the editor of the Unitarian magazine, *Monthly Repository*, hailed *The Precepts* as a work of a 'pure theist' and Sutya-Sadhun, a fellow Indian and a presumed convert to Unitarianism, described Roy as a 'searcher after Christian truth' and appealed to British liberal sense to show 'leniency and not to apply the penal statute against those who deny the divinity to Christ'.[8]

Joshua Marshman, one of the Serampore Baptist missionaries with whom Roy had a cordial relationship until the publication of *The Precepts*, was mildly enthused at the beginning but as the controversy raged on he got suitably angered by it. He was forced to react because Roy had a formidable reputation among the Hindus, and as John Marshman, his son put it 'any treatise from his pen could not fail to exert a powerful influence among his own countrymen, more specially when it harmonized with their own prejudices against Christianity'.[9] While giving 'full credit' to Roy for examining 'the whole of the Sacred Writings in the closest manner' and openly declaring that he was pleased 'by the testimony of an intelligent and unprejudiced Heathen'.[10] Marshman, at the same time, bewailed in the words of the Psalmist 'if the foundations be destroyed what shall the righteous do?'[11] For Marshman, 'the New Testament story has to be accepted as a whole or not at all'. Marshman wondered, without the biblical dogmas dismissed by Roy, 'what is the Gospel?'[12] He reiterated the fact that he belonged to that 'class who think that no one can be a real Christian without believing the Divinity and the Atonement of Jesus Christ, and the Divine authority of the whole of the Holy Scriptures'.[13]

Roy had a head start in this debate. He had already published theological treatises and as such was an experienced past master at handling theological disputes. His editing of the Hindu texts, which was severe and an irritating exposure of polytheism and idolatry, resulted in endless debates with his own pundits. Marshman, on the other hand, looked a mere learner. Although he admitted that he had studied the Bible for more than twenty-five years, he had little experience in engaging in erudite debates. He was candid enough to confess to his son that his response to Roy was the 'only articles in divinity'[14] that he had ever written. Calling Roy, a 'heathen' when he was a formidable intellectual and a serious reformer was an egregious example of Marshman's lack of academic decorum and inexperience in conducting theological debates. Socially, Roy was several notches above Marshman and other Seramapore missionaries. Roy also outsmarted Marshman in another respect. Whereas Roy brought the whole heavy weight of his multicultural background and successfully summoned his comparative exegetical skills, Marshman was restricted by his monocultural, sectarian and dogmatic polemics.

Some of Roy's daring hermeneutical expositions were too much for Marshman who was raised on the solid diet of the pietistic theology of the saving power of the blood of Jesus. Marshman found it uncomfortable when *The Precepts* degraded and reduced the importance of his cherished theological crown jewels. One was the downgrading of Jesus, whom the missionaries proclaimed as the redeemer of the world, by positioning him on a par with Confucius and Mohamed, thus reducing his status to that of a teacher and a founder of a sect. *The Precepts* denied, as Marshman put it, the status of Jesus as 'God over all'[15] and projected him as a gentle moral 'Teacher' rather than an adjudicating 'Judge' who separates the good and the bad ones. This is the Jesus who does not search the hearts of human beings, create guilty feelings and make people submit 'unconditionally to his mere grace for salvation'.[16] Marshman was keen to project the God of Jesus as the one who instils terror in the hearts of sinful humanity. Secondly, *The Precepts* reduced the Holy Book into something on a 'level with the writings of men'. By treating certain parts of the Gospel as valuable, Roy had not only reduced the rest as 'scarcely worthy of notice' but also stripped the Bible of its 'peculiar majesty and authority'.[17] Roy simultaneously challenged their cherished doctrines and at the same time made the Bible, the oracle of God, a culturally relative text. Or, as his missionary opponent put it, *The Precepts* 'depreciate[d] the value of the Christian revelation, and place[d] it, at best, very much on a level with any good book'.[18] Added to these humiliations was trivializing the miracles of Jesus as equivalent to the Hindu sage Ugusti's drinking of the ocean in a fit of passion and causing the Vindhya mountains to prostrate themselves before him. Marshman scornfully smeared *The Precepts* as a 'singularly negative version of Christianity'.[19]

In their methods and motives, there were certain conspicuous convergences. The Roy–Marshman debate is marked by the trading of a huge amount of biblical quotations and allusions by both men. Both seized on biblical passages as evidence of whatever theological position they held. They used biblical quotes to dignify their preconceived theological positions or to tidy up the entrenched exegetical mess they had created for themselves. Both would press into service the entire Bible from Genesis to the Book of Revelation to legitimize and authenticate their adored theological positions. Thus Roy rummaged through the Hebrew Scriptures to demonstrate that Jesus was not the only saviour and that there were many, as attested by Obadiah: 'saviours shall come up on Mount Zion'. In the same vein, Marshman perceived in the angel of Bochim a prototype of Jesus (Judg. 2) and extricated trinitarian ideas entangled in the writings of Isaiah. The whole debate was dense and often cyclic. Roy used the texts to meet the demand of a multireligious context. For him, they were malleable, to suit the occasion, and if some of the narratives were irrelevant, they could be dispensed with. Whereas Marshman understood the biblical texts as containing the inspired word of God, fixed and final and applicable to anywhere irrespective of time and context. They had to be accepted as a 'harmonious whole'.[20] They were basically, decrees for a fallen humanity. Both were assertive and authoritative from their own perspectives but at the same time violating altogether the sense of the text and the origins of the context.

Both resorted to the Scriptures as the final court of appeal. Roy put much stress on the Bible but reinforced by the scientific rational approach: 'I appeal to the Scripture, and also to the common sense,'[21] which he claimed as superior. For Roy, everything had to be proven from the Scripture. In his defence against the missionaries, he used the word 'unscriptural' more than twelve times to show that the doctrines that they were trying to impose were not sanctioned by the Bible but the products of the theological presuppositions and denominational biases of the missionaries and generated largely by the power that the invaders wielded. In his preoccupation with the text, Roy resembled a proto-Protestant. Marshman felt that without recourse to the Bible life was in vain and, more worryingly, that it would be a cause for celebration for the 'many opposers of Divine Revelation,'[22] which no doubt included Roy.

Both unwittingly subscribed to the Protestant principle of interpreting the Scripture by Scripture. Roy was haranguing the missionaries that they should go to the Old Testament first and study it in its canonical sequence, without paying any attention to interpretations given by any Christian denominations, and then approach the New Testament, before comparing them, as this would give an unbiased and a comphrehensive picture. Roy gave Marshman a bold instruction: examine the true strength of the scriptural phrases and expressions without paying attention to any interpretation given by any denominations. In this way, he assured the missionaries that 'Christianity would not any longer be liable to be encroached upon by human opinions.'[23] They both sought for the parallel texts which seemingly addressed their chosen point of view.

Roy and Marshman were engaged in blatantly biased exegesis, while unashamedly blaming each other for being unfairly prejudiced. Their biblical explorations emerged out of heavily loaded prejudices. Marshman's exposition was predetermined by the inerrancy of the Scriptures, the salvific value of Jesus's blood and the trinitarian affirmation of Godhead – the staple diet of Baptist theology at the time. Roy's reading was marked by monotheistic ideals, purest principles of morality and rationalistic thinking. Both forced meaning into the text and read it out of context. They took advantage of both competing texts and counter-narratives in the texts to support their case. Both indulged in an age-old strategy of comparing the most pristine and sophisticated biblical concepts with the worse, decadent thinking of the other.

In Roy the Baptists found a different opponent, an assertive and theologically astute rival. The Baptists, as non-conformists in England, who faced the imperiousness of Anglicanism and engaged in debates centred around kindred doctrinal beliefs, worship practices and church structures, came up against a theological adversary in India, who was not only well versed in various religious texts but also in Christian theology and church history. His proficiency in oriental languages, such as Arabic, Persian and Sanskrit, and philosophies, such as Islamic and Chinese, was well above the Serampore missionaries. They would have found him intimidating and, more troublingly, felt inadequate to face Roy's intellectual and theological prowess.

Marshman likened Roy to one of the numerous meddlesome rationalists in the West whose pastime was to attack the Christian faith. Marshman made the fatal mistake of repeating what the dissenters did at home – the evil thoughts of the heretics had to be expelled by quoting Scripture. His ripostes to Roy were full of biblical citations that did not pay attention to their context. A similar practice was employed by the authors of *A Defence of Some Important Scripture Doctrines*[24] a volume produced by the Baptist missionaries to secure and protect traditional Christianity in the face of *The Precepts*. The volume's essayists used a bombardment of textual retorts with scriptural quotations as their line of argument. Roy, on the other hand, was not denunciatiatory, rather he was declaratory – making clear that the substance of the teaching of Jesus was suffused with a surfeit of scriptural references. To the missionary denunciation, one could add colonial condescension when Roy was addressed in derogatory terms.

When the missionaries insisted that he prove whether his *Precepts* was an inspired work, Roy's answer was that the true test of sacred texts lies not in their designated divine status but in their ability to promote faith in the Supreme Deity and lead human beings to social happiness. A Whig form of liberation hermeneutics in colonial Bengal. For Roy, the legitimacy and trustworthiness of a text was judged by the social comfort they produced. On these grounds, Roy maintained that *The Precepts* was induced by some external creative impulse.

In his First Appeal, Roy concluded with the words that everyone would 'regard the Precepts of Jesus as the sole guide to peace and happiness' and prayed that religion should not become a 'cause of difference between man and man'.[25] As the controversy showed, the missionaries were not in any mood to heed the words of a heathen – a heathen, even by their own admission, who was intelligent.

Notes

1. *A Defence of Some Important Scripture Doctrines*, 98.
2. 'Free Press and Unitarianism in India', *The Monthly Repository* 17, no. 203 (1822): 683.
3. Ibid., 686.
4. C.W. Le Bas, *The Life of the Right Reverend Thomas Fanshaw Middleton Late Lord Bishop of Calcutta in Two Volumes*, vol. 2 (London: C.J.G & F. Rivington, 1831), 408.
5. Le Bas, *The Life of the Right Reverend Thomas Fanshaw Middleton Late Lord Bishop of Calcutta in Two Volumes*, vol. 2, 432.
6. Ibid.
7. F. Lillingston, *The Brahmo Samaj & Arya Samaj in Their Bearing Upon Christianity: A Study in Indian Theism* (London: Macmillan and Co., Limited, 1901), 60.
8. 'Free Press and Unitarianism in India', 685.
9. J.C. Marshman, *The Story of Cary, Marshman and Ward: The Serampore Missionaries* (London: Alexander Strahan and Co., 1864), 308.
10. J. Marshman, *A Defence of the Deity and Atonement of Jesus Christ, in Reply to Ram-Mohun Roy of Calcutta* (London: Kingsbury, Parbury, and Allen, 1822), 3
11. Marshman, *A Defence of the Deity and Atonement of Jesus Christ*, 65.
12. Ibid., 10.
13. Ibid., 6.
14. J.C. Marshman, *The Life and Times of Carey, Marshman, and Ward Embracing the History of the Serampore Mission*, vol. 2 (London: Longman, Brown, Green, Longmans, Roberts, & Green, 1859), 239.
15. Marshman, *A Defence of the Deity and Atonement of Jesus Christ*, 8.
16. Ibid., 3.
17. Ibid., 7.
18. *A Defence of Some Important Scripture Doctrines*, 90.
19. Collet, *The Life and Letters of Raja Rammohun Roy*, 119.
20. Marshman, *A Defence of the Deity and Atonement of Jesus Christ*, 2.
21. Roy, *The English Works of Raja Rammohun Roy*, 825.
22. Marshman, *A Defence of the Deity and Atonement of Jesus Christ*, 4.
23. Roy, *The English Works of Raja Rammohun Roy*, 666.
24. *A Defence of Some Important Scripture Doctrines*.
25. Roy, *The English Works of Raja Rammohun Roy*, 671.

Chapter 5

THE BENGALI AND HIS BIBLICAL ENGAGEMENTS

Roy's first citation of the Bible was in 1816. His introduction to the Ishopanishad ended by quoting the Golden Rule. Roy preferred the biblical version, although there is an equivalent but negatively stated saying in the Mahabharata – 'This is the sum of duty: do not do to others what would cause pain if done to you' (*Mahabharata* 5.1517).

Roy was a keen student of all scriptures and he had an ambition to start a monthly magazine for biblical criticism with a view to putting to the test the fairness of the argument of the Unitarian and Trinitarian doctrines.[1] He even suggested how one should go about assessing these supposed biblical doctrines. He proposed that one should begin with the Book of Genesis and examine its alleged Trinitarian credentials and follow it up with the other books of the Hebrew Scriptures, and then turn to the New Testament writings. Unfortunately, his ambition of starting a biblical journal remained unfulfilled.

Roy was the first Hindu to engage in such noticeable biblical scholarship outside the Semitic circle. There were medieval Muslim scholars who showed a high level of biblical sophistry, especially polemicists such as Ibn Hazm of Cordova (d.1064), whose involvement is well known. Hava Lazarus-Yafeh has competently documented how Jewish or Christian intermediaries engaged with this critical Muslim Bible scholarship, and how he transferred it from the Muslim world to Christian Europe, which paved the way for the development of biblical criticism in the West.[2] Although Roy's impact on the West may not be as far reaching as those of Islamic scholars, his work was a precursor to some of the ideas such as demythologization and narrative criticism, which the West took up without paying any acknowledgement or being aware of his work.

Roy revered all scriptures and showed his reverence by figuring out his religious opinions from the original text, aided by liberal and enlightened criticism. Like most Christians at that time, Roy accepted that the faith of Christians was based on nothing but the Bible. But unlike most Christians, he insisted on using the force of reason and critical resources to arrive at the true version. This meant not blindly accepting every single translated verse of the King James Version. But at the same time, he unwittingly reinforced both Hindu and Christian scriptures. He subscribed to the idea that the validity of theological assertions depended on 'scriptural authority'.[3] Unlike Spinoza and Hobbes, whose criticism of the Bible weakened the authority of the Bible and that of the church, and offered a different authority in the form of the modern state which would have dominion over the people, Roy fervently held on to the ancient texts both Hindu and Christian. He was too conservative to argue for a religion without scriptures but with many stories, not divine oracles but narratives.

Roy did not dismiss the authority of the Bible or his own sacred texts. For him, biblical narratives are not inerrant and therefore they must be investigated by the tools of reason. His position had been that much of the Bible could be treated literally and at the same time much of it could be interpreted allegorically. Once the essence of the message is gleaned the sacred texts have little use. The universal idea of loving god and loving the neighbour will provide humankind with moral and theological guidance. His argument all along had been that the highest truth should be realized not by relying solely on the evidence of the sacred books alone but on the basis of common sense and rationality. In his attempt to arrive at the truth, he cleverly mixed Unitarian and Mimamsa methods. It worked for him like this – start with the text, place it in its original setting and determine whether it is consistent with the context, query its genuineness in the light of other similar sayings, and with the 'benevolence of the Christian dispensation'[4] doubt its strength and legitimacy, and then reassess its usefulness and arrive at the highest understanding and appreciation of the truth with the help of divine assistance.

Roy was insistent that scriptures should be studied looking at the original sources rather than approaching them with preconceived denominational or sectarian prejudices. He drew from the original Hebrew, Greek and Arabic versions of the Bible. He learned the biblical languages to understand the Bible's content better and, more importantly, to allay the accusations of the missionaries that he was not competent enough to argue with them. His contention had been that a close examination of the Greek and Hebrew versions of the Bible would remove the confusion introduced by mistranslation and demystify doctrines such as the Trinity, which was 'a mockery of reason' and went against rational thinking. His plea had been to 'acquire a knowledge of the true force of scriptural phrases and expressions without attending to interpretations given by any sect'. His quarrel with the missionaries was that they were biased and paid 'little or no attention to opposite sentiments' on account of their 'prejudice and partiality'.[5] He urged them to open up to the 'simple enumeration and statement of the respective tenets of different sects'.[6] This way Christianity could be freed from being 'encroached upon by human opinions'.[7]

Roy did not question the use of biblical passages on the grounds of whether they were the words of God but on the basis that it was the missionaries who used them. He contended that these verses were employed by people who were 'conquerors of this country', who were 'eminently elevated by virtue of conquest', and belonged to those who had 'wealth and power'. He understood the pernicious link between power and truth before Western thinkers such as Foucault made it popular in the middle of the twentieth century. For him, truth and religion did not belong to 'high names or lofty palaces'. He claimed that his reading of the Scripture was superior because he 'sought to attain the truths of Christianity from the words of the author of this religion and from the undisputed instructions of his holy Apostles', whereas the missionaries heard it second hand from a parent, a tutor or denominational authorities. He told the missionaries: 'I cannot help refusing my assent to any doctrine which I do not find scriptural.'[8] He found their reading marked by greater reliance 'on a mere dogmatical knowledge of God' rather than on how one attains eternal life by performing one's duty towards one's fellow human beings. He cited the parable of the sheep and goats as a supreme example of one's duty towards one's fellow human beings. In the parlance of liberation theology, what Roy advocated was not orthodoxy but orthopraxis.

His exegetical practice lay in monotonously piling up a series of like-minded relevant scriptural passages to iterate his point – an accusation that equally could be levelled against his missionary opponents. On one occasion, to prove that Jesus disavowed his distinctly divine nature and manifestly subordinated himself to God, Roy cited nineteen sayings of Jesus. The relentless citation of biblical quotations tests one's patience. If one can penetrate through the torrent of quotations, one can discern a hermeneutical purpose in assembling these scriptural passages. He selected texts scattered all over the Bible and, paying scant respect to their context, used them to construct the exegetical point he wished to espouse. He did not mindlessly cite their parallel passages. The idea was to clarify how the terms were used by other Gospel writers in different situations. Another purpose of using parallel passages was to browbeat his opponents with the sheer quantity of the material.

Another interpretative ploy was to redefine most of the biblical doctrine to suit his hermeneutical agenda. As we saw earlier, he reformulated the atonement as service, the Son of man as a metaphor applied to men of power and rank, and the unity between the Father and Son as a moral one. In doing so, he stripped them of their Semitic contents and, in the process, reinforced them. His query besides being that these doctrines were anti-irrational, was that they would not appeal to people who were not tutored in them. Roy was not dislodging these doctrines but rebranding them in humanistic and secular terms.

His argument with the missionaries was that Asian languages, such as Hebrew, 'indulge[s] in metaphor' and 'abounds with expressions which cannot be taken in their literal sense'. Roy, in his inimitable way tutored European Christians that metaphorical meanings were very common among the oriental nations but would cause difficulty to 'European commentators even of profound learning'. He accused them of overlooking the 'idiom of the language of scripture' and altering it to 'suit their peculiar ideas'.[9] He took the scriptures seriously and symbolically whereas his missionary opponents regarded them literally and not figuratively.

Roy set his own interpretative hierarchy. When passages which espouse the idea of the unity of the Godhead were at variance with the narratives which promoted a plurality of Gods, he thought the latter should be stripped of their authority and looked upon as 'altogether unintelligible'.[10] When a biblical writer came up with seemingly contradictory sayings, the one which was most consistent with reason and fitted in with the context should be taken as authentic and the other saying(s) which did not comply with this criteria should be read in a figurative sense. This mode of interpreting the scriptures, he assured the reader, was the universally adopted method.

He had been relentless in reminding the missionaries that when the passages from the Old Testament were used to legitimize the messianic credentials of Jesus, they should be 'accompanied with the respective contexts', otherwise they would be 'misunderstood'. To illustrate his point, he drew attention to Matthew's citation of Hosea: 'Out of Egypt have I called my Son.' Roy conceded that there were certain superficial similarities in Hosea and Matthew. Both Israel and Jesus were carried to Egypt and recalled from there. Both were designated as the Son of God, however Roy pointed out that when read in context the reference would not have been to Jesus. Further, the rest of the verses clearly stated that Israel was sacrificed to Baalim, which Roy reasoned could not justly be ascribed to Jesus.

There is an inborn Biblicism in Roy. He informed his missionary challengers that he derived his opinions 'entirely from the Scriptures themselves'. He constantly declared that his aim was to seek the truth of Christianity from the 'words of the author of this religion' and that he firmly believed that the whole spirit of the teaching of Jesus had been 'faithfully and fully recorded' by the Gospel writers. His dependency on the texts served him in three ways. First, he thought that the textual reliance could guard against 'endless corruption, absurdities, and human caprices'.[11] Second, he was of the conviction that if proved from the scriptures he could convince both his opponents – the Christian clergy and the brahmin pundits. That is why in the battles with his fellow Hindus and Christians there were constant references and citations from Hindu and Christian scriptures. For example, he summoned the Hindu scriptures to support the abolition of sati. Third, once the scriptures had been cleansed of idolatrous, polytheistical and doctrinal impurities, they could regain supreme spiritual status. For him, scriptural texts remained the centre. In the last days of his life in England, he seemed to have said that he considered the internal evidence of Christianity to be stronger than the historical evidence of the New Testament.

Roy's biblical work is a mixture of traditionalism and a conservative progressivism. He worked under the premise that Moses was the author of the first five books of the Hebrew Scriptures. In *Precepts*, Roy retained the passages referred to and upheld their authorship by Moses. He did not question the authorial role of Moses nor engage in philological and historical analysis of the Pentateuch, but he was committed to the moral value of the Bible. Yet there are early signs of form-criticism in Roy's work. He showed how the Gospel accounts had been altered or even created by biblical writers. Unlike the later form critics, he did not conclude that the Synoptic accounts of Jesus were almost useless as an historical record. At a time when thinkers such as Lessing, Semler and Reimarus jettisoned supernatural beliefs and claimed to find falsehood, fakery and forgery in the scriptures, Roy showed much confidence in texts both in his own Vedic scriptures and in the Gospels. His was a kind of narrative criticism but not of the current post-critical variety but the pre-critical one. It is the tracing of the word of God in multiple narratives written by different writers.

Roy was well ahead of biblical scholars when he talked about 'the first and purest ages of Christianity'. It was only thirty years after *Precepts* that the Western biblical scholars were to set what Yii-Jan Li called 'the ultimate goal for New Testament textual criticism: the "original text" the pure, unsullied ancestor".[12] According to her research, it was Karl Lachmann who tried to trace the very original words of Jesus in the text.[13] But Roy sought to separate the essential truth embedded in the scripture from the later accretions even before the Western scholars embraced such an enterprise. What makes him unique is that he did this both to his own scripture and also to the Gospels.

It took another forty years for writers of the *Essays and Reviews* to pronounce the principles of biblical criticism that the Unitarians and Roy were engaged in – treating the biblical texts the same as any other literature, scrutinizing the grammar and philology of the text; situating the text in its context; studying the peculiar phraseology of the writer's culture and country; and examining the doctrinal principles of the author.

Roy was well aware of the current status of biblical scholarship. When he was accused of not using John, Roy showed his knowledge of biblical criticism by saying that the dogmas of the Church had been drawn from this gospel, and this particular gospel was under scrutiny among the most learned scholars in Christendom. He was worried that the 'unprepared understandings' of the Gospels would cause problems for Hindus and Muslims. It was not the historicity of John's gospel that troubled him but its contemplative and doctrinal nature. He blamed the fourth gospel for erecting a stumbling block between the Gospel message and Indians.

At this point, I will briefly look at the facile similarities often made between Bultmann's and Roy's demythologizing projects. It was Kaj Baago, the Danish church historian, who taught at the United Theological College, Bangalore, who first mooted the idea. Incidentally, it was his article that trigged my interest in Roy.[14] Before Bultmann, it was Roy who was engaged in, to use Bultmann's own words, the 'task of stripping the Kerygma from its mythical framework, and of "demythologizing" it'.[15] Both believed that the New Testament lent itself to and invited this kind of divestment of mythical contents. Roy was clear in his thinking that the removal of mythical and supernatural elements was 'founded on and supported by the express authority of Jesus of Nazareth'[16] when Jesus himself chose only the two commandments –to love God and to love fellow human beings – which were sufficient for peace, happiness and improvement of humankind. In Bultmann's case 'the demand for the criticism of mythology comes from a curious contradiction which runs right through the New Testament'.[17]

The demythization agenda of Roy and Bultmann emerged from different contexts. Roy lived among people who had no qualms about accepting a supernatural worldview but would be utterly unimpressed with the biblical miracles. Bultmann lived among people who were trying to adjust to a thoroughly modern and scientific outlook and for whom stories of miracles were simply unbelievable. He tried to make the Gospel relevant to Germans who were now getting used to 'electric light and wireless', and who had the desire to understand the message of Jesus. Both were convinced that, after divesting the Gospels of their supernatural and miraculous contents, the core Gospel was still retrievable, and this retrieved Gospel could speak and act with immediate efficacy: in Roy's case its moral tenets and in Bultmann's case its existential demand for radical discipleship. Roy's audience was wider and multireligious. He was engaged in the service of his fellow Hindus, especially to warn potential converts that there was no point in embracing the imported religion which was not that different from the one they were practising; and also to recover the simple teaching of Jesus contaminated by priests and church officials. Bultmann's constituency was narrow, mono-religious and limited to the German churches. For Roy the sparring partners were the Calvinistic and doctrinally drenched evangelicals who were making the Gospel incomprehensible for Indians. Whereas for Bultmann it was secular ideas such as modernism and freethinking that were making the Gospel almost irrelevant and redundant for Germans.

There are certain perceptible parallels between Bultmann and Roy. Both of them placed much importance on the kerygma and held the view that the historical Jesus was irrelevant for the kerygma. While the church tradition turned the proclaimer into proclaimed, these two men were keen to recover the proclamation behind the proclaimer. For both, the chronological life of Jesus was no longer a priority, but the word he proclaimed was. What Bultmann wrote could well represent the view of Roy: 'the personality of Jesus has no importance for the kerygma'.[18] Their attempts at the lives of Jesus were produced without historical or existential requisites.

But there are crucial differences between the two. To begin with, the authority and status they accord to the Bible was diametrically opposed. For Bultmann, unlike 'Plato or the Bhagavad-Gita' which were discovered through cultural studies, the Bible was 'known through the church' and essentially a church book. For Roy, this was precisely the problem: his accusation against Baptist missionaries was that their understanding of the Bible was poor and defective because they were introduced to the Bible through the prism of church dogmas which prevented them from grasping the authentic words of Jesus. Roy and Bultmann had two different understandings of kerygma. For Roy, unlike Bultmann, the kerygma was not an inner or internal experience, not a decisive event of redemption. It was an outward activity of showing love to God and fellow human beings. While Bultmann placed a high value on the word impinging on one's life from the pulpit or through proclamation, Roy devalued such occurrences. Roy, who witnessed the missionary preaching, had a poor view of the effectiveness of the preached word which, in his experience, was largely denunciatory of Hindu practices and beliefs, or was offering inducements to join the church. For Roy, one does not hear the word. Its efficacy is in its enactment. As in the case of Bultmann, it did not '*address* you' and 'exposes "*your* nothingness, *your* sin"' (italicization in the original).[19] In other words, it did not pass judgement and convict you. It enabled you to move and act humanely towards fellow human beings to bring social happiness and harmony. For Bultmann, who was raised in a monocultural and monotextual context, to hear the 'voice' every other voice had to be silenced, or, as he put it, 'there is room for but one voice'.[20] For Roy, who was part of multicultural, multireligious and multitextual traditions, the divine word, or the voice, was not confined to a single religion or a single text but could only be discerned in a plurality of voices and words.

To bring this chapter to a close: Roy's hermeneutical work was akin to that of the Reformers. The Reformers wrested the Bible from the overbearing control of, and its authoritative interpretation by, the Catholic Church and placed it in the hands of the ordinary Christian faithful. Roy, likewise seized the Bible from the Protestants and placed in the public space made it accessible to ordinary people, but this time it included not only Christians but also Hindus and Muslims.

Roy did not always get it right. Roy accorded only a secondary place to John's Gospel. His position was that, while the Synoptics encouraged the social improvement of the people, John offered only spiritual platitudes. In the history of Indian biblical interpretation, it was the fourth gospel that attracted much attention and, ironically, it was from these spiritual platitudes that Indians drew profitably and worked out innovative interpretations which made Westcott (1825–1901), an Anglican bishop and a biblical scholar, say that the best commentary on John would come from Indians.[21]

Roy was convinced that his version of Christianity was the right one for his people rather than the one propagated by the missionaries, which he described as unscriptural and irrational. In his defence of his understanding of the Christian gospel he acted and argued as if he were a Christian and worked out his own interpretative methods. He wrote as part of the radical Christian tradition and had the ability to speak out within its parameters with both confidence and a civility that has been seldom surpassed in Indian theological circles since.

Sadly, biblical scholars, both Western and Indian, have paid little attention to Roy's biblical interpretation. It has been largely left to researchers who work in the areas of mission studies, church history or interfaith matters. Even here the attempts are scarce and infrequent. This lack of interest among mainstream scholars assumes that the expositions of Roy and other Indians, or, for the matter, anyone who is outside the Western world is treated as the study and exploitation of multitextual cultures and resources rather than making any substantial intellectual and critical contribution to biblical studies. The other assumption is that Western biblical interpretation is universal and other interpretations are local, vernacular and indigenous. Therefore, they are of little interest to the West. This assumed Western universalism, as any postcolonial critic would tell you, is a pretence and a posture, and, more pertinently, it refuses to acquire and get acquainted with the production of knowledge by the 'other'.

Notes

1. Roy, *The English Works of Raja Rammohun Roy*, 681.
2. H. Lazarus-Yafeh *Intertwined Worlds: Medieval Islam and Bible Criticism* (Princeton, NY: Princeton University Press, 1992).
3. Roy, *The English Works of Raja Rammohun Roy*, 113.
4. Ibid., 725.
5. Ibid., 484.
6. Ibid.

7   Ibid., 666.
8   Ibid., 630.
9   Ibid., 664.
10 R. Roy, *Translation of Several Principal Books, Passages, and Texts of the Veds, Some Controversial Works on Brahmunical Theology* (London: Parbury, Allen, & Co., 1832), 46.
11 J.K. Majumdar, ed., *Raja Rammohun Roy and Progressive Movements in India: A Selection from Records (1775–1845)* (Calcutta: Art Press, 1941), 189.
12 Yii-Jan, Lin, *The Erotic Life of Manuscripts: New Testament Textual Criticism and the Biological Sciences* (New York: Oxford University Press, 2016), 9.
13 Ibid., 14.
14 K. Baago, 'Ram Mohun Roy's Christology: An Early Attempt at Demythologization', *Bangalore Theological Forum* 1 (1967): 30–42.
15 R. Bultmann, 'New Testament and Mythology: Mythological Elements in the Message of the New Testament and the Problem of Its Re-Interpretation', in *Kerygma and Myth: A Theological Debate I*, ed. H.W. Bartsch, trans. R.H. Fuller (New York: Harper and Row, [1951] 1962), 3.
16 Roy, *The English Works of Raja Rammohun Roy*, 550.
17 Bultmann, 'New Testament and Mythology', 11.
18 R. Bultmann, *Theology of the New Testament*, vol. 1 (London: SCM Press, 1952), 35.
19 R. Bultmann, *Existence and Faith: Shorter Writings of Rudolf Bultmann*. Selected, trans. and intro. S.M. Ogden (London: Collins, 1964), 199.
20 Ibid., 197.
21 For Indian expositions of the Gospel of John, see A.J. Appasamy, *Christianity as Bhakti Marga: A Study of the Johannine Doctrine of Love* (Madras: Christian Literature Society, 1928), and *What is Moksha: A study in the Johannine Doctrine of Life* (Madras: Christian Literature Society, 1951); C. Duraisingh and C. Hargreaves, *India's Search for Reality and the Relevance of the Gospel of John* (Delhi: SPCK, 1975). M.R. Spindler, 'Indian Studies of the Gospel of John: Puzzling Contextualization', *Exchange* 9, no. 27 (1980): 1–55. Though these are all somewhat dated, they capture expertly the essence of various Indian approaches, themes, methods and personalities involved in Indian Christian appropriations of John's Gospel. In these days of identity-based hermeneutics, such advatic, contemplative attempts are likely to be dismissed as upper-caste indulgences. For the saying ascribed to Westcott on Indians and the John's gospel, see E. Asirvatham, *Christianity in the Indian Crucible* (Calcutta: YMCA Publishing House, 1955), 73.

Chapter 6

VEDAS AND THE VETHAGAMAS

Roy treated the Christian Bible, especially the Gospels, as if they were Hindu puranas consisting of mostly mythical elements, folklores and genealogies of gods and goddesses. Bishop Middleton, the Anglican bishop in Calcutta at that time, was worried that Roy's self-selection of the Gospels might lead his native readers to conclude that the rest of the holy books were like 'Poorans and Tuntras'.[1] To prove the errors of Hinduism, missionaries drew attention to the puranic depictions of Hindu gods having various names and forms, possessing wives and children, and being subject to human feelings and bodily functions. In response Roy pointed to similar descriptions of Jesus found in the Gospels. These Gospel narratives, Roy rightly asserted, document the passions, feelings, birth, death and family life of Jesus, just like the puranic Gods.

Roy also declined to accept the Bible as a revealed text. For him, the Bible was a human construction replete with 'human distortions'. He put the missionaries in an awkward position by posing a question: 'And can any book, which contains an idea that defies the use of the senses, be considered worthy to be ascribed to that Being who has endued the human race with senses and understanding for their use and guidance?'[2]

When pressed to choose between two supreme writings – the Bible and the Vedas – Roy naturally preferred the primeval revelation found in the ancient Hindu text which he declared as 'an inspired work, coeval with the existence of the world'.[3] It was Roy, the proud Indian that he was, who made the Veda the true Bible of India. He claimed that the 'Vedas, our original book', and its doctrines were 'much more rational than the religion which the missionaries profess', and 'in every respect perfectly consistent' and well advanced in matters of spirituality. His small pamphlet, the Universal Religion espoused the cause of the monotheistic ideals of religions. In it he urged the necessity of reading the scriptures of different religions, yet Roy's scriptural selections supporting the universal religion came principally from Hindu scriptural sources which included texts such as the Vishnu-Purana, the Brahma-Sutra and passages from the Upanishads. Roy's preference for the Vedas is plainly evident in the remarks he made to one of his disciples, Chandrasekhar Deb, that – 'the Hindus seem to have made greater progress in the sacred learning than the Jews at least when the Upanishads were written'. He told his disciple that if religion consisted of blessings of self-knowledge, improved notions and attributes of God, and a system of morality, he would 'certainly prefer the Vedas'.[4]

Roy elevated the Vedas over the Christian Bible on four counts. First, its principle doctrine the unity of Godhead: 'The Supreme Being is presented throughout the whole Vedanta System *as the only object of true adoration*.'[5] Vedic phrases such as 'Know "God alone"' and 'Adore God *alone*' were demonstrative of the worship of a single God. Second, the Vedas did not attempt to conceptualize God in anthropomorphic terms as in the case of the Bible. In the Christian Scriptures, God is represented as having arms and fingers, a head with face, mouth, tongue, eyes, nose and ears, heart, bowel, back, thighs and legs; and as exhibiting human feelings such as anger, grief, joy, love and hate; and as performing physical functions such as seeing, being seen, speaking and hearing, slumbering and awaking. Roy was puzzled as to how people of 'sound reasoning' could come up with a picture of God having human features and characteristics when the ultimate reality itself was 'unsearchable, incomprehensible Being'.[6] Third, unlike the Bible, the Hindu scriptures do not reward the good or punish the evil, or await for the eschatological judgement, either in this world or hereafter. But they reveal that human beings suffer or enjoy according to their evil or good deeds in this world – a 'doctrine which' Roy admitted was 'at variance with the first part of the Bible'.[7] Fourth, it taught that the victory over sin is achieved by 'sincere repentance and solemn meditation', whereas the Christian teaching required the blood of the Son of God 'who never participated in our transgressions' to expiate for the sins of humankind.[8] Finally, and more importantly, the Hindu Vedas are almost free of, and untainted by, the doctrinal blemishes – an unfortunate characteristic of Christianity – which Roy found offensive and irrational. For him, the genuine Brahmanical religion is 'taught by the Vedas and as interpreted by the inspired Manu'. He placed his faith ultimately in the Vedas and for him the truth in its purest form was found in them. His social reform and monotheistic ideals were drawn from them. It was the missionaries' determined attempts to 'stigmatize the Veda'[9] that motivated Roy to reclaim the Vedas as the foundational text for Hinduism.

In Roy's reading the Veda became as good as the Bible. It encouraged monotheism, scorned idolatry, disregarded caste, proscribed the burning of widows and looked as 'true, pure, and as perfect as Christianity' itself. Roy did not hesitate to acknowledge that the unity and incomprehensibility of God found in the Vedas was also manifest in the biblical texts. He cited from the Kenopanishad – 'Hence no vision can approach him, no language can describe him, no intellectual power can compass or determine him: we know nothing how the Supreme Being should be explained' – and found corresponding verses in the Bible: 'Behold God is great, and we know him not' (Job 36.26), and 'His greatness is unsearchable.' (Ps. 145.3)[10] For Roy, the God that Christians worshipped was the same as his own and, in fact, worshipped in all religions.

He was not uncritical towards his own Vedas. He freely conceded that some sections of the Vedas represented 'the Hindu religion as very base'[11] and exhibited 'allegorical representations of the attributes of the Supreme Being, by means of earthly objects, animate or inanimate'.[12] His outlook on the Vedas was akin to his approach to the Bible – unintelligible teachings had to be discarded. He rejected the concept of maya and was indifferent to the Hindu view of asceticism as a means of salvation. He also sought to distance himself from the renunciatory advocacy of classical Vedanta which was at odds with the democratic principles of Hindu teachings.[13] Unlike some Hindu reformers who privileged ascetic life and revered sannyasins who turn away from the world, Roy's ideal was the godly householder who worships the supreme being while carrying out civic and worldly duties. He transformed the conservative teaching of world renunciation of the Vedanta into a world affirming principle.

For Roy, revelation was not confined to one particular scripture. The same virtues found in the Vedic scriptures were also manifested in the Christian Testaments, in the Qur'an, in the Zend Avesta, and in any sacred book of any nation. He stated that this disclosure had to be acknowledged and looked upon as emanating from the 'God of truth', and had to be treated as a demonstration of the yearnings of the human spirit and the cravings of the human heart. However, when it came to determining the soundness and strength of any sacred texts, Roy did not have any qualms about disregarding the authority of other scriptures when they clashed or disagreed with the Vedas.

Notes

1 Le Bas, *The Life of the Right Reverend Thomas Fanshaw Middleton*, vol. 2, 409.
2 Roy, *The English Works of Raja Rammohun Roy*, 172.
3 Roy, *Translation of Several Principal Books*, 45.
4 Rammohun Roy, *The Correspondence of Raja Rammohun Roy*, vol. 1, *1809–1831*, ed. D.K. Biswas (Calcutta: Sarawat Library, 1960), 305.
5 Roy, *The English Works of Raja Rammohun Roy* 186.
6 Ibid., 564.
7 Ibid., 185.
8 Ibid.
9 Ibid., 186.
10 Ibid., 563.
11 Ibid., 162.
12 Roy, *Translation of Several Principal Books*, 45.
13 B.A. Hatcher, *Bourgeois Hinduism, or Faith of the Modern Vedantists: Rare Discourses from Early Colonial Bengal* (New York: Oxford University Press, 2008), 25.

Chapter 7

GOSPEL HARMONIES, BIBLE VERSIONS AND TRANSLATIONS

The Gospel harmonies

The Gospel harmonies, an effort to compress all four Gospels into a single narrative, are not new. It has been an ongoing enterprise ever since the early followers of Jesus were left with a plurality of Gospels. It was Tatian, a second-century Syrian Christian, who initiated the compression of the Gospel in his *Diatessaron* (Harmony of Four). Since then there have been many such compositions which peaked in the sixteenth century. McArthur, in his survey of the Gospel harmonies, reckoned that it was this century that produced 'more harmonies' than the combined efforts of the preceding centuries.[1] While ecclesiastical authorities tried to control the unwieldy and awkward texts and make them into a suitable shape, the same century saw the emergence of Spain and Portugal as colonial powers on a mission to conquer, count, measure and improve the wild and unruly people and to make them conform to Western civilizational norms.

While *The Precepts* was the first single account of Gospel narratives to be produced outside Europe, Roy seemed to be aware of the existence of such Gospel compilations. He argued that his motivation was not that different from these Western Gospel harmonies. But with his characteristically upper-class confidence Roy claimed that the 'parts so selected' in his *Precepts* were 'superior' to the existing Gospel harmonies. The earlier European harmonies were largely devotions and meditations. They had fourfold aims. One, to edify the faithful by presenting a chronological and a comprehensive picture of Jesus; two, to streamline multiple, especially duplicate textual traditions into a single narrative; and third, to refute the critics who exposed the inconsistencies of the Gospels by pointing out their palpable similarities; and fourth, to demonstrate the astonishing trustworthiness of the accounts of the life of Jesus in spite of their contradictions.

But there was one significant difference between Roy's and the European compilations. Whereas a seventeenth-century harmonist offered his work as an apologetic defence against 'Jews and Turks',[2] Roy was trying to safeguard the Gospels from Christians, who in his view wrongfully presented the message, especially the Baptist missionaries who were obsessed with Trinitarian beliefs, heathenish notions of miracles and fiendish ideas of blood sacrifice. While the European compilations were basically an answer to the critics from outside the Church, with a view to offering comfort to traditional believers, Roy, a Hindu outsider, freed the Gospels from the Christian interpreters who injected the narratives with heathenish notions and unscriptural elements, and presented his *Precepts* as a means of improving the 'the hearts and minds of men of different persuasions and degrees or understanding'.[3] He claimed that his *Precepts* had a useful and noble aim. He saw his single Gospel narrative as a potential instrument for instructing Hindus of their 'civil duties' and directing Christians to the genuine words of the founder of their religion.

Unlike the Gospel harmonies of the West, Roy was not keen on weeding out duplicates and repetitions found across the Gospel narratives. The retention of Matthew's and Mark's versions of the Parable of the Sower, Mark and Luke's tellings of Widow's mites, and Matthew's and Luke's version of the Lord's Prayer is illustrative of this trend. The repetition of the widow's story could be attributed to his own experience of witnessing the exploitation of widows by his own Brahmanical leadership, and his championing of their cause. His declaration that he had found no other prayer which is 'so brief, so comprehensive, and suitable to man's wants' could be the reason for his preservation of both Matthew's and Luke's version of the Lord's Prayer.[4]

Roy's *Precepts* emerged before biblical critics developed source criticism and two-source theories. He collapsed all the four Gospels into one comprehensive tract, thus erasing the individuality of each of the Gospel writers, their diverse theological stances and the variety of communities for whom they were composed. Thus the individual Gospels were reduced to virtually indistinguishable entities containing ethical codes.

The Improved Version

The Bible versions that Roy used reveal both his familiarity with various versions of the Bible and the easy availability and access of these versions in colonial India. Although his *Precepts* was a straightforward reproduction of the King James Bible, which was marketed by the British and Foreign Bible Society as the book which the emperor read, Roy cited from the Improved Version – a controversial text produced by the Unitarians in 1808 – in his scriptural disagreements with the missionaries. He summoned this text at least ten times to support his theological arguments which resonated with this Unitarian version. Apparently, the Improved Version was in use in the Unitarian circles in Calcutta. Roy, in his letter to Thomas Belsham, under whose editorship the version was published, called it 'as unquestionably the best of all versions' and stated that the 'numerous essential benefits'[5] he had gained from this version were impossible to estimate, and he wished that there were more copies available. He even expressed his gratitude to the editors by stating that 'the Christian world is indebted to its eminently learned authors'.[6]

The purpose of this contentious version, as the introduction put it, was to provide the English reader with (a) a more accurate text of the New Testament, which was 'as nearly to the apostolical and evangelical originals',[7] (b) to take advantage of the then emerging modern textual criticism and especially divest the text of its doctrinal components, such as the Trinity, which had no foundation in the Scriptures, and (c) to emphasize the human dignity of Jesus, which made all humans aspire to 'the consummate humanity of Christ'.[8] Apart from questioning the divine status of Jesus, the editors of the version challenged several of the stock creedal statements, which included the atonement and the accompanying doctrine of Christ's vicarious suffering, and they also rejected the scriptural notion that salvation was limited to a few. The editors also disputed the authenticity of some of the books in the received canon such as the Epistle to the Hebrews, the Letter of James, 2 Peter, 2 and 3 John, Jude and Revelation. Students of biblical studies would be familiar with the long drawn out ecclesiastical battles before these books were accepted into the canon. The editors, in their generosity, permitted reading of these books in public assemblies but warned that they were not to be taken as a 'sufficient proof of any doctrine'.[9]

What is crucial to our current concern is the comment made by the anonymous author in his introduction to the Improved Version regarding the canon and the choice of the books, which would have had some impact on Roy when he was engaged in compiling *The Precepts*. Although the author declared that no person had any right to determine the canonical or apostolical authority of any biblical book, he also gave freedom to the reader: 'every sincere and diligent inquirer has a right to judge for himself, after due examination, what he is to receive as the rule of his faith and practice'.[10] Especially the last line might have been swirling in Roy's mind while he was preparing his tract.

This Improved Version could have been influential in Roy leaving out the early chapters of Matthew and Luke, which the editors of the Improved Version assuredly affirmed were later insertions, especially the miraculous conception of Jesus as 'probably the fiction of some early gentile convert, who hoped, by elevating the dignity of the Founder, to abate the popular prejudice against the sect'.[11] While the Improved Version formatted these passages in italics and placed them within brackets, Roy simply removed them.

Roy made use of the Improved Version to substantiate his claim that the unity of the Father and Son were not oneness of nature but 'perfect concord of will'.[12] Roy was not as adventurous as the Unitarians' Bible. He never expressed 'the least doubt as to the truth of any part of the Gospels'[13] but simply reproduced the KJV text without challenging its veracity. Whereas the Improved Version not only vigorously questioned the doctrinal claims of the text even before the Jesus Seminar came out with different colour codes to determine the relative reliability of the sayings of Jesus, the creators of the Improved version used different fonts to highlight the texts which they deemed as fake. Roy did not attempt any such inventive methods that caused much annoyance to the purists but he saved their agony by simply redacting them.

Translations

Roy was an inveterate translator. His translation efforts put him slightly above biblical translators such as Wycliffe. Whereas Wycliffe rendered the Bible into English, Roy was involved in translating both his own scriptures into English and the English Bible into his mother tongue. He faced a similar linguistic conservatism from his own Bengalees when he translated Sanskrit texts into Bengali. Just as the early European translators were accused of rendering the Bible into vulgar languages such as English and German, Roy was indicted for rendering 'chaste ornate language' such as Sanskrit into Bengali, seen as an 'undisciplined vulgar tongue'.[14] Roy desired that his people understand and examine their own scriptures in their own language.

Roy was blatantly harsh about the English translation of the Bible. He found the English version full of 'mistranslations' and 'errors'. He blamed this on the doctrinal and linguistic biases of English translators. These inaccuracies were due to the preoccupation of the translators with 'the idiom of English language' rather than with the original meaning. He castigated the English Bible translators for violating the original texts by adding their own phrases. A notable example, he drew attention to was Gen. 27. When the text said 'God created man in his image', the translation became, 'in his *own* image'. He wondered whether the addition was simply an 'energy of expression'? Of several erroneous renditions, Roy noted a couple of examples. One was Isa. 9.6. Roy showed how translating a definite article in Hebrew into an indefinite article in the Greek version gave the contemporary event an appearance of a prediction. The passage, he pointed out, referred to Hezekiah, the son of Ahaz, emblematically designated as the son of the virgin. This had nothing to do with Jesus. His argument was that once Hebrew texts were placed in their original historical contexts, the Gospel stories would lose their prophetic import and implications. Other examples included the biblical phrases 'everlasting fire' and 'everlasting punishments'. Much to the annoyance of Roy, these expressions found their way into the missionary preaching of the time, which terrorized the hapless Bengalis. He clarified that the original Greek term denoted duration or ages and as such these terms should have been rendered as 'durable fire' or 'durable punishments'. To buttress his case he also pointed out that when 'everlasting' was applied to an object which was not divine it 'implied long duration'. A vivid example of this was the verse from the book of Genesis: 'And I will give unto thee, and to thy seed after thee, the land wherein thou art a stranger, all the land of Canaan, for an everlasting possession' (17.8).

He also found the Bengali Bible translation wanting. He collaborated with two Baptist missionaries, Adams and Yeats, in translating the Bengali Bible. He admitted that in his life he had not undertaken such a 'difficult task as the translation of the New Testament into Benglee'.[15] It was so difficult that he often left many passages for future consideration. He conceded that it was not easy to find suitable Asiatic terminologies for English or Semitic idioms and ideas. He also disputed with the *Proposed Version of Theological Terms* planned by William Hodge Mill and Horace Hayman Wilson for Bible translation. He found that their proposal relied too much on the occidental use of the terms as employed in ancient writings than using the current usage of terms by Indians. One of the terms he questioned was Deva for *theos*, which he felt was vague and general.[16]

His translations of the Vedas had several hermeneutical intentions aimed at convincing both Christians and his fellow Hindus. He was keen to prove to his

'European friends' that the superstitious practices which discredit Hindu religion had 'nothing to do with the pure spirit of its dictates!'[17] He perceived his mission as reminding the West that what was projected as Hinduism had no sanction from the Hindu scriptures. He also wanted to introduce Europeans to Hindu 'doctrinal scriptures' which they 'seldom translate[d]' and to which they paid less attention largely due to Western Orientalists' over excessive interest in the Puranas, prurient moral tales. He reprimanded Western Orientalists who had a penchant for all Smritis (that which is remembered) to the superior Śrutis (that which is revealed). He called the former the 'atheistical works' which were in contradiction to the Vedas, and, worse still, they were not conducive to 'future happiness'.[18] He also wanted to wean the attention of the missionaries away 'from the superstitious rites and habits daily encouraged and fostered by their self-interested leaders'.[19]

Roy believed that efforts in translation would be beneficial to his fellow Bengalees. He strongly felt that if his people read the scriptures in their own mother tongue they would come to know that '*the real spirit of the Hindu scriptures which is but the declaration of the unity of God*' (emphasis in original)[20] and that the unity of the Godhead was innate to their scriptures. He also expected that reading the scriptures for themselves would help his fellow Hindus to realize that idolatry was not the norm and that the Vedas tolerated it as the 'last provision'[21] for those who were totally unable to train their minds to contemplate the incomprehensible character of the God of Nature and that the Vedas inculcated only the enlightened worship of one God. Roy offered his translations as a way out of the divisive corruptions while retaining Indian self-respect by rediscovering Hindu monotheism and the truth of one Supreme Being.

Roy hoped that reading the ancient texts in the vernacular would have another benefit. It would make his fellow Bengalese understand, examine and compare their own scriptures with that of the Christian Bible and reflect for themselves 'in what respect one excels the other in purity'[22] and thus make them 'happy and comfortable both here and hereafter'.[23] Roy also had a vested interest in translating these ancestral texts. He believed that if his fellow Bangalis read the scriptures in their own language, they would appreciate the type of Hinduism he was trying to recover and promote rather than doubt his version and fall prey to the wilful misinterpretations of the crafty priests.

As he wrote in the *Brahmanical Magazine*, it was the 'compassion' that he had for his fellow Hindus that compelled him to produce these vernacular versions. His desire was to 'use every possible effort to awaken them from their dream of error, and by making them acquainted with their scriptures, enable them to contemplate with true devotion the unity and omnipresence of Nature's God'.[24] He hoped that his labours to translate the texts would make Hindus come to know the pure essence of the Hindu religion that was depicted in the Vedas. He resolutely believed that his own people should not be kept in ignorance and that the true foundation of their belief should be made known to all.

Roy's Bengali renditions had both credit and debit sides. His translations of the Vedic texts gave access to the textual and philosophical glories of India's past which went unnoticed and were underplayed during the Mughal rule. These textual resources have now become available to those who had forgotten the past and did not have the benefit of Sanskrit to appreciate the ancient glories. Unfortunately, access is limited to a particular group of high-class Bengalis.

Notes

1. H.K. McArthur, *The Quest Through the Centuries: The Search for the Historical Jesus* (Philadelphia, PA: Fortress Press, 1966), 86.
2. Ibid., 88.
3. Roy, *The English Works of Raja Rammohun Roy*, 686.
4. M. Monier-Williams, 'Indian Theistic Reformers', *Journal of the Royal Asiatic Society of Great Britain and Ireland New Series* 13, no. 1 (1881): 10.
5. Roy, *The Correspondence of Raja Rammohun Roy*, vol. 1, 174.
6. Roy, *The English Works of Raja Rammohun Roy*, 832.
7. T. Belsham, 'Introduction', in *The New Testament in an Improved Version, Upon the Basis of Archbishop Newcome's New Translation; with a Corrected Text, and Notes Critical and Explanatory*, xxvi (Boston, MA: Society for Promoting Christian Knowledge and Practice of virtue by the Distribution of Books, 1809).
8. Ibid., v.
9. Ibid., vii.
10. Ibid., vi.
11. *The New Testament in an Improved Version, Upon the Basis of Archbishop Newcome's New Translation; with a Corrected Text, and Notes Critical and Explanatory* (Boston: Thomas B.Wait and Company, 1809), 2.
12. Roy, *The English Works of Raja Rammohun Roy*, 822.
13. Ibid., 567.
14. S.K. Das, 'Rammohun: His Religious Thought', in *Rammohun Roy: A Bi-Centenary Tribute*, ed. R. Niharranjan (New Dehli: National Book Trust, 1974), 73.
15. Roy, *The English Works of Raja Rammohun Roy* 885.
16. Roy, *The Correspondence of Raja Rammohun Roy*, vol. 1, unpaginated.
17. Roy, *Translation of Several Principal Books*, 4.
18. Roy, *The English Works of Raja Rammohun Roy*, 162.
19. Roy, *Translation of Several Principal Books*, 57.
20. Roy, *The English Works of Raja Rammohun Roy*, 90.
21. Ibid., 21.
22. Ibid., 907.
23. Ibid., 929.
24. Ibid., 5.

Chapter 8

HEATHENISH AND IRRATIONAL DOCTRINES

The Baptist missionaries bore the brunt of Roy's ire when he accused them of making up doctrines which were not part of the teachings of Jesus and were a challenge to reason and logic. What the missionaries hailed as the 'grand doctrines',[1] Roy treated sniffily as 'self-contradictory creeds' and 'strange doctrines'. These complicated creedal statements were, in his view, both a deterrent to Indians understanding the truths of Christianity and an embarrassment to the intelligence of Western Christians.

Incarnation

Roy not only questioned the claim of the missionaries that the incarnation of Christ was a unique event but also undermined it further by placing the incarnated Jesus within the pantheon of Hindu avatars. Roy stated with his usual confidence that the incarnations of Ram and Jesus were foretold in the holy books of the Hindus and Christians, especially that of Ram more than 4,000 years ago 'in the most precise and intelligible language; not in those ambiguous and equivocal terms found in the Old Testament', which had undoubtedly caused reservations about Christ being the real manifestation of God. Roy delineated the parallels between these two saviour figures. Ram was the divine son of Dushuruth of the tribe of Ragu, whereas Jesus was the reputed son of Joseph of the tribe of Judah. Both were tempted while on earth, performed wonderful miracles suspected by the unbelievers as the work of *asuri sakti* (demonical spirit) in the case of Ram and by the power of Beelzebub in the case of Jesus. Both ascended up to heaven and are worshiped even today by millions. Such simplistic correspondences between Ram and Jesus simultaneously helped Hindus who were unfamiliar with this Semitic figure to recognize and welcome him as one of their incarnations and at the same time downgraded him to the status of the multiple Indian avatars. These over simple resemblances signalled a crucial theological point – that the manifestation of God was not confined to Judea alone but also extended 'to all places and persons'. Stated differently, God's disclosure was not strictly confined to the land of the Israelites only. Roy remarked in his sharp way that if Christians claimed that God could take the form of man and even that of a dove in Judea then there was 'every possibility that the deity also should design to appear in the human shape for similar reasons in India'.[2] Hindus, as believers in incarnations, would not have doubted for a moment that a God who had assumed the form of an Israelite would not manifest in another part of Asia. It was in his dispute with Tytler, an East India Company doctor, that Roy was forced to demonstrate and clarify the parallels between Ram and Jesus. Otherwise, he was not keen to project Jesus as another Hindu avatar with all the paraphernalia that would have fitted in well with popular Hindu avatar stories. Such a framing of Jesus as an incarnated being, Roy feared, would undermine Jesus's moral teachings, which he earnestly believed India needed badly and urgently for her political and social rejuvenation.

For Roy, all incarnated beings including Jesus were sent by the Almighty from time to time 'to afford mental rest to mankind' and to 'impart to them the comforts of divine revelation'. These incarnated figures, in Roy's reckoning, never considered themselves as the 'incarnations of the divine essence' but only as fulfilling 'the commission given them by God'. Roy was not averse to the adoration of Jesus. Although he was sceptical about the idea of incarnation, he urged his fellow Hindus to treat Christians who believed in such a phenomenon in the same friendly manner as they would act towards their own who meditate upon Rama and other supposed incarnations without forming any external images of them.[3]

All these clarifications and commendations of Roy would have looked reckless to Marshman. Horrified by Roy's outlandish perceptions of incarnation, Marshman, in his predictable denunciatory tone, accused Roy, this 'intelligent heathen', of opposing the '*grand design* of the Saviour's becoming incarnate'.[4]

Atonement

Roy raised a number of objections to one of the fundamental doctrines of the Baptists – the atonement. Firstly, it was unscriptural. He drew attention to the fact that atonement as a divine sacrificial institution was 'not represented in any of the sacred books'. He maintained that even when sacrifices were mentioned, they were intended for people who were 'unaccustomed to the worship of God in truth and spirit'.[5] Secondly, he found the idea of the atoning power of death incompatible with the nature of God. He argued that the two-nature theory of Jesus being both God and Man was used as a way of justifying this baffling doctrine. With tongue firmly in cheek, Roy posed a question to the missionaries: in what form – human or divine – was the saving work of Jesus carried out? If Jesus suffered vicariously in his divine form, this would be 'highly inconsistent with the nature of God, which' is 'above being rendered liable to death or pain'. If, on other hand, Jesus sacrificed himself in his human capacity, this would go against the notion of divine justice by putting an 'innocent person to a painful death' – an innocent man who never transgressed the will of God being sacrificed on the cross for the crimes committed by others. Thirdly, it was inconsistent with the idea of human justice. It was an infringement of human justice that God should wash away the sins of theft, robbery and murder, thus disregarding 'individual sufferings' of the victims. If the sins had been washed away, then Roy reckoned that it was presumptuous on the part of Christians to punish criminals whose sins had already been forgiven through the vicarious death of Jesus. Roy drew attention to the Gospel accounts such as the scenes in Gethsemane which showed very clearly how Jesus who was offering himself as a sacrifice agonized over it and was hesitant to go through with it.

The atonement also went against the mercy of God and was restricted to those who placed their faith in God. It was seen as a bargaining process and 'proceeded from a reciprocal consideration'. This meant millions of people were damned to die in sin for not being prepared to enter into the necessary bargain by putting their faith in him in return for his forgiveness of their sins. The doctrine also discriminated against those who were 'saved through a virtuous life and sincere repentance'.[6]

Roy was not simply critical of the doctrine of Atonement but recast it in a number of new ways. First, using his expertise in Oriental languages, he clarified that the ransom of God in Hebrew, Arabic or Persian expressed 'extreme attachment or obedience, without implying an actual sacrifice as an atonement for sins'.[7] He cited different translations to support his case. For instance, to clear the confusion caused by the rendition of Zech. 12.10, he referred to the Arabic Bible and the Septuagint to bolster his argument. Second, he turned one of the foundations of evangelical Christianity into an act of practical help and moral duty rather than pacifying a wrathful God. He reminded the missionaries that Jesus himself frequently declared that he saved the people 'solely through the inculcation of the word of God': 'Now ye are clean through the word which I have spoken unto you' (Jn 15.3). Third, he revamped atonement not as a reparation done by someone on behalf of others but as something done by people themselves. It is a kind of a practical, mutual help Christianity. He redefined one's duty to God and to our fellow human beings as the 'most acceptable atonement on our part to the All-merciful'. He reconfigured the doctrine of atonement in terms of practical help and moral duty rather than through juridical images of expiation. Now God can be propitiated by works. One could be saved on account of good deeds. Finally, Roy revised the atonement not as a stand-in suffering but as an illustration of Jesus's courage in 'executing the commands of God' and his death as a 'self-devotion or sacrifice' which no Jewish high priest had ever surpassed. The sacrifice of Jesus was not a vicarious suffering but a striking illustration of his bravery in fulfilling God's commission. This, Roy firmly believed, was what the Scriptures taught.

For Roy what procures salvation is not the ritual sacrifice of someone or taking refuge in the cross but sincere repentance alone as required by the redeemer. Roy cited the Parable of the Prodigal Son as the supreme example of the contrition which led to his redemption. Roy reminded the missionaries that the chief object of the mission of Jesus was calling sinners to repent. To support his claim that it was not sacrifice but repentance that was the central message, Roy provided a string of quotations from Jesus and also from the Hebrew prophets. The argument of Marshman had been that to lead a life of 'peace and happiness' mere moral commandments or examples of self-devotions were not enough. What was needed was a saviour to judge humanity for its depraved state. In other words, Marshman wanted a Christ who could convict sinners.

To summarize: the idea that God in human form should atone for the sins of humanity had no scriptural sanction. The Scriptures have examples of God forgiving righteous and good people. The way to achieve salvation and to find favour with God is an uncomplicated human activity which does not involve sacrificial death. For Roy, the best and the only means of obtaining the forgiveness of our sins is 'to keep his commandments'.[8] Or, as Jesus told the lawyer 'This do and THOU SHALT Live'[9] (Lk. 10.28). What was clearly an action of God, Roy turned into an action of human beings.

The Trinity

In his debate with the missionaries, Roy expressed his exasperation with the doctrine of the Trinity: 'I regret that notwithstanding very great mental exertions, I am unable to attain a comprehension of this creed.'[10] Roy challenged a doctrine, which was a punishable offence. At least eight people were burnt at the stake between 1548 and 1612 for questioning it.[11] Roy regarded the doctrine as the case of the divine setting forth a 'system of perfect polytheism'. He clearly stated that his 'reverence for Christianity and for the author of this religion', had prompted him 'to vindicate it from the charge of polytheism'.[12]

As with the other doctrines, Roy dismissed the Trinity as unscriptural stating that he had 'attentively read the Bible of the Christians', and to his great astonishment he did not 'find any explanation of the Trinity in that book'.[13] Roy wondered why Marshman, who fondly called it the 'Ever-blessed Trinity', should consider this creed as an essential and integral part of the apostolical preaching, when there was no evidence of it in their discourses to the early converts. Roy blamed the fourth Gospel for being the source for this mysterious doctrine, which proved to be an obstacle to Hindus, Muslims and Chinese: he remarked that the Chinese would find the Christian claim that there are three gods, one of whom died, 'bewildering and ridiculous'.[14]

Roy also felt that the idea of God in three persons went against the 'self-evident perfection of God's nature'. The spirit of the Bible was, he repeatedly stressed, 'The Lord our God is one Lord.' He also disputed some of the biblical verses used for justifying the triune nature of God. One such example was 'our likeness', 'our image' found in Gen. 1.26, used as proof of the doctrine, which in Roy's view showed total disregard for the idiomatic nuances of Hebraic, Arabic and Asiatic languages in which the plural was used instead of the singular to express respect to a person. In any case, such a claim was contradicted in the next verse which was in the singular: 'So God created man in his own image.'

Roy envisaged his task as vindicating the Gospel 'from the charge of polytheism'. Using his knowledge of church history based on the work of Johann Mosheim's *Institutes of Ecclesiastical History Ancient and Modern,* he argued that the doctrine was a late comer and introduced only in the fourth century after violent discussion supported by the 'authority of a monarch'. The approval of the Council of Nicaea in favour of three persons in the Godhead could be easily accounted for. The majority of the converts including the emperor were Gentiles for whom the idea of a plurality of God was perfectly acceptable. Roy feared that the idea of God in three persons would encourage the Hindu sects who profess polytheistic ideas to believe that it is reasonable to hold on to these ideas.

Roy found the missionaries 'deficient in discretion'. The more zeal they showed in support of the Triune God, the more they exposed Christianity to the ridicule of Hindus and Muslims. He had pity for the Chinese. His argument was that one cannot give a satisfactory rational explanation for the doctrine of the Trinity. He wondered how Christians who claimed that they had a 'cultivated understanding' in spiritual matters could justify and mislead the Indian people. His advice to Christians was that it was profitable to give up the doctrine altogether rather than advancing convoluted augments to validate it. Roy's unequivocal verdict was that people with 'possession of senses' would find it 'morally impossible' to get converted to the Trinitarian Christianity which the missionaries were keen to promote and determined to defend.

Holy Spirit

Roy refused to grant the Holy Spirit an equal status with God, or as one of the persons of Godhead. In other words, he refused to treat the Holy Spirit as a deity possessing a separate personality, as the missionaries believed. He claimed that there was no single passage in the whole of the Scriptures that advocated such an assertion. To think of the Holy Spirit as a 'distinct personage' would result in forming a 'very strange notion of the theology of the Bible', he told the missionaries. The title he gave to the chapter on the Holy Spirit in his Second Appeal – 'The Impersonality of the Holy Spirit' – is very revealing and indicative of his thinking. Harnessing a swathe of biblical texts, he proved that the Holy Spirit did not have any separate existence or any distinct personality. The Holy Spirit, in his view, did not have any particular bodily form or shape. In his habitual fashion, he rightly posed an awkward question to the missionaries: 'For, if we believe that the Spirit, in the form of a dove, or in any other *bodily shape*, was really the third person of the Godhead, how can we justly charge with absurdity the Hindoo legends of the Divinity having the form of a fish or of any other animal?'[15]

As with the doctrine of the atonement, Roy did not simply criticize the idea of the Holy Spirit, but he came up with his own reconfiguration of it, obviously resonating with his hermeneutical needs and ideals. For him, the Holy Spirit represented simply the 'holy influence of God', the power of God. A noticeable example of such a miraculous influence of God was when it came upon Mary resulting in the birth of a child. Roy informed the missionaries that this way of interpreting the Holy Spirit as influence and power of God, would be consistent with and strengthen the belief in the Divine Power without damaging the unity and the purity of the deity. In Roy's envisioning, the Holy Spirit was the influence of God which directed the righteous to truth and enabled them to seek heartily

God's will. He was quick to remind the missionaries that such examples of divine power and God's influence were found in India as well.

Roy even daringly suggested how to reconstruct biblical sentences which were inconsistent with the unity of the Godhead and posed theological awkwardness in presenting Jesus as the second person of the Triad relationship. He suggested alternative renditions and was willing to rewrite the Word of God. Illustrative of some of his alternative suggestions are: to change 'He shall baptize you with the Holy Ghost and with power' to 'He shall baptize you with the spirit of truth and power'; 'God anointed Jesus of Nazareth with Holy Ghost and with power' to ' God anointed Jesus of Nazareth with his holy influence and power'; 'blasphemy against the Holy Ghost shall not be forgiven unto men' to 'blasphemy against the power of God shall not be forgiven to men'; and 'Jesus being full of the Holy Ghost, returned from Jordan' to 'Jesus being full of the influence of God, returned from Jordan.'

To bring this chapter to a close, there are four principal reasons that led Roy to challenge the creedal statements of Christianity that he thought were more a hinderance than a help for the Christian cause. One, as he repeatedly reminded the missionaries, these Christian creeds had no scriptural authorization. His constant mantra was: 'I cannot help refusing my assent to any doctrine which I do not find scriptural.'[16]

Two, these doctrines were thrust on people who were totally unprepared to receive them. He accused the missionaries of completely counteracting their own noble efforts by introducing dogmas and mysteries taught in Western churches to 'people by no means prepared to receive them'. He felt that his fellow Bengalis were unable to reconcile these dogmas because they had totally 'unprepared understandings' of them. Three, doctrinal affirmations were the cause of division and discord among Western Christians and he did not want these dissensions to be replicated in India. He contended that it was unreasonable to subject the people of India to Western doctrinal battles in which they had no part or interest. Knowing church history well, he drew attention to the disputes among the followers of Jesus, triggered by different interpretations of the doctrines. He believed that such doctrinal disputes had destroyed harmony and union among various Christian denominations which resulted in wars and bloodshed more dreadful than between Christians and infidels. Fourth, he found it offensive and shameful when several of the Christian creedal phrases were used in an irreverent manner by Bengalese in their vernacular writings and literature.

All that Roy wanted to do was to cleanse the 'pure religion of Jesus' from doctrinal 'stigma'. For Roy, 'the idea of a Triune God, a man-God, and also the idea of the appearance of God in the bodily shape of a dove, or that of the blood of God shed for the payment of a debt, seem entirely heathenish and absurd, consequently their conversion to Trinitarian Christianity is morally impossible.'[17] He was very clear that any Indian with 'common sense and common honesty' would never be persuaded to 'believe in their self-contradictory creed[s]'. Another of his statements captures this point very intensely: 'The doctrines which the missionaries maintain and preach are less conformable with reason than those professed by Moosulmans, and in several points equally absurd with the popular Hindu creed.'[18]

8. Heathenish and Irrational Doctrines

Finally, let me recapitulate the position of the missionaries and Roy. The response of Marshman, who believed in the sufficiency of the Scriptures, was that since these doctrines were taught in the 'Sacred Word', people should not 'cavil against them' but 'manifest the most cordial submission' to them. In other words, submit to the Scriptures. Roy's apposite retort, which he uttered in annoyance at the obduracy of the missionaries, was: 'how far *their* doctrines are agreeable to reason', when most of them were unscriptural. He took it upon himself to introduce the idea of reason and logic to religion, and urged especially his fellow Bengalese to use their intellectual powers in such matters.

Notes

1. *A Defence of Some Important Scripture Doctrines*, 108.
2. Roy, *The Correspondence of Raja Rammohun Roy*, vol. 1, 328.
3. Roy, *The English Works of Raja Rammohun Roy*, 212.
4. Marshman, *A Defence of the Deity and Atonement of Jesus Christ*, 1, italics in original.
5. Roy, *The English Works of Raja Rammohun Roy*, 700.
6. Ibid., 196.
7. Ibid., 717.
8. Roy, *The English Works of Raja Rammohun Roy*, 552.
9. Capitalization in original.
10. Ibid., 188.
11. F.E. Mineka, *The Dissidence of Dissent: The Monthly Repository, 1806–1838* (Chapel Hill: University of North Carolina Press, 1944), 7.
12. Roy, *The English Works of Raja Rammohun Roy*, 665.
13. Ibid., 187.
14. Ibid., 558.
15. Ibid., 620, italics in original.
16. Ibid., 630.
17. Ibid., 881–882.
18. Ibid., 881.

Chapter 9

MODEST PROPOSALS, UNEXPLAINED PROPOSITIONS

Roy had the habit of advancing ideas and then failing to expound them explicitly in detail. One is monotheism and the other is the moral precepts of Jesus, both of which he was passionate about and keen to promote.

Roy claimed that monotheism was superior but never explained why. There is no clue as to where he picked up the idea. Probably at Patna where he was supposed to have spent time at a Madrasa. By insisting on monotheism as a single centre, Roy deprived many who found themselves comfortable with a pluralistic, polytheistical way of experiencing religiosity. He was condescendingly dismissive of those involved in such practices as incapable of comprehending the worship of one true god without any discernible physical objects. Roy was not the first Hindu to discover or advocate monotheistic ideals. Monotheism was not new in India as Müller remarked in his *A History of Ancient Sanskrit Literature*: 'There is a monotheism which precedes the polytheism of the Veda, and even in the invocations, of their innumerable gods, the remembrance of a God, one and finite, breaks through the midst of an idolatrous phraseology, like the blue sky that is hidden by passing clouds.'[1] Before Roy, there were the sixteenth- and seventeenth-century bhakti poets who had an unshakable belief in one, non-incarnate, eternal, formless and indescribable God. They followed the path independent of the dominant religions of the time – Islam or Hinduism. They criticised superstitious Hindu practices and the caste system, and they questioned Brahminism and their scriptures. The difference was that Roy and his Hindu adherents in colonial India faced a new threat – Christianity, the religion of the conquers of Hindustan. More specifically, they faced incessant slanderous misrepresentation of Hinduism by the missionaries.

The monotheistic God that Roy so fervently promoted was a remote and a transcendent being to be extolled and adored from afar without any chance of mystical union which later Hindu reformers and Christian theologians advocated and cherished. This deity, which Roy endorsed eagerly, remained a detached one and did not emerge as an ethical exemplar to be emulated or to be followed. The theological sophistication that he found in monotheistic ideals failed to recognize that the Greeks with their plurality of Gods and Goddesses were far more superior philosophically and cerebrally than the Jews with their notion of a single God. His advocacy of love towards fellow human beings sounded like an abstract principle of universal benevolence. It was devoid of any romantic or filial love. It was rational, compassionate, being of service to one another without any personal, familial or sexual ties or special relationships.

Roy's abstract, impersonal monotheistic ideal appealed only to a few in the Hindu elite. Instead of exclusively championing a single revered centre such as monotheism, Roy, knowing very well the pluralistic context of India, should have worked out a paradigm in which monotheism was not at war with polytheism but sat alongside it. Thus, providing options for people with different levels of spirituality to experience the divine. A polytheistic mode of thinking has one added advantage in that it can accommodate monotheistic ideals within its framework. Roy, who scrupulously catalogued the evils of polytheism, did not name a single atrocity done on behalf of the monotheistic god. The well-worn cliché example is the warmongering monotheistic god of the Christian crusaders.

Roy's other idea that went undefined was the morality of Jesus. Roy was convinced that his fellow Indians should know the moral teachings of Jesus but he was quite reticent about identifying what these morals were. In his frugal explanation, he confined himself to a few sentences from Jesus.

His choice was limited to two sets of sayings of Jesus totalling nearly thirty-six words. One, the Golden Rule – 'do unto others as you would be done by',[2] which he first mentioned in his translation of Isha Upanishad and referred to in the introduction to *The Precepts* and again in his Second Appeal. The other is the greatest Commandment – 'love the Lord thy God with all thy heart, and with all thy soul, and with all thy mind, and Thou shalt love thy neighbour as thyself' – which is the summation of the law and the prophets. He was persuaded that these teachings would transform humanity at large. In his customary confident tone he declared that these teachings would help to 'reconcile us to human nature, and tend to render our existence agreeable to ourselves and profitable to the rest'.[3]

Roy acknowledged that the Golden Rule, which he called 'a grand and comprehensive moral principle', was not unique to Jesus but was 'partially taught also in every system of religion' that he was acquainted with, but he claimed that there was a difference in that it was 'principally inculcated by Christianity'.[4] But he did not provide any evidence as to how it was implemented in the Christian church. Like the Synoptic writers from whom he borrowed the code, Roy hardly clarified its content. The Golden Rule is rather a one-sided moral responsibility which obliges one to take care of one another without any reciprocal return. He never explained what these duties entailed and whether it included helping an elderly person to cross the road. He might have been attracted by the positive rendition of the Golden Rule in the Synoptics, whereas the Indian and Chinese versions formulate it negatively: 'That which you do not wish that people do to you, do not do to them.'

The other moral teaching that Roy referred to and characteristically did not develop in detail was the great Commandment to love thy God and love thy neighbour, which anyone familiar with biblical matters knows is a combination of Deuteronomy – 'You shall love the Lord your God with all your heart, and with all your soul, and with all your might' (6.5) – and Leviticus – 'love your neighbour as yourself' (19.18). Here again, he defined morals and moral duties in a vague sense to include 'our conduct to God, to each other, and to ourselves' that were 'calculated to elevate man's ideas to high and liberal notions of one God'. This is a simple morality which speaks about duty to God, duty to society and one's responsibility to communities. He was convinced that: 'Nothing so sublime as the precepts taught by Christ and that there is nothing equal to the simple doctrines he inculcated.'[5] Further, he failed to explain how this injunction is uniquely Christian. Although this maxim has various proximate correlated sayings in a number of world religions, Roy, in his inimitable pedantic way, declared to his Unitarian friends that this 'morality is no other than that of the gospel'.[6]

Besides these moral codes, Roy also referred to 'the blessed and benign moral doctrines taught in the Sermon on the Mount (containing the 5th, 6th, and 7th chapters of Matthew) which include therefore every duty of man, and all that is necessary to salvation'. Unlike Gandhi who explicitly stated that among the teachings of Jesus he was fond of the Sermon on the Mount and provided textual examples, Roy did not furnish any specific teaching of the Sermon on the Mount but only mentioned chapter numbers. There is no discussion as to why the Sermon on the Mount was attractive to him.

There could be two reasons for Roy's preference for the Golden Rule, the Greatest Commandment and the Sermon on the Mount: one, they were rationally and easily communicable but more pertinently practicable. They were all love in action in the world and not a retreat from the world which one strand of Hinduism advocated and that Roy opposed. Two, these ethical enactments were not linked to eschatology. Their potential did not depend on the realization of the kingdom of God which Roy eschewed but on the human ability to enact them.

A closer look at Roy's ethical proposal will reveal that it is Semitic in origin. The morality that Roy proposed was not original or unique to Jesus, but has roots in the Jewish tradition. The Golden Rule was seen as 'the sum of the Torah'. Nearly at the end of the Sermon on the Mount, the Golden Rule ends with the words 'for this is the Law and the Prophets'.

The placement and prominence accorded to the Law and the Prophets in the Sermon on the Mount was an indication of how much it is linked to the Jewish scriptures. The summation of the Greatest Commandment, too, concludes with a similar saying 'On these two commandments depend all the Law and the Prophets.' The Law and the Prophets meant the scriptures of the Jews – the first five books of Moses and the books of the prophets. What Jesus had reinforced was Moses's exhortation in Deut. 6 where it was required that love for God was to be lived in social obligation and obedience. In turn, Roy re-introduced, accidently or wilfully, the Jewish morality which is embedded in Jewish scriptural traditions. Roy need not have spent his energy looking for inspiration from the Jewish Scriptures. What is extolled by the Hebrew Scriptures is in all religious texts. The Qur'an with which he was familiar has a similar saying: 'Do good to near of kin, the neighbour, the companion at your side who is a stranger, and to the traveller' (4.36). All moral codes, including the Golden Rule and the Great Commandment are an ideal to aspire to and not easily realizable ethical principles.

Roy profoundly had an idealistic belief in the Golden Rule and the Great Commandment. In upholding the moral precepts Roy strengthened the idea that religious faith was an essential requisite for moral behaviour. The fact that one needs a mystical power to impel one to act morally is based on the assumption that human beings need some higher divine power to move them to act ethically. Humans do not need to invoke the name of gods or goddesses to live a moral life. The wisdom books of the Bible have plenty of examples of experiencing God through nature and one could learn about the human cooperation, social bonding and fortitude from the world of ants. For example, the good book says, look at the ants and learn from them (Prov. 6.6).

Notes

1. M.F. Müller, *A History Ancient Sanskrit Literature as so far it illustrates the Primitive Religion of the Brahmans*, 2nd rev. edn. (London: Williams and Norgate, 1860), 559.
2. Roy, *The English Works of Raja Rammohun Roy*, 74
3. Ibid., 483.
4. Ibid., 483.
5. Collet, *The Life and Letters of Raja Rammohun Roy*, 213.
6. 'An Account of the Life and Writings of Rammohun Roy', *The Monthly Repository* 15, no. 169 (1820): 2.

Chapter 10

TO CONVERT OR NOT TO CONVERT

Roy was exasperated and incensed by the unfair methods that missionaries used for converting Indians. He witnessed a great number of converted Indian Christians offering petitions to the highest ecclesiastical authorities stating how they were given inducements to give up their ancient religion through the 'false promises of advancement'.[1] Furthermore, he was unhappy with the threating language employed by Christian missionaries against those Hindus who refused to heed the Christian message. He was offended by words like 'hell fire and still hotter fire', awaiting those unrepentant Hindus. He pitied the Hindus who were poor and vulnerable and, more worryingly, lacked the spirit and theological and intellectual resources to withstand the relentless onslaught of the institutional might of various Christian denominations. Roy blamed the money and power of the missionaries which had blinded them from appreciating other perspectives or detecting their own doctrinal weaknesses. In the face of such harsh homiletical threats and duplicitous means of conversion, Roy felt that the Hindus were helpless and had to be protected.

Roy's knowledge of different religions enabled him to demonstrate to his fellow Hindus that there were no substantial differences between Hindu creeds and rituals and the majority of Christian doctrines and practices. Roy's familiarity with various religions provided him with enough expertise to pronounce confidently that virtues and falsehoods were 'common to all religions without distinction'.[2] Roy's deterrent memorandum to his fellow Hindus was that if the missionary message was simply about a triune God, an incarnated saviour figure and a vicarious sacrificial redeemer, then this Western imported faith had nothing new to say to India, and, more reassuringly, Indians need not needlessly worry about this invader's creed.

His message to Hindus was that there was no special spiritual benefit in converting to the type of Christianity presented by missionaries which was perceptibly no different from Hindu practices. A Hindu converting to Christianity, as he put it sharply, was like exchanging 'one set of polytheistical sentiments as a substitute for another set'.[3] He declared that the change would be like 'substituting the blood of God for the water of the Ganges as a purifying substance'.[4] For him, the popular practices of the majority of Christians such as idols, crucifixes, saints, miracles, relics, holy water, transubstantiation and other idolatrous machinery[5] were all similar to the ones followed by Hindus. He was convinced that the idolatrous gratifications of Hindus were no worse than those of Christians in Europe and America.

The Precepts and the controversy that followed enabled Roy to show that the Christianity practised by the missionaries was as polytheistic, irrational and immoral as the Hinduism that the missionaries criticized. His implied message to vulnerable Hindus was that there was no need for them to exchange one irrational system for another. His reply to Bishop Middleton who offered to make him the Apostle of India if he gave up his ancestral faith might sound apocryphal but it encapsulated what he stood for: 'My Lord, you are under a mistake. I have not laid down one superstition to take up another.'[6]

He argued throughout his debate with the missionaries that reason and the Bible did not encourage such a transfer of faith. The Bible was clear that a simple faith in the unity of God and moral conduct towards fellow human beings was enough to be accepted by God. He declared that these very precepts were found in all religions. When he was pushed by the American Unitarian Henry Ware, he wrote that reason had led him to believe what was stipulated in the Scripture, that 'in every nation he that *feareth* God and worketh *righteousness* is accepted with him'. He had no qualms in conceding that Christianity had a certain edge because of its involvement with progressive movements in the West. He went on to write that 'Nevertheless, I presume to think, that Christianity, if properly inculcated, has a greater tendency to improve the moral, and political state of mankind, than any other known religious system.'[7] He was clear about what was to be properly inculcated. It meant preaching pure theism without any encumbrances of doctrinal peculiarities and being good to fellow human beings.

It is often said that Roy was hospitable towards missionary work, but he extended his cooperation with some qualifications. He said that those who believed in one absolute Godhead and worshipped God in spirit, and showed compassion to fellow human being – the ultimate service to God – 'should be regarded by us with affection, on the ground of the object of their worship being same with us'. Roy informed his fellow Hindus that they should not be deterred by the fact that Christians claimed that Jesus was the messenger of God and their spiritual teacher. The faith in a singular God and service to humanity should 'produce attachment'[8] between Hindus and Christians. He condescendingly looked upon those Christians who ennobled and elevated Jesus to the status of a supreme God, and who constructed various images of him and used such images to convert Indians. He righteously instructed his country people that these misguided Christians should not be hated but must be shown 'compassion on account of their blindness to the errors into which they themselves have fallen'.[9]

Roy redefined who a Christian was and it was into this definition that he was trying to fit in the Hindus. Roy identified three types of Christians: those who believed the divine Trinity; those who acknowledged the Bible as the revealed word of God; and those who adhered to the doctrines of Christ, as taught by Jesus himself.[10] The last one went beyond the narrow definition imposed by the missionaries. It was into this broadest definition that Roy was willing to accommodate Indians. While Christian missionaries wanted to make Hindus into

Christians, Roy had a different objective. He anticipated the ethical energising of the Hindus through the moral teachings of Jesus while they held on to their Hindu beliefs.

Roy knew from history that the invader's religion would last a long time. Learning from the Mughal occupation of India and the impact of the Islamic faith that they brought with them had on the Indians, Roy anticipated that the Christianity that came with the British invaders would gradually envelop the Indian religious landscape. He was clear about the type of Christianity that would be suitable to Hindus without undermining their inherited Hindu tradition. He simultaneously opened the minds of Hindus to a *mleccha*[11] morality and at the same time firmly shut the door for Christian conversion and expansion.

Roy had his own vision of Christianity which was far from the narrowly defined faith offered by the Baptists at that time. He urged that the Christianity that missionaries proclaimed should represent 'all mankind as children of one eternal father' and it should 'enjoin them to love one another, without making any distinction of country, caste, colour, or creed' and manifest 'their respect towards each other, according to the property of their actions, and the reasonableness of their religious opinions and observance'.[12]

Notes

1. Roy, *The English Works of Raja Rammohun Roy*, 558.
2. Ibid., 943.
3. Ibid., 172.
4. Ibid., 882.
5. Ibid., 194.
6. Sen, *Rammohun Roy*, 86.
7. Roy, *The English Works of Raja Rammohun Roy*, 875.
8. Ibid., 212.
9. Ibid., 212.
10. Ibid., 483.
11. Mleccha, a Sanskrit term used in ancient India for people of foreign origin, not often favourably, just as the Greeks used barbarian.
12. Roy, *The English Works of Raja Rammohun Roy*, 920.

Chapter 11

THE MLECCHA AND HIS MORAL CODES

The date of Roy's first encounter with Jesus is not easy to determine. It is possible that Roy initially come across him not through the preaching of the missionaries but through his knowledge of the Qur'an, where Jesus is mentioned twenty-five times and the prophet Mohammed is referred to only four times. His *Tuhfat ul Muwahidin*, published before he encountered the missionaries, has references to the Koran, demonstrating his familiarity with Islamic learning and the work of Muslim rationalists. His three Appeals in defence of *The Precepts* also showed his knowledge of the Islamic holy book. He was supposed to have studied in a Patna Madrasa, but what sort of education he had remains a mystery. It is reasonable to assume that his early impression of Jesus could have been influenced by Islamic thinking. Although there is no direct textual evidence, it is possible that his idea of the oneness of God and Jesus as God's accredited messenger might have come through his familiarity with Koranic knowledge.

What is clear from his writings is that his intention was not to make Jesus another moral philosopher teaching 'God, virtue and immortality', as the missionaries envisaged. He did not want to turn the Jesus story into one of the mythological stories of India of which India had plenty. Such magical portrayals would weaken the moral message of Jesus, which Roy felt India needed urgently. Roy also did not want another redeemer in a country crowded with saviour figures. Instead, he fashioned a Jesus whose moral teachings could rejuvenate their spiritual slothfulness, social degradation, political apathy and usher in a new humanity without caste and religious distinctions.

Roy identified four prevailing opinions of Jesus: an expounder of the laws of God; a mediator between man and God; one of the three mysterious persons of the Godhead; and for Jews, a mere man. Roy's perception of Jesus comes nearer to the Jewish one. The Jesus that emerges in *The Precepts* is a complicated figure. The general perception is that Roy's Jesus is a harmless simple moral teacher. This is far from the truth. His Jesus, drawn from all four Gospels does not appear as an innocent dispenser of plain morals but a complex character exhibiting both virtuous and villainous characteristics. Besides the moral teachings of Jesus, *The Precepts* includes passages in which Jesus tells his hearers that the purpose of his coming was to bring disunity. He demands allegiance to him. It did not occur to Roy, who was full of admiration for the moral teachings of Jesus, that the same

Jesus was asking his followers to abandon families, kith and kin including children. This Jesus demands deference and discipleship. This is not the Jesus who preached social comfort, happiness and harmony but anticipated friction, tension and deep discord that his preaching would bring. He stipulates that his followers should give up personal and family obligations. He does not tolerate weak and flimsy excuses. Attending to creaturely needs, fulfilling filial duties and demonstrating love and loyalty were all frowned upon. His message of love your neighbour is mixed with curses and rebukes. Yes, certainly, he was a morally good, compassionate and self-giving man, but at the same time he was often aggressive, petulant and encouraged divisions within family. He is judgemental and divides people into saved and not saved. In *The Precepts*, Jesus comes across as a stern, humourless and almost a pedant Brahmin pundit. He constantly talks. *The Precepts* begins with the Sermon on the Mount and ends with the command: 'Ye are my friends, if ye do whatsoever I command you ... Ye have not chosen me, but I have chosen you, and ordained you, that ye should go and bring forth fruit, ... These things I command you, that ye love one another.' In between there is a continual torrent of one-sided dialogue with his disciples. Roy's Jesus comes across almost as an argumentative Indian.

Roy's admiration for Jesus and attraction to his teachings remained undiminished regardless of (1) his protracted and bitter disputes with the missionaries; and (2) the mixture of mythical and speculative elements in the Gospels' narrative life of Jesus. Unlike the later nineteenth-century Jesus questers, Roy was not attempting to discover a historical Jesus who would be the standard by which to appraise what Schweitzer called the 'Jesus Christ of the doctrine.'[1] For him, the norm was not the flesh and blood historical Jesus but the kerygma, the proclamation of Jesus. Before Käsemann, who revived the search for the historical Jesus through the kerygma after the impasse caused by historical criticism, Roy identified Jesus through his moral kerygma. But this kerygma, of course, had to be rescued and rinsed of its mythical and supernatural entanglements.

What is remarkable about *The Precepts* is the total absence of the stock orthodox images generally associated with Jesus. *The Precepts* does not announce the coming of Jesus, nor does it portray him as the only way to salvation. Roy's Jesus neither asserted any divine status nor possessed any divinity. This Jesus does not preach the Kingdom but 'obedience and love' towards God 'evinced by the practice of beneficence towards their fellow creatures'. He was not a saviour and did not vicariously suffer on behalf of people. He was not the risen Lord who dramatically impacted himself on believers and who induced dramatic internal changes in the lives of people.

Roy effortlessly dismissed Christological titles which had any semblance to Jesus's divine status or his divine connections such as the 'only begotten of God', 'the first born of God', 'the Holy One', 'the saviour' and 'the Messiah'. In his painstaking reading of the biblical texts and in a densely argued case, Roy was able to demonstrate that these titles were not exclusively conferred on Jesus. To the horror of the missionaries, he reminded them that the epithets such as 'the first born of God' and 'the Holy One' had already been applied to Jewish biblical figures like David and as such there was nothing unique about them. Roy made the missionaries aware that the 'Most Holy' need not refer to a person and could also mean inanimate objects such as an altar or an eating place. He identified a number of Saviours like Jesus who were 'human individuals' endowed with the power to save people by inculcating teaching or offering protection without the need for an atoning death. Roy cited Obadiah and Nehemiah who spoke of saviours who, unlike Jesus, redeemed people without shedding blood. He listed several Israelite kings on whom the title 'Messiah' was bestowed including Hezekiah. His point being that the 'use of this appellation does not serve to prove the deity of any of them'. The most that Roy was willing to grant Jesus was the title the Son of God, which he insisted should be interpreted in a non-mythical way. He conceded that this honour Jesus "*alone* deserves".[2] While endorsing this designation, Roy at the same time undermined it by claiming that the title Son of God was metaphorically applied to people of 'power and exalted rank'. Just like judges were called Lord, although they did not come from noble families. Jesus was such a person. The title Son of God was a conferment of a gift of God to Jesus rather than his innate inborn status.

Roy comes out with his own descriptions of Jesus which are a confusing picture of him as a mere human being while attributing to him divine qualities. Roy honours Jesus and at the same time desacralizes him. He is 'Superior' yet a subordinated and an inferior being. He is 'anointed and exalted' even 'above the angels of God' but seen as 'still a created being'. He dwelt with God 'before the creation of the world', loved by God 'before the foundation of the world', nonetheless, he was 'inferior to his Maker'. Roy quoted the Colossian verse to strengthen his argument that Jesus was the 'image of the invisible God, the first born of every creature' (Col. 1.15). But at the same time this laudable claim was diluted by listing a range of sayings which effectively removed the agency of Jesus and created the Father as the one who glorified Jesus and had given him power over all humanity.

Roy never accorded the divine status to Jesus that the missionaries invested him with but saw him only as 'the founder of truth and true religion', the 'author of Christianity', a 'guide to peace and happiness', 'an inspired teacher of righteousness', 'an accredited messenger from God',[3] the 'greatest prophet of God'[4] and in 'whom dwelt all truth.' He quotes several biblical passages to prove the natural 'inferiority of the Son to the Father'. The biggest accolade Roy bestowed on Jesus was that he was the 'spiritual Lord and King of Jews and Gentiles'. Roy's thesis all along had been that the doctrinal formulations about Jesus were 'introduced by some heathen writers to suit their polytheistic prejudices'.

Roy utilized to his advantage the self-description of Jesus and the perceptions of those who were closer to him to firm up his argument that he was not a divine figure. Roy recalled how Jesus spoke of himself 'throughout all the Scriptures only as the promised Messiah',[5] often 'compared himself to David or some of the other prophets'[6] and even the disciples called him 'prophet' after the crucifixion. All these were sufficient evidence of his human character. Roy interpreted the instances of worship or adoration of Jesus accorded to him in the Gospels by a blind person, a leper and by his own disciples, as the external marks of 'religious reverence' or a 'token of civil respect due to superiors'.

Although Roy was unapologetic in his belief in the moral authority of Jesus and not his divinity, he did not rule it out altogether, according some supernatural status to him. Roy subscribed to the idea of the pre-existence of Jesus, which described that 'Christ lived in the divine purpose and decree before the world was'. In Roy's estimation, Jesus was a great man, even a supernatural being but not God himself. He was endowed with the 'supernatural wisdom'. Whatever Jesus achieved, Roy declared that he 'accomplished as instrument in the hands of God'. Jesus was created by God but subordinate to God. Nonetheless, he had divine qualities and was a proper object of worship.

For Roy, Jesus was not divine but on a divine commission. Deifying Christ, for Roy, was both an 'affront to God and an *antichristian* doctrine'.[7] The divine status of Jesus, in Roy's assessment, was based on a 'perverted interpretation' of verses like 'the Father in me, and I am in him'. He cautioned that there were similar verses applied by disciples of Jesus that would his 'increase the number of persons of the Godhead much beyond the three'. He was on earth to do his father's business, namely to 'preach and impart divine instructions'. John's Jesus says: 'For I have given unto them the words which thou gavest me; and they have Deceived them, and have known surely that I came out from thee, and they have believed that thou didst send me' (Jn. 17.8). He was greatly esteemed as a saviour for instructing people about the divine will and law as 'never before so fully revealed'. He completed and brought to 'perfection' the laws of Moses and other prophets. This does not degrade Jesus or depreciate his dignity. The clear manifestation of Jesus rendering the law perfect was evident in his repeated assertion that 'you have heard' followed with the words 'but I say unto you'. He was a 'Redeemer, Mediator, and Intercessor with God in behalf of his followers', but Roy was quick to add that such a mediating office did not 'prove the deity of or the atonement of Jesus'.

Roy's Jesus was not only on a divine commission to preach the word but also had another commitment, this time to judge the world. He not only delivered moral precepts but also dispensed judgement. Roy claimed that the 'heavenly Father had committed to Jesus the final judgement of all who have lived since the creation'. It was the Father himself who had given him the authority to '*execute judgement*'.[8] In one rare occasion, Roy openly admitted that he agreed with Marshman: 'I agree also with the Reverend Editor, in esteeming the nature of this office.' In other words, Roy subscribed to the idea that when the fate of humankind was decided, the judge who would take that decision would be none other than Jesus. God committed the 'final judgement' of the humanity to him.

But there is one caveat. Whereas Marshman claimed the Son had the knowledge of the day of the final judgement, Roy denied Jesus having any such prior knowledge. He cited the Markan saying to bolster his claim: 'But of that day and that hour knoweth no man' (Mk 13.33). Roy did not provide any clue as to on what basis one would be judged except to say that the 'wisdom of God' would decide one's fate. If one would hazard a guess it would be on the deeds done by people to each other. Roy's Jesus judges, but unlike Marshman's he does not condemn and convict people for their sins and depravity but for their failure to owe allegiance to him: 'Whosoever therefore shall confess me before men, him will I confess also before my Father which is in heaven. But whosoever shall deny me before men, him will I also deny before my Father which is in heaven.'

The Father and the Son

Roy was probably the first Indian to articulate that there was a strong but a different kind of unity that existed between the Father and the Son. Roy treated the notion of the Son being of the same nature with the Father as a matter of 'small importance, and as little connected with the fundamental essential doctrine' of Christianity.[9] This unity was not a metaphysical or material one but one of 'concord of will and design'.[10] While Marshman and the Baptist missionaries held on to the traditional position worked out at Chalcedon that Christ had the same substance as the Father, Roy interpreted this union as the Son conforming to the Father's will and expectations. In his forceful words, this union was 'one in design, action, agreement, affection'. He reminded his missionary opponents that when the unity of the Father and Son was mentioned in the Scriptures it referred to 'perfect concord of will' and by 'no means oneness of nature'. This union was strengthened and given added profundity by the Son being perfect in obedience, but the Father and Son remained distinct. For Roy, this unity was no different from the same unity that existed between Jesus and his disciples. It was Roy's interpretation of 'I and my Father are one' in personal and performing terms, which later Indian theologians enthusiastically plagiarized without acknowledging Roy's contribution. Roy not only challenged the same substance theory of orthodox Christianity but was also dismissive of the metaphysical unity of *atman* and *brahman* expounded by Sankara's advaita which was enthusiastically advocated by some of the Hindu reformers. Roy did not subscribe to the view that the human soul was absorbed into Godhead. Such an idea, he contended, might be of comfort to Hindu philosophers but was 'inconsistent with the belief of every Christian'.

Roy was dismissive of the two-nature theory that Jesus was 'at once complete in Godhead and complete in manhood, truly God and truly man', declared since the days of the Council of Chalcedon (451 CE). He found the union of two natures, human and divine, in one person as incongruous to 'both revelation and common sense'.[11] With a genuine tone of regret, he opined that the idea of a two- or threefold nature of God was 'very much calculated to lower the reputation of Britons both as a learned and a religious people'.[12] He wished that Western Christians would discover that the 'idea of a *Mangod* or *Godman* to be unnatural and pregnant with absurdity, and not a mere innocent speculation'.[13] His warning to the Christians was that however they couched the doctrine in theological sophistry, it would not convince or earn respect in the world.

The popular conception is that Roy rejected the birth and the resurrection of Jesus and omitted the miracle stories because he was a rationalist and found such narratives contrary to reason. Like all perceptions about him, these perceptions are not as straightforward as they appear. The liberal theological stance he often took in his *Precepts* was not followed through nor did it match with ideas expressed in his controversy with the missionaries. In a number of cases he takes a relaxed view, or redesigned his ideas to suit his mercurial theological position. Roy duly left out the birth narratives in his *Precepts* but later acknowledged that Jesus had a miraculous birth not by 'Godhead having had intercourse'[14] with a virgin but by a 'miraculous influence of God',[15] which came upon Mary so that she could bear a child.[16] Similarly, his sceptical views on the resurrection, evident in his prompt editing out of any reference to such passages in *The Precepts*, seem to have undergone a change. In his last days in England, it appeared that Roy had modified his views. He was reported to have said that he believed in the resurrection, which was the 'foundation of the Christian faith', and on this great fact 'rested his own hopes of a resurrection'.[17]

Roy felt that the message of Jesus itself was divine enough and the divine status that the missionaries claimed for Jesus did not add any extra credence to his personality. Roy was respectful to Jesus as he would be to any prophets of religion. He counted himself as one of the followers of Jesus without any firm commitment. He did not have any qualms about calling Jesus as 'our gracious Saviour', 'our Saviour', 'our Saviour and King'. Roy in a confessional tone, which would have warmed the hearts of any TV evangelists, admitted that the Scriptures represented Jesus as pure light, innocent as a lamb, as a bread of life and great as the angels of God.

Roy was so assured of the venerable status of Jesus that he was able to openly acknowledge that he was one 'in whose veracity, candour, and perfection, we have happily been persuaded to place implicit confidence'.[18] He routinely used reverential terms, such as Lord and Master, but made it clear that nowhere in the Gospels was Jesus presented as God but simply as a God-conscious but deeply flawed man.

Roy's Jesus was a mild dispenser of moral precepts which look useful but idealistic. He appears as a remote, impersonal adjudicator who expected loyalty and commitment. What make Roy's Jesus different is that, unlike the later Western liberal theologians, Roy posited a Jesus who could be understood apart from his own expectation of the imminent end of the world. Roy's Jesus dispensed ethics without eschatology. His counsel to the missionaries was that, instead of paying 'greater attention to the inquiries after his nature', they should 'confine their instructions to the practical parts of Christianity'.[19] In other words, observe his commandments.[20] His Jesus also differed from that of the European lives of Jesus of the time. Whereas European construals of Christ worked out by Reimarus (1694–1768), D.F. Strauss (1808–1874) and Ernest Renan (1832–1892) were marked by cynicism, doubt and at times by anti-Christian feeling, Roy and other Bengali reformers who came after him, such as Keshub Chunder Sen (1838–1884) and P.C. Mazoomdar (1840–1905), projected a self-confident, optimistic picture of Jesus. He was not the miserable, mistaken, miscalculating crusader of these Western imaginations but a person with a moral message without requiring any allegiance to him.

What Roy offered was not a 'Unitarian' Jesus, as an exasperated Müller put it,[21] or a Thakur – a feudal title indicating chief or a person of rank – as an irritated Tytler, Roy's fiercest critic who accused him of degrading the status of Jesus, stated. What Roy conveyed to his fellow Hindus was not a Jesus of impeccable Jewish heritage but a figure alienated from his own people. A rootless dispenser of moral teachings, like wondering Hindu sadhus that Indians could subscribe to without making any firm commitment to him or affirming his salvific potency. Finally, it was Roy who not only first mooted the idea of Jesus as an Asiatic but loftily claimed that Roy himself being an Asiatic had the inherent cultural credentials to grasp the life, work and teachings of Jesus. A kind of insider privilege which would come under severe reproof from postcolonial critics.

Notes

1. A. Schweitzer, *The Quest of the Historical Jesus: A Critical Study of its progress from Reimarus to Wrede* (London: A.C. Black, 1910), 4.
2. Roy, *The English Works of Raja Rammohun Roy*, 577, emphasis in original.
3. Carpenter, *The Last Days in England of the Raja Rammohun Roy*, 137.
4. Roy, *The English Works of Raja Rammohun Roy*, 840.
5. Ibid., 575.
6. Ibid., 642.
7. Ibid., 873, emphasis in original.
8. Ibid., 591, emphasis in original.
9. Ibid., 629.
10. Ibid., 577.
11. Ibid., 675.
12. Ibid., 193.
13. Ibid., 193, emphasis in original.
14. Ibid., 618.
15. Ibid., 619.
16. Ibid., 593.
17. Ibid.
18. Ibid., 570.
19. Ibid., 193.
20. Ibid., 920.
21. M.F. Müller, *Biographical Essays* (London: Longmans, Green, & Co, 1884), 23.

Chapter 12

THE INDIAN REFORMER, THE AMERICAN PRESIDENT AND THEIR DESIGNER GOSPELS

In 1820 when Roy's *Precepts* appeared, nearly 8,000 miles away from Calcutta, in the same year, a similar compilation was brought to completion. The compiler was the third president of the United States of America, Thomas Jefferson. Roy was the citizen of a country which was about to change from a Mughal occupied colony to one occupied by newly invading English forces. Jefferson was a newly decolonized citizen who was at the forefront in getting rid of the British. Both were upper-class men and involved in the politics of their respective countries. Their extracts of the Gospels were not harmonizations of the Gospels but, on the contrary, distinguished by a motive to provide a moral code for a new republic, in the case of Jefferson, and, in the case of Roy, for an ancient country which was creaking under Mughal rule and about to come under that of the British. Eusebius of Caesarea, a fourth-century ecclesiastical historian and a biblical exegete, would have accused them of doing what his perceived unbelievers did with ancient texts: 'They have treated the Divine Scriptures recklessly and without fear ... Therefore they have laid their hands boldly upon the Divine Scriptures, alleging that they have corrected them.'[1]

Jefferson called his composition 'The Life and Morals of Jesus of Nazareth', but it was popularly known as the Jefferson Bible. This is the only record of what Jefferson thought about his faith and his reasons for choosing the ethical teachings of Jesus found in the Gospels above all other moral teaching.

Jefferson's Bible was in the making for a long time and had gone through several incarnations. First, as an outline in *Syllabus* in 1803 and a year later it took the form of the lesser known *Philosophy of Jesus*, which he called a 'wee little book' consisting of forty-six pages compiled strictly for his 'private moral instruction and education'.[2] The original copy was nowhere to be found and the present version is a reconstruction based on the notes he left behind. It took him another seventeen years before he compiled his *The Life and Morals of Jesus*. The whole process was a slow and more gradual development. Jefferson completed *The Life and Morals of Jesus* when he was seventy-seven, whereas Roy was comparatively younger and was in his late forties when *The Precepts* rolled off the Baptist Mission Press in Calcutta, a press owned by the Baptists, one-time friends of Roy who later became his enemies, trigged by the contents of this small booklet. Roy does not provide any clues as to whether he had any other earlier rough drafts of Gospel compilations before he came to produce *The Precepts*.

Roy and Jefferson produced these compilations for diametrically opposite motives and purposes. Jefferson envisaged his cut and paste version only for his personal use. As a child of the European Enlightenment, religion for Jefferson was a private affair between him and God alone. On its completion, he wrote: 'I have performed the operation for my own use.' He might have produced his little scrap book Bible for his personal use, yet he might also have secretly harboured the notion that his fellow Americans would benefit from the morals of Jesus. The wording on the front page of his personal Bible was indicative of this secret missional ambition: 'I am a real Christian, that is to say, a disciple of the doctrines of Jesus. I have little doubt that our whole country will soon be rallied to the unity of our creator.'[3] While for the president, the compilation was purely a personal exercise, for the Roy the production of *The Precepts* was a public act, more significantly, a duty towards his people, and it was intentionally aimed at a multireligious community. Roy, for whom private and personal spheres overlapped, envisaged *The Precepts* as a public document containing all the essence 'necessary to instruct mankind' and the morals of Jesus as a 'simple code ... well fitted to regulate the conduct of the human race in the discharge of their various duties to God, to themselves, and to society'. He had the double intention of repairing the distorted faith of the Christians and introducing to Hindus a set of moral codes which could revitalize their lives. While Roy had Christians, Hindus and Muslims in mind, Jefferson's target was mainly white middle-class men.

Jefferson had two other additional reasons. One was to provide documentary evidence to prove his religious identity as a 'real Christian' and a 'disciple of the doctrines of Jesus Christ'.[4] His interference in the state–church issue, especially his attempt to disestablish the church in Virginia and his accommodation of the non-conformists and Jews, did not endear him to the Anglican clergy. The antagonism became evident during the 1800 election year when he was accused of being an infidel, an atheist and a womanizer. He, in turn, accused them of making a muddle of the simple teachings of Jesus in order to maintain their power and position. The compilation of the teachings of Jesus was his way of establishing his credentials as a good Christian. Secondly, the *Life and Morals of Jesus* was an act of redemption for his earlier persuit of secular ideals and philosophies. In his earlier days, he maintained that the morals drawn from the ancient philosophers such as Seneca and Epictetus were 'more full, more entire, more coherent and more clearly deduced from the unquestionable principles of knowledge' than the ones drawn from the teachings of Jesus. From such a revered sceptical position, and discarding his earlier shyness of declaring his faith publicly, he wrote candidly that he had not seen a 'more beautiful or precious morsel of ethics' than that expounded by Jesus.[5] He was moved to confess that the moral teachings of Jesus were 'eminently more perfect than those of any ancient philosophers' and were 'the most sublime and benevolent code of morals which ha[d] ever been offered to man'.[6] How and what made Jefferson move from his admiration of 'heathen moralists' to Jesus is not clear. Roy, being a Hindu, did not have any such conversion experience nor did he have to make any public declaration of his faith. As pointed out earlier, his *Precepts* did not emerge from his personal needs but arose as a response to the religious, political and cultural needs of colonial India, which was being transferred from a Muslim empire to a Christian empire.

Roy and Jefferson sliced off histories, dogmas and myths in the Gospels, not with the intention of weakening the potency of the Bible but of privileging their version of Christianity. The hermeneutical practice at work here was to weed out the elements which were a hinderance to the perception of the Christian message they wanted to promote. Both conceived their task as a righteous cause in removing any components which would be in Roy's view, 'destructive of the comforts of life, or injurious to the texture of society'. In Jefferson's case, weeding out 'hay from the stubble'.[7] They imagined themselves as honourable men engaged in a virtuous endeavour.

Roy and Jefferson subscribed to the view that the original message of Jesus had been corrupted by subsequent generations of Christians. Roy blamed the Greek, Roman and Barbarian converts for contaminating the religion of Jesus with absurd, idolatrous doctrines and practices. Jefferson had a long hit list which included ecclesiastical figures such as Athanasius, Ignatius Loyola and Calvin, who introduced absurdities. His special opprobrium was reserved for Calvin whose writings Jefferson described as 'maniac ravings'.[8] He wrote:

> Our savior did not come into the world to save metaphysicians only. His doctrines are levelled to the simplest understandings and it is only by banishing Hierophantic mysteries and Scholastic subtleties, which have nick-named Christianity, and getting back to the plain and unsophisticated precepts of Christ, that we become *real* Christians.[9]

Both wanted to restore the original, 'primitive Christianity, in all the simplicity in which it came from the lips of Jesus'.[10]

Roy and Jefferson, both being deists, concurred in another respect, namely, the application of reason to the study of the Scriptures. To their way of thinking, the highest spiritual truth could only be grasped, not by relying solely on the evidence of the sacred books but on the basis of common sense and rationality and the study of nature. While Roy put it this way: 'The only test of the validity of any doctrine was its conformity to the natural and healthy working of man's reason, and the intuitions and cravings of the human heart',[11] Jefferson urged in his letter to Peter Carr: 'Fix reason firmly in her seat, and call to her tribunal every fact, every opinion.'[12] Both exhibited a naturalistic outlook and left out any supernatural references in the Gospels.

Both showed deep disrespect for organized religion and displayed particular distaste towards priests. As Hinduism was structurally a loosely-knit faith, Roy, unlike Jefferson, did not face the heavy weight of the institutional power of Hinduism. Yet Roy had endless disputes with his Brahmanical communities as well as with Christian missionaries. He attacked the priests for introducing 'hundreds of useless hardships' and rites motivated both by gaining monetary advantage and maintaining their authority by 'self-interested leadership'.[13] For Jefferson, religion was a matter solely between believer and God, and the legislative powers of government should not make law for the establishment of religion or 'prohibition of the free exercise of it.' He supported erecting a wall between church and state.

Both held the view that the fundamental tenets of the Christian faith were the central distractions and they showed a healthy scepticism towards them. For Jefferson, the immaculate conception of Jesus, his miraculous powers, his resurrection and ascension, his bodily presence in the Lord's Supper, the Christian doctrines such as the Trinity, atonement and the Holy Spirit were all 'artificial systems' invented by different sects 'unauthorized by any single word' uttered by Jesus. Roy relentlessly repeated in his controversy with Marshman that these creeds had no scriptural sanctions. These doctrinal statements were all fabricated with one purpose – of making lay people depend on priests and increasing the financial revenue of the institutional churches.

Both respected the religious beliefs of others and had no intention of converting them. Jefferson wrote to Margret Bayard Smith, an author and a political commentator in the early days of the republic, that he 'never attempted to make a convert, nor wished to change another's creed' and went on to say that he had 'judged the religion of others by their lives'.[14] As we saw earlier, Roy only wanted Hindus to benefit from the moral precepts of Jesus and never encouraged conversion. For both, what mattered ultimately was not what the people of other faiths believed but how they conducted themselves towards God and towards their fellow human beings.

Both had somewhat similar views of what it meant to be a Christian. For Roy, it was those who adhered to the 'doctrines of Christ as taught by him'. A similar view was taken by Jefferson: 'I am a Christian in the only sense in which he wished any one to be; sincerely attached to his doctrines, in preference to all others.'[15]

Roy and Jefferson were inspired by, and drew on, a wide range of sources and thinkers. While Roy was influenced by Hindu and Islamic philosophers, Vedic traditions, Unitarianism and Enlightenment thinkers such as Locke, it was both classical Greek and modern thinkers who affected Jefferson's thinking. Both were in search of the very essence of the religion which they thought was distorted, overlooked or downplayed over the years. Both subscribed to the orientalists' notion of 'back to the beginning' and, in their case, to the words of Jesus as a way of weighing up later accretions imposed by priests and Church authorities. Roy perceived his task as seeking 'to attain the truths of Christianity from the words of the author of this religion',[16] while Jefferson declared that the 'greater purity' was found in the precepts of Jesus and in 'his discourses'.[17] He envisaged his mission in terms of restoring the Gospel of Jesus to the 'primitive simplicity of its founder'.[18]

Slicing the Scriptures, condensing the Gospels

Jefferson embraced the Bible reluctantly and gave importance to it quite late in his life. In his *Notes on the State of Virginia*, he advised not placing the Bible in the hands of school children. Instead, he urged them to study Greek, Roman, European and American history. He perceived the Bible as a human document and he earnestly counselled Peter Carr, one of his nephews, to read the Bible 'as you would read Livy or Tacitus'.[19] In other words, he accorded the same status to and treated the Bible like any other secular text – a classic Enlightenment mindset. There is no record to say when Roy first encountered the Bible. The possibility is that he would have known about biblical materials through his reading of the Qur'an. Roy, too, thought of the Bible as a document full of 'human distortions' and regarded the Christian Bible like any other sacred text and placed it below his own Hindu scriptures and thus diminished its unique status as claimed by the missionaries. Both reflected and reinforced the mood of the Enlightenment of the time – the Christian Bible as one more book to be investigated or, to paraphrase Edward Said speaking of the orient, it had to be studied, structured and subjugated.[20]

In this post-critical era, Roy and Jefferson would be regarded as biblical literalists, but they were not simply literalists. They were much more nuanced. Yes, they did not question the integrity of the redacted texts but only the extraneous interpretations imposed on them over time. They were inferential comprehenders of the texts. They made textual judgements based on information embedded in the narratives. For them, the original, authentic words of Jesus were reliably stored in the texts. But they challenged the notion of a fixed and finalized form of the Christian text. For them, the Bible was a book that could be tampered with and improved upon. They treated the Gospel texts as mouldable material about Jesus which had their own integrity without any reference to any vested theological interests or church traditions. Jefferson's method was to 'cut verse by verse out of the printed book' and arrange the matter distinctively belonging to Jesus, which was as easily distinguishable as 'diamonds in a dunghill'. There is no clue as to how Roy physically put together his *Precepts*. It looks as if he simply discarded the ones which did not meet with his hermeneutical expectations.

The Bible, as far as these two gentlemen were concerned, was not a divine word manifested in print form but a book that could be cut up and glued onto paper as Jefferson did. Of the two, Jefferson was more adventurous.[21] He freely moved texts even between the Gospels without paying much attention to the canonical order or the context of a text. A notable example of Jefferson's daring rearrangement was the way he reshuffled Mt. 27. Whereas in Matthew the suicide of Judas and returning of the thirty pieces of silver were placed at the beginning of the chapter, Jefferson removed them to the end after Pilate had handed over Jesus for crucifixion. This cut and paste method had serious consequences. It omitted the newly born baby Jesus without the rejoicing of the angels; the shepherds failed to turn up at his birth; the man born blind was still waiting to get his sight back; Malchus's cut-off ear still remained unpatched, and Lazarus was left decaying in the tomb. Roy did not engage in such drastic rejigging but faithfully adhered to the canonical and chronological order of the Gospel narratives, slicing off passages which did not suit his hermeneutical agenda.

Female biblical characters play only marginal roles in the compilations of these two men. Where they do figure they were chosen for their generosity, vulnerability or as an example to be emulated. The woman caught in adultery features both in *The Precepts* and the *Life and Morals of Jesus*, but she is seen as a trend setter for good behaviour and as offering an opportunity for Jesus to expound his morality. Jefferson's choice of the Luke's version of the anointing is instructive. While the other three Gospel writers present the action of the woman as a preparation for Jesus's death, an event in which Jefferson had no interest, Luke's portrayal of the action of the woman is as an affectionate gesture of an adventurous woman fitted in with his hermeneutical interest. The prime purpose of including her is to inspire men to act like her. *The Precepts* contains both Mark's and Luke's version of the widow's contribution to the temple treasury and her generosity is idealized as an act of selfless giving. The Samaritan woman figures partially in Roy's compilation. Her questions are edited out, but Roy included the answers of Jesus to her questions about how the new worship in truth and spirit would replace the old ritualistic practices – the very practices about which Roy himself had endless quarrels with his own Hindu pundits. The strong women characters such as the Syrophoenician woman who daringly challenges Jesus, are left out in both versions. These selected biblical women were fitted in to suit the hermeneutical needs of Roy and Jefferson while having their own voices and distinctiveness erased.

Apart from the Synoptic writers, Roy and Jefferson had a minimal relationship with other biblical authors. We saw earlier, Roy's limited use of John and his reasons for not utilizing him. While *The Precepts* contained around fifty-six verses of John, the *Life and Morals of Jesus* had three times more than that, and it was largely due to Jefferson's inclusion of the trial and the crucifixion narratives. Both were careful to leave out Johannine statements which sounded triumphalistic such as 'I am the way, the truth and the life' which made him the sole saviour of humankind. Also left out was any reference in the fourth Gospel to the divine status of Jesus: 'the Father is in me and I am in him'. Another conspicuous example of this exclusion was Jesus's saying of the glorification of the Son of man. This is scissored off in Jefferson's construction of the Last Supper. What would have appealed to Jefferson about this episode was the ethical injunction of Jesus: 'That ye love one another; as I have loved you, that ye also love one another' as well as the washing of the feet as an example of love expressed through humility and servanthood.

Roy and Jefferson had their own pecking order of biblical books. For Jefferson, the Gospels, which were seen as the true depositories of the teachings of Jesus, were placed at the top. The New Testament epistles were demoted to secondary status. For Jefferson, they were occasional writings written to those who had already become Christians and to meet their contextual needs. They simply replicate the essentials of Christianity which had been already expressed in the Gospels. In spite of the fact that they contained the fundamentals of the Gospels, Jefferson found them to be 'promiscuously mixed with other truths'. The other truths that Jefferson referred to here were the explanations about moral behaviour and worship which Jefferson dismissed as not 'fundamental' to the message of Jesus.[22] His most severe scorn was reserved for Paul's writings. Jefferson described Paul as 'the great Coryphaeus and first corrupter of the doctrines of Jesus'. Roy would have instinctively concurred with Jefferson. While acknowledging that Paul was the 'most exalted among the primitive Christians', Roy dismissed his cross-centric theology as unscriptural.

Roy, too, accorded primary status to the first three Gospels and found the fourth one theologically and doctrinally incompatible with the simple moral teachings of Jesus. He found its triumphalistic tone and the divine status accorded to Jesus in John, unpalatable to his hermeneutical stance. Another matter that irritated Roy about John's Gospel was its incomprehensibility to those not schooled in the thought patterns of the author of the fourth Gospel, which proved a big stumbling block for Indian readers.

Roy and Jefferson had different perceptions of the Bible. For one it was a theological document and for the other it was a historical depository. For Roy, sacred writings were theological texts which encouraged faith in a supreme deity and prescribed moral duties that lead humanity to eternal happiness. Their legitimacy and usefulness were measured by the type of social comfort and cohesion they endorsed and promoted. Whereas Jefferson viewed the Bible as a historical document. When he was asked by Robert Skipwirth, a neighbour, to suggest books for his library, Jefferson interestingly itemized the Bible under history and strangely listed the writings of Locke, Xenophon, Epictetus, Seneca, Cicero, Bolingbroke and the sermons of Sterne under religion. The religious books that his nephew was asked to read included Middleton and Voltaire, but not the Bible. In the same letter he informed his nephew that he viewed the New Testament as 'the history of a personage called Jesus'.[23]

Roy and Jefferson believed that the scriptural truths in themselves had no purchase unless they were put into practice. Their energy depended on enacting the great commandments. For Roy, there was no other means of attaining eternal life except performing duties towards God and in obeying his commandments.[24] Jefferson took a similar stance when he wrote to Margret Bayard Smith that 'it is in our lives, and not from our words that our religion must be read'.[25]

Jesus the preacher of moral precepts

The Jesus that these two men came up with is a forced and an artificial construct. Just as any portrayals of Jesus, their Jesus is filtered and recovered for their own theological purposes. Roy, a Hindu, reaches out to borrow a hero of another religion in order to reinforce his hermeneutical agenda, and in the process he retrieves him from the needless dogmatical garb in which he was wrapped. Whereas Jefferson, an agnostic, rescues Jesus from church clerics who had obscured and distorted his image and, more crucially, to prove his credentials as a Christian.

The Jesus that emerges out of the writings of Roy and Jefferson is not the familiar figure that Christians are acquainted with. There is no story of the annunciation, the virgin birth or the appearance of the angels to the shepherds. The resurrection is not even mentioned. This is the Christ who neither fulfils the Hebrew prophecies nor emerges as victorious after Satan's temptations. There was no sign of the spirit of the Lord being upon him.

There is a difference between Roy and Jefferson in their use of the historical aspects of Jesus's life. Some of the historical events that happened to Jesus find their way into the president's texts which included the birth of Jesus minus angels and Gabriel explaining to Mary about the miraculous conception, his circumcision, his baptism sans the supernatural events linked to it, his visit to the temple, the entry into Jerusalem, the last days before his arrest, his trial and death. He included them presumably as they were illustrative of the human side of Jesus rather than his divine ranking. A rare historical event that crept into Roy's edition was the Caesarea Philippi incident where Peter confessed Jesus as the Messiah. But the Messiah that Roy had in mind was not the Messiah of Jewish expectation but an Asiatic one with Asiatic sensibilities.

For both, Jesus was a great teacher of wisdom, compassion and a person with an incredible sense of divine consciousness but never a divine person. They both did not believe that Jesus was, nor that Jesus claimed to be, the Son of God. They were convinced that Jesus was divinely 'inspired from above'.[26] Roy was very firm in his conviction that Jesus was brought forth by the supreme being as a 'created being'.[27] Jefferson was equally convinced that Jesus was not a 'divine being' but 'a first wise and good being'.[28] He went on to describe him as a 'man, of illegitimate birth, of a benevolent heart, [and an] enthusiastic mind',[29] who did not claim any divine status for himself. If he had any such idea, it was inculcated into him in his younger days.

For Roy and Jefferson, Jesus was basically a teacher who preached simple moral truths which were later complicated by meddlesome church authorities and theologians. Roy maintained that Jesus preached a 'simple code of religion and morality' but it was obscured by puzzling doctrines and historical details created by Roman converts in the fourth and fifth centuries. Jefferson, too, emphasized a similar kind of understanding. He held on to the belief that the 'simple doctrines' preached by Jesus were made incomprehensible by his 'pseudo-priests' and 'pseudo-followers' who infused his teachings with Platonist ideas. For both, the moral teaching of Jesus is summed up in the two commandments – belief in a single deity and the love for this deity to be expressed through active compassion towards neighbours. Basically, they reduced the message of Jesus to absolute love and service. This did not prevent Roy and Jefferson from regarding Jesus as a saviour. Jefferson addressed him as 'our saviour',[30] a description, as we saw earlier, Roy himself did not have any hesitation in using.

Roy and Jefferson did not subscribe to the atoning power of Jesus's death, a cardinal teaching of the church. The vicarious suffering of an innocent man for the guilt of others did not find favour with them. For Jefferson, Jesus was a good man, killed ultimately not for the sins of the humanity but for sedition. He was the victim first of Roman authorities and later of the church. Jefferson's extracts ended coldly and impassively with the burial descriptions of Matthew and John. He sliced off the resurrection narratives because he believed that they went against the original Gospel. Roy who did not believe in the need for 'the human blood, or that of God in human form, as an indispensable atonement for sin', viewed the death of Jesus as an innocent who was persecuted presumably for teaching the divine will and the law. He saved 'the people solely thorough the inculcation of the word of God'. He perceived the death as an innocent 'subjected to persecution'. As we saw earlier,

Roy also rejected the doctrine of atonement as unscriptural, and he reframed it as service and obedience. He kept on reminding his missionary opponents that there was not a single passage from Jesus which upheld the idea that the cross was 'all sufficient or indispensable for salvation'.

Both perceived Jesus as a reformer of the Mosaic religion. For Roy, Jesus rendered the law 'perfect' – 'the unity of God and obedience to his will and commandments' – initiated through Moses and continued via a line of faithful messengers appointed by God from time to time. In Jefferson's view, Jesus was basically the 'greatest of all the reformers of the depraved religion of his own country' and the one who refined the 'Hebrew code of religion'.[31] For Jefferson, Jesus was not a mere imitator of Moses but drastically different from the Jewish law giver on three counts. One, Moses did not believe in life after death, whereas Jesus 'inculcated that doctrine with emphasis and precision'. Two, Moses encouraged many 'idle ceremonies', while Jesus dismissed them as futile and irrelevant. Three, while Moses instilled among his people 'anti-social spirit towards other nations', Jesus preached 'philanthropy and universal charity and benevolence'.[32]

Jefferson envisaged Jesus following in the line of great Greek moral philosophers and surpassing them, whereas Roy pictured him as one of the cohorts of the Indian sages complementing and reinforcing their vision and message. While Jefferson saw Jesus as a Jew and placed him within his Jewish milieu, Roy perceived him from a broader perspective and situated him within a wider geographical context and identified him as an Asiatic.

While Jefferson attempted to make Jesus a moral philosopher, a closer reading of Roy's writings will reveal that his intention was not to make Jesus another moral philosopher teaching 'God, virtue and immortality' as the missionaries envisaged. He did not want to turn the Jesus story into one of the mythological stories in India which had plenty of such stories. Instead, he fashioned Jesus as a harbinger of the new humanity, the one who breaks down caste, communities and brings people together.

Both men were engaged in what is now known in scholarly circles as the search for the historical Jesus without the paraphernalia of the modern search. Such a search earnestly began only three decades after these extracts appeared with the publication of David Strauss's *The Life of Jesus* (1835). Unlike the later nineteenth-century lives of Jesus, Roy and Jefferson did not engage in detailed excursive studies of the linguistic evidence nor address the complex question of the Gospel sources. They were content to deal with texts at the redacted level.

These two men were accidental searchers for the historical Jesus without any of the academic pretensions which marked the modern search. Albert Schweitzer himself, who wrote a magisterial although Eurocentric history of the quest for the historical Jesus, conceded that to 'know Jesus and understand him requires no scholarly initiation'.[33] Neither Roy nor the president questioned whether Jesus was an authentic historical person. What they were looking for was not the historical Jesus but the meaningful Jesus of the Gospels. These two men came up with a Jesus who was consistent with their predetermined hermeneutical presuppositions and so did the modern questers who despite claiming academic neutrality arrived at a Jesus who fitted their theological, philosophical and nationalistic expectations. Where these two men differed from Schweitzer's vision was that they did not subscribe to his eschatological Jesus of Jewish apocalypticism. They embraced the ethics of Jesus without the eschatological lexicon in which it was framed. They also differed in one more respect. Encountering Jesus for them was not, as Schweitzer claimed, an experience 'ultimately of a mystical kind' but an aural experience of listening to his moral message, which both believed would uplift humankind. Roy, who took a characteristically Indian position, was not enamoured by the personality of Jesus but was more interested in his moral principles and the ethical values that he represented. Jefferson, on the other hand, was in awe of his personality as is exemplified by his inclusion of the details of Jesus's life in his compilation. In one respect, however, they would have agreed with Schweitzer – to follow Jesus meant fulfilling the tasks he gave us to do.

Roy and Jefferson rejoiced at Jesus's great contributions, especially in certain areas. Firstly, his monotheistic ideal. Jesus preached what Jefferson called the 'pure and simple unity of the creator of the universe', which helped to get rid of the polytheistic notions of the ancient world. Roy repeated Jesus's employment of the First Commandment – the 'Lord our God is one' three times in his *Precepts*. Secondly, the universal appositeness of Jesus's morality. Both were convinced that the morality Jesus preached had relevance beyond his narrow constituency and had an appeal for the whole of humankind. It was a system designed, in Roy's words, to bring 'social comfort' and, in Jefferson's vocabulary, 'social concord'[34] and harmony among citizens. Finally, only in Jefferson's case, his teachings on the future life, for which Roy had little time.

It is a cliché to say that portrayals of Jesus almost mirror the one who investigates him. This is true of these two men. The Jesus that emerges is not the Jesus who transforms Roy or Jefferson but a Jesus who was transformed by these two men to match their existing view of him as the greatest moral teacher in the world. Neither of them was anti-Jesus. What they opposed was, as Jefferson put it, the 'corruption of Christianity' and not the 'genuine precepts of Jesus himself'.[35]

Both were unambiguous in identifying Jesus as a human person, but they hardly mention his human frailties and emotional outbursts. The severe and harsh sayings of Jesus are conveniently left out. A case in point is the cursing of the fig tree. Both men's principle assertion that one should love one's neighbour because the text says so may look a bit vacuous in a post-Christian and post-scriptural world. One should love a fellow human being not because a text or a divine figure tells us to do so but because one identifies with and understands the feelings of other human beings.

To bring this chapter to a close, let me try to resolve two conundrums. One is the persistent and intriguing question: did Roy and Jefferson know each other's work? The chances are that it is very unlikely. Jefferson completed *Life and Morals* in 1820 – the same year Roy published his *Precepts*. Jefferson's Bible was not known to the public for a long time, whereas Roy's *Precepts* was in the public domain and generated open arguments and debates. Jefferson was adamant that the *Life and Morals* should not be published during his life, and there was no reference to it in his correspondence or any mention of its existence by his family members. It became known only after his death.[36] A synopsis of an earlier version titled 'Syllabus of an Estimate of the Doctrine of Jesus, compared with those of others' was published in 1816 in *The Monthly Repository,* an English Unitarian journal. It was an outline of what Jefferson was planning to do and appeared without his name. Sadly, the piece did not spark any debate, and the fact that the journal had poor circulation and that it was little known in America, meant that Jefferson's effort went unnoticed even in his own country. *The Monthly Repository* in the January 1820 issue published an account of the life of Roy, interestingly from a French pamphlet. The Jefferson Bible remained largely unknown beyond a close circle of relatives and friends until 1904, when its publication was ordered by Congress. About 9,000 copies were issued and distributed in the Senate and the House. Therefore, it is highly doubtful that they knew each other's work.

The other conundrum is how do we account for their similar hermeneutical standpoints – fervent faith in monotheistic ideals; human reason as a valid instrument to assess the truth; an anti-Trinitarian stance; the endorsement of the morality of Jesus; misgivings about the biblical revelation; the irrationality of Christian doctrines; distrust of the clergy and the pundits? What the philosopher and former president of India Radhakrishnan reasoned said of the parallels and correspondences in the teachings of Buddha and Jesus could well be applicable to the work of these two men. Radhakrishnan reasoned that such coincidences were the natural outcome of the human mind's search for truth. These spiritual yearnings and religious quests of humankind are the 'same on the banks of the Ganges as on the shores of the Lake of Galilee',[37] or, in this case the Mississippi River. *The Precepts* and the *Life and Morals of Jesus* were twin expressions of the same spiritual longing.

Notes

1. 'Eusebius - The Two Theodoti: Historia Ecclesiastica, 5.28', *Early Church Texts*. Available online: https://earlychurchtexts.com/public/eusebius_theodotus_monarchianism.htm (accessed 10 February 2019).
2. D.W. Adams, ed., *Jefferson's Extracts from the Gospels: 'The Philosophy of Jesus' and 'The Life and Morals of Jesus'* (Princeton, NJ: Princeton University Press, 1983), 30.
3. 'Thomas Jefferson', *Faith of Our Fathers*. Available online: http://www.faithofourfathers.net/jefferson.html (accessed on 10 February 2019).
4. Adams, *Jefferson's Extracts from the Gospels*, 384.
5. Ibid., 365.
6. T. Jefferson, *The Jefferson Bible: The Life and Morals of Jesus of Nazareth* (Boston, MA: Beacon Press, 1989), 17.
7. Adams, *Jefferson's Extracts from the Gospels*, 388.
8. Ibid., 413.
9. Ibid., 385, italics in original.
10. Ibid., 413.
11. Lillingston, *The Brahmo Samaj & Arya Samaj in Their Bearing Upon Christianity*, 58.

12 J.P. Boyd, ed., *The Papers of Thomas Jefferson*, vol. 12, *7 August 1787 to 31 March 1788* (Princeton, NJ: Princeton University Press, 1955), 15.
13 Roy, *Translation of Several Principal Books*, 57.
14 Adams, *Jefferson's Extracts from the Gospels*, 376.
15 Ibid., 331.
16 Roy, *The English Works of Raja Rammohun Roy*, 630.
17 G. Chinard, ed., *The Literary Bible of Thomas Jefferson: His Commonplace Book of Philosophers and Poets* (Baltimore: John Hopkins Press, 1928), 35.
18 Adams, *Jefferson's Extracts from the Gospels*, 32.
19 Ibid., 7.
20 E.W. Said, *Orientalism* (London: Penguin Books, 1978), 3.
21 For a list of passages Roy included, see, A.A.-A. Ghazi, *Raja Rammohun Roy: An Encounter with Islam and Christianity and the Articulation of Hindu Self-consciousness* (Bloomington, IN: Xlibris Corporation, 2010), 293–302; and for the passages left out by Jefferson, see C. Haus, *The Reverse Jefferson Bible: What the President Left Out* (Clear Words.org, 2009).
22 J.P. Boyd, ed., *The Papers of Thomas Jefferson*, vol. 1, *1760–1776* (Princeton, NJ: Princeton University Press, 1950), 550.
23 Boyd, *The Papers of Thomas Jefferson*, vol. 12, 16.
24 Roy, *The English Works of Raja Rammohun Roy*, 553.
25 Adams, *Jefferson's Extracts from the Gospels*, 376.
26 Ibid., 397.
27 Roy, *The English Works of Raja Rammohun Roy*, 584.
28 Adams, *Jefferson's Extracts from the Gospels*, 370.
29 Boyd, *The Papers of Thomas Jefferson*, vol. 12, 16.
30 Adams, *Jefferson's Extracts from the Gospels*, 385.
31 Ibid., 388.
32 Ibid., 396.
33 A. Schweitzer, *The Quest of the Historical Jesus: The First Complete Edition Edited by John Bowden* (London: SCM Press, 2000), 480.
34 Adams, *Jefferson's Extracts from the Gospels*, 24.
35 Ibid., 331.
36 Ibid., 38.
37 S. Radhakrishnan, *Eastern Religions and Western Thought* (Oxford: Clarendon Press, 1939), 184.

Chapter 13

HERMENEUTICAL ACHIEVEMENTS: STRENGTHS AND SHORTCOMINGS

Max Müller, the controversial yet compelling Orientalist, saw in Roy a fellow Aryan engaged in similar work to his own, namely, restoring the 'old religion of India, as contained in the Veda'.[1] Both were involved in unearthing what they imagined to be the original message of the Vedas, but Roy went one step further in identifying the pure essence of the Gospels. While Müller made available sacred texts of the East to Westerners,[2] Roy's vernacular translations opened the ancient wisdom to his own people which until then had been inaccessible to them. But Roy offered something that Müller could not do. While his fellow Hindus perpetuated the tradition in the name of shastric authority, Roy began privately to generate interpretations which challenged the accepted wisdom and priestly authority. He moved the debate, which was largely based on shared core values, faith, tradition and authority, to one in which everything regardless of its deeply rooted nature was questioned from the perspective of thoughtful reason and logic.

In another important respect, Roy's interpretative work surpassed Müller's. Roy was involved in stripping off mythological elements in the Gospels which was of little interest to Müller. Roy was engaged in isolating Jesus from later doctrinal accretions, wresting the Bible from manipulative Church authorities, and weeding out Christian doctrines manipulated by crafty clergy. Müller did not engage with any of these. Roy went even further, something which Müller could not have emulated. He subjected his own Hindu tradition to a similar scrutiny. He recovered a pure and elevated form of theism from the Vedantic texts amidst dualist, non-dualist and pantheistic passages interwoven in them. In doing so, he reinstated an enlightened adoration of the one true divine from the idolatrous worship encouraged by his fellow Brahmin pundits. Roy never thought himself as a reformer or discoverer of the doctrine of the unity of God: 'I have urged in every work that I have hitherto published, that the doctrines of the unity of God are real Hindooism, as that religion was practised by our ancestors, and as it is well known even at the present age to many learned Brahmins.'[3]

It's worth recalling that Roy did not fight against Christians, but he fought for purifying Christianity from institutional accretions. He attributed the decadence of both Christianity and Hinduism to the influence of Church authorities and the priestly caste of both religions. He was not against Christians or missionaries but disputed their doctrinal form of Christianity. He did not attack Christian believers but defended the Bible against the narrow interpretations of the missionaries. Similarly, he did not quarrel with Hindus but resisted the Brahmanical elements which introduced images and polytheistic worship and meaningless rituals. Roy had all along claimed that his dispute was not with Brahminism but with the perversion of it. All his disagreements were with the religious leaders who put aside 'justice and honesty' and invented passages to support their doctrines which were 'absurd and contradictory assertion'.

Roy's *Precepts* showed his Hindu compatriots that Semitic images found in the foreign religion were not something alien that they had to be protected from. Roy assured them that the ethical precepts of Jesus would enrich their tradition rather than enervate it. The message of Jesus had to be understood for its moral content and utility and, more specifically, for its potential to uplift India from her moral inertia. He encouraged his fellow Hindus and also Indian Muslims to read the Bible and evaluate it for themselves. He firmly believed that the study of the scriptures of other people and the embracing of biblical ethics would not undermine their religious heritage but enrich it. Unlike the current Hindu nationalists, Roy wanted to remove the fear of other religions among the Hindus. The confidence he had in his own faith enabled him to advocate this. When the distribution of the Bible caused uneasiness among students, he reassured them that Horace Hyman Wilson, who studied Hindu scriptures, remained a Christian, and Roy himself had read the Qur'an and the Bible and had neither become a Musalman nor a Christian. He asked them 'why then do you fear to read it? Read it and judge for yourself'.[4]

Roy never opposed religion as such but he had his own vision of it. The core of authentic religion, for Roy, was the belief in one ultimate Being who is 'the animating and regulating principle of the whole collective body of the universe' and who is the 'origin of all individual souls'. All that was required to worship such a Being was compassion or 'benevolence towards each other'.[5] In one of the last letters that Roy wrote before his death to Robert Dale Owen, a freethinker, he told him that religion promoted 'social, domestic and political welfare'. In his reckoning it is a system which promoted 'love and charity' and is capable of 'furthering our happiness, facilitating our reciprocal transactions and curbing our obnoxious feelings and passions'. But he had his own criterion for evaluating a religion. His judging principle, whether it was Christianity or Vedantism, was none other than the generic, global ethical practices of love and charity. Even before Gandhi who made religion into a public discourse, Roy's modest proposal encouraged such intervention of religion in public life.[6]

He wrote little about salvation and constantly challenged the missionaries' view of vicarious redemption, a person dying on behalf of humankind. While missionaries were talking about human depravity and the need for salvation, he was promoting the moral improvement of his fellow Indians and their social well-being. This is what made him different from missionary preachers of the time. His initial attack on polytheism, image worship and popular expressions of Hindu faith was based on his conviction that these destroyed 'every humane and social feeling' and 'texture of society', and he deeply believed that such practices led to immorality. He blamed the stories of Krishna, which encouraged nakedness, licentiousness and murder. He found kali worship even more obnoxious, for it included human sacrifice. His drive against *sati* (immolation of widows on the funeral pyre of their husbands) was an example of bringing about social change. His vision of obtaining salvation was limited to 'spiritual devotion, benevolence, and self-control, as the only means of securing bliss'.[7] He rejected the Hindu frugal way of living with strict dietary rules regarding food and drink and the Hindu notion of asceticism which crucially prevented people from taking care of the needs of others. He declared that the 'faith in the Supreme being, when united with moral works, leads men to eternal happiness'.[8] More importantly, while Christianity offered other worldly salvation, he emphasized salvation as this worldly. The persistent criticism that was levelled against him by his critics was whether the moral sayings alone were sufficient for salvation without doctrinal support. He was not seriously concerned about salvation and he never speculated on the problem.

Roy detected very early the insidious connection between knowledge and power, which is common in current discourse analysis. The missionary interpretation for him was about the assertion of power bolstered by the 'virtue of conquest'. He maintained that the 'truth and true religion did not always belong to wealth and power, high names or lofty palaces'. He perceived this hermeneutical control in binary terms as a battle between 'reason, scripture and common sense' and 'wealth, power and prejudice'. What the interconnection between power and position did was to make it impossible for those in authority to 'perceive their own defects'. Roy exposed the view that there was an innate link between political power, scientific advancement and religious truth. He informed his fellow Indians that the way the English conducted their political affairs and made scientific inventions did not mean that their religious doctrines would be 'equally reasonable', and their religious truth had 'no connection with political success'.

Roy alerted the Hindus to the fact that their own culture and religious heritage were under attack by two invading forces – Muslim Mughals and the Christian British. Though he was enthused by the foreign religions which accompanied these occupiers, he was also exasperated by them. He reminded them that as a people they were cultured, compassionate and charitable, and worthy. While he did not feel the need to get rid of these foreign occupiers, he acted as an inspiration for his fellow Hindus, not to feel inferior but, rather, to be proud and superior to these invaders. He inculcated a fair amount of national pride but disassociated himself from the virulence and viciousness that routinely went with such patriotic aspirations. Though Roy did not use the language of identity politics, he inadvertently sowed the seeds of Hindu self-consciousness which in Modi's modern-day India has taken sinister and brutal forms.

Roy was instrumental in reminding Indians of their traditional riches and offering them future hopes. He reminded them that the world was 'indebted *to our ancestors* for the first dawn of knowledge, which sprang up in the East and thanks to Goddess of Wisdom'.[9] He told them that they still had Sanskrit, a 'philosophical and copious language' which distinguished them from other nations, who cannot express scientific or abstract ideas without borrowing the language of a foreigner – a clear hint at English, which had borrowed vocabularies from other European languages.[10] Such monumental value ascribed to India would later come under heavy postcolonial accusations of re-orientalizing the orient.

He offered Vedic religion as a formidable rival to the biblical tradition as the oldest and profoundest record of human spiritual strength. He seemed to have recovered Sankara's *advaita*, which had been somewhat marginalized by the Hindus of Bengal at that time. He would not have imagined that the advaita Vedanta that he moderately advocated would one day be repurposed for Hindu nationalism. Roy would not have anticipated that this eighth-century philosophy meant for an ascetic way of life would, like Semitic monotheism, swallow up all rival and diverse theological perceptions and become a colonizing tool to herd all Hindus under one single system.

While his missionary opponents tried to emphasize the strength and uniqueness of the Christian faith, Roy took a different approach altogether. He spoke of the broadmindedness and universality of the Hindu tradition which made the religion of the missionaries look like a stern, mean, judgemental and narrow faith. Roy made monotheistic ideals and service to humanity not exclusive to Christianity but also part of the Hindu system. He wrote with his usual confidence that his travels in many lands and studying many scriptures had led him to the conclusion that it was natural and common for all human beings to turn towards One Eternal Being.

Roy was probably the first Indian to offer an intellectual response from a Hindu perspective and a critique of the theology of the missionaries in India. There were earlier protests in India about the missionaries' activities, which were mainly in the form of violent agitation, as evidenced in the 1806 Vellore Mutiny. Up until this point it had been the Christian missionaries who attacked the follies of the Hindus. Now more horrifying to the missionaries, a Hindu had come forward to expose the discrepancies and prejudices of Christianity, and aimed to reform the missionaries' view of Christianity from the outside. He criticized the missionaries for teaching their dogmas and mysteries to people as if they had been brought up in a Christian country and had been acquainted with them from their infancy.

Roy did not let the missionary charges and the defamation of Hinduism go unanswered. He forensically analysed their accusations and found that the version of Christianity propagated by the missionaries was not only irrational but also encouraged immoral practices. He blamed the missionaries who zealously ascribed 'unreasonableness to every other system of religion' and tended to close their eyes to 'the total want of reason and irrationality in the faith which they themselves profess and preach'. If there is any notion at all which is 'unreasonable and conducive to immoral practices' it is the idea of an atoning God 'that God *has blood*, and the blood is offered *by God* to reconcile to God'.[11] He was totally convinced that his version and method of promoting Christianity in India was likely to be more effective and successful than the exclusive, strident and illiberal one advocated by the missionaries.

Roy was wounded by the ferocious attack of his missionary and Christian opponents. Undaunted, he worked out a superior sense of Hindu universality and originality which matched, or even outclassed, such western claims. While expressing gratitude for the introduction of science from the West, the proud

Indian that he was, he acknowledged indebtedness to his Hindu ancestors in the field of science, literature and religion.

Müller, who offered a cautious welcome to the interpretative efforts of Roy, commented that his expositions were 'half true, half false',[12] and no one was in a position to challenge or criticize him. Though Müller saw Roy as a kindred spirit, this was the Western Orientalists' stock dismissal and distrust of natives. Roy's greatest advantage was that he knew biblical languages, such as Hebrew and Greek, and vernacular languages, such as Bengali and Sanskrit, which allowed him to make his own independent judgement on the biblical books as well as on his own Vedic texts and their contexts, and to dispute the exegesis of the missionaries and fellow Bengali pundits.

Unlike the countless Hindu reformers and Christian thinkers who came after him, Roy was not in the business of indigenizing Christianity and transforming its unfamiliar cultural trappings into identifiable Indian idioms. Roy was the first one to call Jesus an Asiatic, but he did not attempt to frame Jesus within Indian images as a jivanmukta (one who attained liberation while alive) or a satyagrahi (lover and fighter for truth). Rather, his was an earlier attempt at the Semeticization of the Vedic tradition. His insistence on the monotheistic ideal is a conspicuous example. The ideal moral teachings he singled out – the Golden Rule and the Great Commandments, love thy god and love thy neighbour – was nothing but the 'sum of the Torah'.[13] He was a partial initiator of the Semeiticizing process which Romila Thapar theorized later. A single God (one Supreme Being), a single text (the Upanishads) and a single community (Brahmo Samaj). Far from reconceptualizing human-divine encounters of Asia, Roy did the opposite by strengthening Semitic images.

Roy's articulations are far from perfect. There are a number of inconsistencies in his writings. He insisted that there was no necessity for 'intermediate agencies' such as 'prophets or revelation' for guidance in attaining spiritual salvation. But he repeatedly acknowledged Jesus as the 'Redeemer, Mediator and the Intercessor with God on behalf of his followers.' Another notion that Roy undermined was that of Jesus as a unique Messiah, pointing out that there were many before like him, but then he hailed Jesus as a long awaited Messiah destined to 'suffer death and difficulties like other prophets'. Similarly, Roy disputed Jesus as the Son of God but did not hesitate to perceive him as a Son of God in human capacity as someone who was honoured and sanctified by God.

While Roy dismissed the miracles of Jesus as an ineffective means to attract the Hindus, he conceded the value that the supernatural deeds of Jesus had for the Jews. He reckoned that they prompted a great number of Jews to a belief in Jesus as the promised Messiah and further enabled his disciples to confirm their already acquired faith in the Saviour: 'Then those men, when they had seen the miracle that Jesus did, said, This is of a truth that prophet that should come into the world' (Jn 6.14). Roy implicitly acknowledged the power of the miracles of Jesus.

He also often resorted to a mixture of humour, threat, paternalism and compassion. His dry wit comes out when he debated with an irate East India Company doctor called Tytler who was concerned about Roy's anti-Trinitarian stance. In the course of their exchanges when the doctor became more wilfully obstinate, Roy teased him saying that the same omnipotent God who can 'make three ONE and one THREE, can equally reconcile the unity and plurality of three hundred and thirty millions, both being supported by a sublime mystery which far transcends all human comprehension'.[14] His point being that the numerical differences between three persons of the Trinity and the Hindu belief in three thousand gods were founded on frail human reason and were fallible. He suggested that those who hold on to the Trinitarian belief should be shown 'compassion' rather than resentment on account of their 'errors' into which they had fallen blindly. While suggesting benevolence to his opponents, he could be exegetically vicious and sarcastic when Hindu beliefs and practices were attacked and challenged. He warned that if the missionaries ridiculed the rituals of the Vedas, he would be forced to refer to 'ceremonies of similar character in the Christian Scriptures' and if they should dwell on the corruptions that had crept into modern Hinduism, he would remind them of the 'corruptions introduced by various sects into Christianity'. He would compare what missionaries called corruptions in Hinduism with similar corruptions prevalent in Protestant, Catholic, Armenian and Greek churches. He would cite the examples of 'idols, crucifixes, saints, miracles, pecuniary absolutions from sins, trinity, transubstantiation, relics, holy water, other idolatrous machinery' prevalent in these churches to demonstrate that they were not different from those practised in Hinduism. When the Hindu belief of God appearing in animal forms came under missionary ridicule, he asked them how they could possibly make a mockery of Hindu gods appearing in the shape of a fish or a cow when the Gospels claimed the appearance of God in the form a dove to testify the appointment of Jesus as God's son. He taunted them: 'Is not a fish as innocent as a dove? Is not a cow more useful than a pigeon?' When missionaries become unreasonable and showed utter contempt for Hinduism, his method was to offer counter foibles for all the allegations missionaries levelled against Hinduism.

It is not easy to figure out Roy's hermeneutical influences. This is largely complicated by Roy's annoyingly reticent habit of not clearly articulating his intellectual sources. According to *The Monthly Repository,* he had prepared himself for his 'polemical career from the logic of the Arabians which he regard[ed] as superior to every other'.[15] The influence of Islamic thought was evident in *Tuhfat*, which he was supposed to have written in his teenage days. Traditional Hindu philosophical knowledge was also a significant factor in Roy's intellectual world. He found an ally in the Unitarians who advocated this-worldly salvation and took an anti-Trinitarian stance. Roy's intellectual and rational approach to religion chimed with that of the Unitarians. His method showed a clever use of Unitarian rationality and localized it for his Indian audience. His writings are suffused with Western enlightenment writers, such as Locke and Newton, despite his admission that he 'found nothing in European books equal to the scholastic philosophy of the Hindoos'.[16]

Roy's work is a conspicuous case of what Edward Said called 'Late Style'. Studying the works of artists, authors and musicians, Said noted that at the end of their careers they exhibited two kinds of response: (1) anarchy and anomaly, and (2) a sense of mellowness and maturity and an attempt to cleanse earlier recklessness and rebelliousness.[17] Roy's writings fall within the second category and show a sense of mellowness, harmony and a streak of conservativism. Roy, who was relentless in advocating that the best method of interpretation was not in surrendering exclusively to the texts and vehement that one should 'appeal to reason', ended up confessing that one should rely on 'the goodness of the Almighty Power, which alone enables us to attain that which we earnestly and diligently seek for'.[18] Or, as he put it, the 'best method was not to surrender' oneself 'completely in the hands of sastras and reasoning' but to be 'dependent upon the beneficence of the Almighty God'. In general research into theological truth, reason is not a 'sure sign' because it serves to 'generate a universal doubt'. His message was to trust 'in the mercy of that Being to whom the motives of our actions and secrets of our hearts are well known'.[19] It was the same Roy who in his rebellious first pamphlet had castigated the religious leaders when their theological claims clashed with reason, who then responded with the stock answer that 'affairs of religion depend upon faith and Divine Help'.[20] He even chastised them with Quranic phrases. His persistent opposition to idol worship and multiple gods and goddesses seemed to soften in his later days, and he recommended that such practices were for people who were 'incapable of adoring the invisible Supreme Being'. The final blow for reason as a valid resource came when he composed songs for the Brahma Sabha which were marked by emotion and intuition.

It was Roy's comparative religious engagements and intertextual study of various scriptures that gave impetus to the succeeding generation of both Hindu reformers and Christian thinkers to stretch their imaginations to the utmost for the hermeneutical task of India. It was Roy's audacious assertion that Jesus was an Asiatic that paved the way for later reformers such as Keshub Chunder Sen to claim that 'I am an Asiatic, was not Jesus an Asiatic'[21] and Swami Vivekananda to remind the missionaries that despite all their 'attempts to paint him with blue eyes and yellow hair, the Nazarene was still an oriental'.[22] Similarly, it was Roy's comparative study of the scriptures which acted as an incentive for people such as K.M. Banerjea, at times forcefully or in violation of the original context, to demonstrate closer ties between Vedic texts and a Mosaic dispensation.[23] Chunder Sen's use of a variety of scriptures in his Dispensation Church and Gandhi's engagement with multireligious texts in his prayer meetings would not have been possible without Roy's hospitality towards the sacred texts of other people. It was Roy's international outlook and his perception of the world as one family and vision of a borderless world that enabled Gandhi to say 'I do not want my house to be walled in on all sides and my windows to be stuffed. I want the culture of all lands to be blown about my house as freely as possible. But I refuse to be blown off my feet by any.'[24] It was Roy who gave the confidence that, as Asiatics, they were in a better position to figure out Jesus and understand the Gospels which were the products and heritage of West Asia. Christianity meant much more to Roy. He took hold of the religion of the West and almost made it his own. He came up with his own definition of who a Christian was, reconfigured Jesus as an Asiatic and took away the monopoly of the Westerners as the sole interpreters of Christianity. In Roy's revisioning, Christianity hardly looked like a white man's religion and the blue-eyed Nazarene resembled a dusky Asiatic.

Notes

1. Müller, *Biographical Essays*, 3.
2. A fifty volume set of religious text of the east published between 1879 and 1910 by Oxford University Press.
3. Roy, *Translation of Several Principal Books*, 136.
4. Collet, *The Life and Letters of Raja Rammohun Roy*, 281.
5. Roy, *The English Works of Raja Rammohun Roy*, 198.
6. For the full text of the letter, see Collet, *The Life and Letters of Raja Rammohun Roy*, 494–495.
7. Roy, *The English Works of Raja Rammohun Roy*, 222.
8. Ibid., 106.
9. Ibid., 906.
10. Ibid.
11. Ibid., 197, emphasis in original.
12. Müller, *Biographical Essays*, 19.
13. U. Luz, *Matthew 1–7: A Commentary* (Edinburgh: T & T Clark, 1990), 426.
14. Roy, *The English Works of Raja Rammohun Roy*, 893.
15. 'An Account of the Life and Writings of Rammohun Roy', 3.
16. Ibid.
17. E.W. Said, *On Late Style* (London: Bloomsbury, 2006), 5–7.
18. Roy, *The English Works of Raja Rammohun Roy*, 37.
19. Roy, *Translation of Several Principal Books*, 58.
20. Roy, *The English Works of Raja Rammohun Roy*, 950.
21. K.C. Sen, *Keshub Chunder Sen's Lectures in India* (London: Cassell and Company, 1901), 33.
22. Swami Vivekananda, *The Complete Works of Swami Vivekananda. Mayavati Memorial Edition*, vol. 4 (Almora: Advaita Ashrama, 1923), 138.
23. K.M. Banerjea, *The Arian Witness: Or the Testimony of Arian Scriptures in Corroboration of Biblical History and the Rudiments of Christian Doctrine, Including Dissertations on the Original and Early Adventures of Indo-Arians* (Calcutta: Thacker, Spink & Co., 1875).
24. *Collected Works of Mahatma Gandhi*, vol. 23, *6 April 1921–21 July 1921*, 215. Available online: https://www.gandhiashramsevagram.org/gandhi-literature/mahatma-gandhi-collected-works-volume-23.pdf (accessed 20 June 2019).

Chapter 14

READING RAMMOHUN ROY TODAY

There are no settled views on Rammohun Roy. They vary from complimentary to cautiously reserved about his accomplishments. The often tediously repeated epithet is that he is the father of modern India. His groundbreaking progressive social reforms have resulted in this term being routinely applied to his work and career. 'First' and 'pioneer' are often attached to his name and rightly so. Monier-Williams's identification of him as 'perhaps the first-earnest minded investigator of the science of comparative religion that world has produced' is suitably apposite for the central concern of this volume. Roy had his fair share of uncharitable critics too. He was perceived as a pliable personality wanting to please all of the people all of the time. James Sutherland, his friend, put it thus: 'no matter what the creed of the parties with whom he conversed on such subjects', he was sure to impress upon them that 'they had converted him to it'.[1] He was smeared as a 'privileged native informant and a mouthpiece for British rule in India'.[2] Fellow Hindu Bengalis called him an 'apostate' and a 'renegade' for compromising the Vedas to suit theistic notions from the Bible. While an upper-class Brahmin dismissed him for being totally removed from his own people, an Indian Christian discounted him as an 'inconsistent and reprehensible'[3] reformer. For Hindus and Christians he was a meddlesome and serial interventionist in religious matters. There is some truth in all these plaudits and accusations.

What Roy achieved in nineteenth-century colonial Bengal has some resonances for postcolonial India. As it has been noted earlier, his interventions are too vast and enormous and go well beyond the principal focus of this volume. More to the point, I am not the right person to undertake such an enterprise. Therefore, I will restrict myself to issues pertaining to this volume.

Roy's striking contribution was to make Indians realize that no real benefit could come to India by merely embracing Western values. He asserted with energetic fervour that no Western import could be of any genuine worth except in so far it was naturalized. Intellectually and in his lifestyle Roy was westernized but continued to be a Hindu. He wanted Indians to remain Indian while being open to the riches of other cultures. He desired the removal of all barriers and encouraged and facilitated the free movement of people 'in order to promote reciprocal advantage and enjoyment of the whole human race'.[4] Roy's firm commitment to Indian ideals placed him as an ideal explainer and go-between for Indians and English people.

In these post-empire days, there is a temptation to portray Roy as a plucky subaltern voice as some postcolonial critics would prefer or tend to depict him. Roy was not an oppressed subject of an occupying force. He was far from that. He was part of the Indian intelligentsia which transformed itself into a westernized intellectual elite through colonial service. He occupied the highest position a native could aspire to. Müller mentions in his biographical essay that 'a special clause had to be inserted in his Agreement that he should not be kept standing in the presence of his employer'.[5] Not only professionally but also intellectually he imagined himself as one of the Western freethinkers on religion and wanted his missionary opponents to see him as part of the questioning world of Locke and Newton whose Christianity, like his, contained no doctrine of the Trinity. Unlike the current Hindu traditionalists, Roy's reframing of Hindu ideals was not born from victimhood or an inferiority complex but from strength and status.

He was not even an anti-colonial figure. Progressive and emancipatory ideas like 'independence' and 'national freedom' were not part of the Indian discourse at that time. The person who supported the Irish peasants against their absentee landlords and celebrated when constitutional governments were established in Spanish-controlled South America did not think in terms of India's freedom. He welcomed the British as a sign of divine providence to 'break the yoke of those tyrants [i.e. Mughal rule] and to receive the oppressed Bengal under its protection'.[6] He even thanked the 'Supreme Disposer of the Universe' for the British who delivered India 'from the long continued tyranny of its former rulers'.[7] He genuinely welcomed the English as 'deliverers' rather than as 'a body of conquerors'.[8] His deference to the British rulers was so cringingly reprehensible that he described the Indians as the 'lowest of your subjects'. In fact, he offered support and prayed for the continuation of British rule and presence. He was willing to 'reconcile to the present state of things', however uncomfortable they were, for the advantages, promises and permanent benefits to the posterity of India derived from the 'connection with the Great Britain'.[9] In an attempt to please, he also heaped an exaggerated praise on the British for the abolition of sati – an abolition in which he played a considerable role – and he gave an inflated credit to them saying that it would not have been possible without their help. He hoped for gradual and lasting improvement under British rule. This was the same Roy, who in his younger days was apprehensive about the British presence. In his autobiographical note he wrote that he felt 'great aversion to the establishment of the British power in India'.[10]

Some of the theological issues that Roy raised still have relevance for Christians. Roy, nearly two hundred years ago, identified Jesus as an Asiatic, and except for sporadic individual attempts, the Indian Church has yet to exploit the Asianness of Jesus. Institutional and ecumenical documents are still couched in Semitic and Hellenistic images. One of the descriptions of Jesus he hinted at and predictably did develop was Jesus as the Wisdom of God. Indian Christians could explore more the image of Jesus as a sage rather than portraying him in royal and triumphalistic tones which was redundant in a country overpopulated with princely warrior gods and goddesses. Jesus as a sage would be a barricade against an imperial Jesus who encouraged subjugation and slavery to a monotheistic god, a god who eventually subdues everyone in the Kingdom of God – the universal empire. The lesson to the Indian Christians is to tell the Gospel story in a non-coercive way.

Roy has another message for Christians. The doctrinal and mythological language in which Christianity was presented would confuse people, but worse it had nothing new to say to India. His counsel to the missionaries had been that there was no point in employing convoluted strategies to prop them up. The current theological fraternity should take note of Roy's plea to Marshman and his compatriots that Christians should stick with the simple and sensible moral precepts of Jesus rather than imposing muddled and messy dogmas.

Roy's lay status and his persisting hermeneutical interventions as a non-professional theologian are a call to Indian Christians to recover the amateur tradition of doing theology. This was a virtuous trait of earlier Indian theological discourse, now completely lost. It was the writings of laypersons such as Pandipeddi Chenchiah, Vengal Chakkarai, M. M. Thomas, J. C. Kumarappa, Pandita Ramabai (all high caste) and Sarojini Pakiamuttu that illuminated Indian Christian theology. Now we have seminary-trained specialists and technical formalists who churn out minutely detailed, excruciating work which has little purpose other than advancing their careers. Roy is an apt example for Indian laypeople for recapturing the bygone days of doing theology with care and affection rather than dabbling with showy methods and splashy techniques.

There are certain areas where Roy and the current Hindu nationalists seem to align. But a close reading will reveal that although there are some close affinities between the two, they are beset with serious disagreements. Both believe that an inquiry into India's past and the multiplicity of its ancient traditions would make India proud again. Roy's reverential reference to 'our books and our example', his robust declaration that the Hindus were the 'original inhabitants' of India, his popularization of the notion that Hindus were the most tolerant of all people and that all were 'equally within the reach of Divine',[11] could be seen as not only providing profitable fodder for the Hindutva cause but could also prompt Hindu nationalists to think that he was one of their own. What the Hindu nationalists would conveniently overlook is that Roy's retrieval of India's glorious past occurred in a context in which the morale and morality of Hindus were abysmally low. His reclamation was undertaken solely to induce self-confidence to already intellectually and spiritually weakened Indians. Such a monumental value ascribed to India's fabled past would not only fall into wrong hands but also lend itself to the postcolonial accusation of re-orientalizing the orient.

Roy and Hindu nationalists concur on another point – the thorny issue of conversion. Roy, too, raised his opposition to the conversion of Hindus. He knew very well how vulnerable people were exploited and coerced into the Christian faith by the provision of material help. Thus far he and the Hindutva were on the same page, but where he differed was the reason for their disapproval. He opposed conversions not because Christianity was a foreign religion, or because it came with the colonialists as deplored by current Hindu apologists, but because the new faith presented by the missionaries was no different from Hinduism. It was disturbingly similar to it and hence there was no need to embrace the foreign faith.

Roy's anti-Christian stance was not motivated by xenophobia – that the converts would be a threat to national interests – but by the pointlessness and uselessness of converting to a religion which was as bad as Hinduism. Unlike the current Hindu nationalists, Roy did not entertain the idea that conversion was a lapse from Hinduism and a dilution of an authentic Indian identity. He never imagined it as an un-Indian or an un-Hindu activity.

But there are also other stark differences between Roy and current Hindu nationalists. Roy delved into the past with a view to inspiring pride and implanting an awareness of the 'fabled India' in the face of missionaries thrusting Christianity with the involvement and collusion of the invading power. Hinduism then looked weak and vulnerable and was passing through a weary and sterile phase fuelled by the missionaries discounting and discrediting Hinduism, coupled with useless rites confected by crafty Hindu priests. It was under these circumstances that Roy's retrieval of the ancient past took place. Today the denunciation of Hinduism that was propelled by subtle support for colonial rule is no more. Now Hindus are the dominant majority in India and Christians and other religious minorities are at the receiving end of the ire of Hindu nationalists. Whereas Roy looked to the ancient texts to instil pride and self-worth in fellow Hindus who were intellectually too vulnerable to withstand the missionary onslaught, the current Hindu nationalists dredge the Vedic scriptures to gloat about the spiritual prowess and scientific expertise of ancient India, and in order to demonstrate how Indians were much more advanced than the West and used algorithms and performed cataract operations in the Vedic period even before these things were invented in the West.

This leads neatly into another contentious issue for Roy and Hindu nationalists – the use and manipulation of the Vedanta. Roy offered Vedic religion as a formidable rival to the biblical tradition as the oldest and profoundest record of humanity's spiritual quest. He recovered Sankara's advaita, bypassing a fellow Vaishnavite philosopher Ramanuja, which had been somewhat marginalized by the Hindus of Bengal at that time. He would not have imagined that the advaita Vedanta that he moderately advocated would one day be repurposed for Hindu nationalism. He would not have envisaged that this ancient philosophy worked out for the ascetic life of a certain group of people would now be in the hands of Hindu nationalists and turned into a colonizing and tyrannical single value system. Just as Semitic monotheism swallowed up and dethroned all rival theological thinking and perspectives, advaita has become a single unifying template for Hindu nationalists, which absorbed enormous diversity within Hinduism.

Although the current Hindu nationalists may be drawn to Roy's advaita Vedanta as a national ideal, they will find it difficult to embrace him enthusiastically for their twisted Hindu vision. What Roy encouraged was Vedantic philosophy but not Vedantic education. He would have found it difficult to accept Vedic roots for plastic surgery or the construction of aeroplanes as claimed by *Bharatiya Vidya Saar*, a textbook produced by the All India Council of Technical Education (AICTE).[12] Roy would have dismissed such outrageous claims as 'imaginary learning'. In his view, such an education was loading the minds of the youth with 'grammatical niceties and metaphysical distinctions' with 'no practical use'[13] and 'calculated to keep this country in darkness.'[14]

Roy and Hindu traditionalists are keen on revering and reverting to ancient scriptures. Roy chose the Upanishads as the text for the Brahma Samaj (a monotheistic reform movement within Hinduism), but he would not have nominated or singled it out as the national book of India, as Sushma Swaraj, a cabinet member in Modi's government, has done. Her decision was based not on lofty spiritual ideals but on a bizarre logic that Prime Minister Modi presented the book to President Obama. Roy did not believe that any one book had the monopoly of truth. As seen earlier he professed that whatever was good in the Vedas was found in other scriptures and should be acknowledged as equally valid revelation and emanating from the 'God of Truth'. He encouraged his fellow Hindus as well as Indian Muslims to follow his practice of reading the Bible and one another's scriptures, and to evaluate them for themselves. He firmly believed that such a comparative intertextual study of other peoples' scriptures and embracing the ethics of the Bible would not undermine the religious heritage of India but would enrich it. Unlike the current Hindu nationalists, he removed the fear among Hindus of the 'other' religions. The confidence he had in his own faith enabled him to do this.

Related to the above point is the question of borrowing from other scriptural traditions. Roy, as an avid reader of various religious texts, realized that creative borrowing from other religious traditions enhances one's thinking and outlook. Unlike the Hindu nationalists, for him borrowing was not a sign of weakness but an enhancing activity. His appropriation of biblical monotheism was a conspicuous case in point. It was an exemplary illustration of how acquisition from other texts or from other cultures illuminates and offers a fresh perspective to one's own texts and viewpoint. His bibliocentric monotheistic reading of the Upanishads yielded a different perception that helped to strengthen and create a new awareness among Hindus of their faith which was at a very low point at that time. What Roy did was to make the monotheistic ideal one of his 'crowning achievements'.[15] He used it to reiterate monotheism as part of the Hindu system and not something exclusive to Christianity. Such a borrowing from non-Hindu sources would be anathema to current Hindu reformers.

Roy would also have parted company with the Hindu religionists who act as cultural police and impose strident dietary habits and dress codes. When an anonymous defender of Hinduism who called himself the Establisher of Religion and posed questions to Roy about a certain well-known person from the Vaishnava tradition (one of the major sects within Hinduism), who ignored these injunctions and cut off his hair, ate fish, drank wine and consorted with infidels, Roy shot back at him contrasting him with the people who outwardly fulfilled strict prescriptions of religion but were abusive at home. He was concerned that people should spend time on 'judging of the propriety and impropriety of certain foods without reflecting on the science or Divine Truth', and he added a sardonic remark that the current food fascists and anti-beef eating Hindu fanatics should take note that 'it is certainly far more profitable to adorn the mind than think of purifying the belly'.[16] For him, mental and spiritual peace were more important than these useless external observations. He advocated that such regulations must be freed from the textual restrictions and hindrances and must be seen mainly from the principle of utility as well as the happiness and harmony that they could bring within and across religious communities. Roy firmly believed that the vitality and robustness of any religion depended on its ability to acclimatize to new situations. For him, in fulfilling the religious principles, the Hindu Smriti, Muslim sharia and the Christian canonical laws must accustom themselves to the ongoing revelations of God's truth in science and the laws of nature.

Unlike present-day Hindu nationalists, Roy did not valorize Aryans or Aryan culture. Roy in his English writings, seldom used the word Aryan. This was largely due to the fact that the idea of Aryan was not in existence at that time. It took nearly another thirty years before Aryan became a racial descriptor when Max Müller erroneously confused linguistic connections with race. Roy used generic terms such as pan-continental, Asiatic or wider regional, oriental or familial ancestors. Likewise, Roy never claimed India as a special place of God's revelation. For him God's revelation took place in Asia. In one of his letters, he informed one Mr French, a barrister in England, that God manifested 'in flesh in no other quarter of the world but in Asia'.[17] In other words, he did not restrict God's manifestation to a narrow subcontinent but the entire Asian continent. Similarly, Roy hardly claimed any special privilege for Indians or Hindus as God's chosen people but accorded that status to Asians as a whole who always had been God's 'most favourite and peculiar people'.[18]

Roy often used Hindustan not in the religious but in the geographical sense, which indicated lands that lay beyond the river Indus. He described Hindustan as a country of three-fifths Hindus and two-fifths Muslims, unjustifiably ignoring the presence of Christians, Sikhs, Parsees and Buddhists. But more tellingly, he did not see these communities as 'internal threats'. In his minute to a select committee appointed by the British Parliament on the question of the renewal of the charter of the East India Company, his description of India was mainly geographical and not about its people. In this deposition, he referred to Manu, maker of law codes, naming India as Aryavarta, which Roy found 'obscure' and 'wholly unintelligible'. Roy rendered the term not in a racial sense, which the current Hindu nationalists would like to do, but as a 'land inhabited by respectable people'.[19] In fact, he envisioned a borderless world and perceived humankind as 'one great family'.[20]

There are enough materials in Roy's writings which could play into the hands of the Hindu nationalists who would like to villainize these long dead and gone Mughal kings and treat them as substitutes for present-day Indian Muslims in order to whip up anti-Muslim feeling. Roy's attitude to Islamic learning, Muslim rule and Muslim character is a complex one – a mixture of drawing inspiration from Islamic theology and depressingly condemnatory of Mughal rule. He described the Mughal rulers as 'savage conquerors', 'despotic', 'cruel' and those who trampled upon the 'civil and religious rights of its original inhabitants', and he spoke of the 'religious horror of Muhammudans'. These negative representations are all grist to the mill for Hindu nationalists. Such an attitude is inexplicable and indefensible. What the Hindu traditionalists will overlook is that in the same Questions and Answers on the Judicial System of India in which Roy came up with these disappointingly negative images of Muslim rulers, Roy also praised the fairness of the Mughal rule and listed the benefits that the Hindus enjoyed under the Mughals, which included, among other things, high offices of state and the commanding of armies. He had a high regard for the honesty of Muslim lawyers and recommended that Muslim lawyers should be appointed to the criminal courts because they had the expertise and experience till 'other classes' (his term) acquired such qualifications. At the same time, Roy openly stated that Hindu lawyers did not enjoy the confidence of the public and are 'in general not well spoken of'. Given this, it is even more surprising that such negative images should come from Roy who learned about Islam not from the Western Orientalists but from Madrasas. His passion for monotheism, his opposition to idolatry and his depiction of Jesus as the messenger of God all came from his profitable learning of Islamic theology. Roy's anti-Muslim sentiment was the result of the combination of centuries of Muslim rule in India and the disintegration and ineffectiveness of Hinduism to provide hermeneutical resources to withstand those trying times. Whereas present-day India is not under Muslim rule but at the mercy of the majority Hindu rule which perceives Muslims as a threat.

Roy is a flawless exemplar of how to engage in inter-religious dialogue. In his writings, he was civil and courteous to his religious adversaries. Roy acts as a magnificent model for the current Hindu religionists as to how to conduct a religious debate. In his bitter controversy with Marshman and other Christian opponents, he was always courteous and showed no venom in his writings. He even praised the Serampore Baptist missionaries, once friends but later turned enemies as the 'best qualified' and the 'most careful observers' of Indian affairs.[21] While he was being 'vilified and abused', he continued to offer 'reason and argument'. This civil behaviour of Roy stands in contrast to the present-day Hindu writers such as Rajaram, Goel and Ram Swarup, to name a few, whose writings are marked by antagonism and vitriolic fulminations. For instance, Roy would not have used phrases such as 'foul mouthed', 'stark mad' – phrases employed by Goel to describe Jesus.[22] Roy conducted the debate with dignity and in a well-mannered way. He prayed for their well-being and empathized with them for toiling in a climate which was 'generally inimical to European constitutions'. One cannot imagine the current Hindutva brigade exhibiting civility to Christians and Muslims.

There is a temptation to turn Roy into a heroic figure for our times. Some of his articulations, especially his exegesis, have a valedictory tone about them now. His social interventions could strike home today, for the current generation of Indians. Some of the social and religious issues that Roy addressed are increasingly problematic in India today – even more so than in his own time. His fight against social evils, his support for the socially oppressed, especially women, and his warning against priestly manipulated religious practices and dogmas, his acceptance of various nations and tribes as branches of one human family, and his cosmopolitan vision are exemplary and worth emulating. At a time when there is a crude form of nationalism, poisonous popularism, perverted nativism and toxic religionism, Roy's call to free oneself from 'rustic uncatholicity', to recognize fulfilment in each other's traditions and heritage, and in this fulfilment to perceive interconnections among all humans, is a well-meaning principle to be matched and supported.

Notes

1. Collet, *The Life and Letters of Raja Rammohun Roy*, 370.
2. B. Joseph, *Reading the East India Company, 1720–1840: Colonial Currencies of Gender* (Chicago: Chicago University Press, 2004), 154.
3. R.C. Bose, *Brahmoism; or, History of Reformed Hinduism from Its Origins in 1830 Under Rajah Mohun Roy to the Present Time* (New York: Funk and Wagnalls, 1884), 39.
4. For his letter to Prince Talleyrand, see Collet, *The Life and Letters of Raja Rammohun Roy*, 502.
5. Müller, *Biographical Essays*, 16.
6. Roy, *The English Works of Raja Rammohun Roy*, 446.
7. Ibid., 447.
8. Ibid., 446.
9. R. Roy, *Selected Works of Raja Rammohun Roy* (Ahmedabad: Publications Division, Ministry of Information and Broadcasting, Government of India, 1958), 42.
10. Roy, *The English Works of Raja Rammohun Roy*, 224.
11. Ibid., 148.
12. Z. Us Salam, 'Now, Vedic Science', *Frontline*, 23 November 2018. Available online: https://www.frontline.in/the-nation/article25437649.ece?homepage=true (accessed 13 November 2018).
13. Roy, *The English Works of Raja Rammohun Roy*, 472.
14. Ibid., 474.
15. Hatcher, *Bourgeois Hinduism, or Faith of the Modern Vedantists*, 22.
16. Roy, *The English Works of Raja Rammohun Roy*, 138.
17. Roy, *The Correspondence of Raja Rammohun Roy*, vol. 1, 328.
18. Ibid.
19. Roy, *Selected Works of Raja Rammohun Roy*, 2.
20. Collet, *The Life and Letters of Raja Rammohun Roy*, 502.
21. Roy, *The English Works of Raja Rammohun Roy*, 447.
22. S.R. Goel, *Jesus Christ: An Artifice for Aggression* (New Delhi: Voice of India, 1994), 67.

THE

PRECEPTS OF JESUS

THE

GUIDE TO PEACE AND HAPPINESS;

EXTRACTED FROM

THE BOOKS OF THE NEW TESTAMENT,

ASCRIBED TO THE FOUR EVANGELISTS.

WITH

TRANSLATIONS INTO SUNGSCRIT AND BENGALEE.

CALCUTTA:

PRINTED AT THE BAPTIST MISSION PRESS,
CIRCULAR ROAD.

1820.

INTRODUCTION

A CONVICTION in the mind of its total ignorance of the nature and of the specific attributes of the Godhead, and a sense of doubt respecting the real essence of the soul, give rise to feelings of great dissatisfaction with our limited powers, as well as with all human acquirements which fail to inform us on these interesting points.—On the other hand, a notion of the existence of a supreme superintending power, the author and preserver of this harmonious system, who has organized and who regulates such an infinity of celestial and terrestrial objects; and a due estimation of that law which teaches that man should do unto others as he would wish to be done by, reconcile us to human nature, and tend to render our existence agreeable to ourselves and profitable to the rest of mankind.—The former of these sources of satisfaction, viz. a belief in God, prevails generally; being derived either from tradition and instruction, or from an attentive survey of the wonderful skill and contrivance displayed in the works of nature.—The latter, although it is partially taught also in every system of religion with which I am acquainted, is principally inculcated by Christianity. This essential characteristic of the Christian religion I was for a long time unable to distinguish as such, amidst the various doctrines I found insisted upon in the writings of Christian authors, and in the conversation of those teachers of Christianity with whom I have had the honor of holding communication. Amongst those opinions the most prevalent seems to be, that no one is justly entitled to the appellation of Christian who does not believe in the divinity of Christ and of the Holy Ghost, as well as in the divine nature of God the Father of all created beings. Many allow a much greater latitude to the term Christian, and consider it as comprehending all who acknowledge the Bible to contain the revealed will of God, however they may differ from others in their interpretations of particular passages of scripture; whilst some require from him who claims the title of Christian only an adherence to the doctrines of Christ, as taught by himself, without insisting on implicit confidence in those of the Apostles, as being, except when speaking from inspiration, like other men, liable to mistake and error.—That they were so is obvious from the several instances of differences of opinion amongst the Apostles recorded in the Acts Epistles.*

---

* Vide Acts, Chap. xi. 2, 3. Chap. xv. 2, 7. 1st Corinthians, Chap. i. 12. Galatians, Chap. ii. 11, 12, 13.

Voluminous works written by learned men of particular sects for the purpose of establishing the truth, consistency, rationality, and priority of their own peculiar doctrines, contain such a variety of arguments that I cannot hope to be able to adduce here any new reasonings of sufficient novelty and force to attract the notice of my readers; besides, in matters of religion particularly, men in general, through prejudice and partiality to the opinions which they once form, pay little or no attention to opposite sentiments (however reasonable they may be), and often turn a deaf ear to what is most consistent with the laws of nature, and conformable to the dictates of human reason and divine revelation. At the same time, to those who are not biassed by prejudice, and who are by the grace of God open to conviction, a simple enumeration and statement of the respective tenets of different sects may be a sufficient guide to direct their enquiries, in ascertaining which of them is the most consistent with the sacred traditions, and most acceptable to common sense.—For these reasons I decline entering into any discussion on those points, and confine my attention at present to the task of laying before my fellow creatures the words of Christ, with a translation from the English into Sungskrit and the language of Bengal. I feel persuaded that by separating from the other matters contained in the New Testament the moral precepts found in that book, these will be more likely to produce the desirable effect of improving the hearts and minds of men of different persuasions and degrees of understanding.—For historical and some other passages are liable to the doubts and disputes of free-thinkers and antichristians, especially miraculous relations, which are much less wonderful than the fabricated tales handed down to the natives of Asia*, and consequently would be apt at best to carry little weight with them.—On the contrary moral doctrines, tending evidently to the maintenance of the peace and harmony of mankind at large, are beyond the reach of metaphysical perversion, and intelligible alike to the learned and to the unlearned.— This simple code of Religion and morality is so admirably calculated to elevate men's ideas to high and liberal notions of one GOD, who has equally subjected all living creatures, without distinction of cast, rank, or wealth, to change, disappointment, pain, and death; and has equally admitted all to be partakers of the bountiful mercies which he has lavished over nature: and is also so well fitted to regulate the conduct of the human race in the discharge of their various duties to GOD, to themselves, and to Society, that I cannot but hope the best effects from its promulgation in the present form.

---

* Ugasti is famed for having swallowed the ocean, when it had given him offence, and having restored it by urinary evacuation: at his command also, the Vindhyu range of mountains prostrated itself, and so, remains. (Wilson's Dictionary.)

THE PRECEPTS OF JESUS
THE
GUIDE TO PEACE AND HAPPINESS.

* AND seeing the multitudes, he went up into a mountain: and when he was set, his disciples came unto him: and he opened his mouth, and taught them, saying, Blessed *are* the poor in spirit: for theirs is the kingdom of heaven. Blessed *are* they that mourn: for they shall be comforted. Blessed *are* the meek: for they shall inherit the earth. Blessed *are* they which do hunger and thirst after righteousness: for they shall be filled. Blessed *are* the merciful: for they shall obtain mercy. Blessed *are* the pure in heart: for they shall see God. Blessed *are* the peacemakers: for they shall be called the children of God. Blessed *are* they which are persecuted for righteousness' sake: for theirs is the kingdom of heaven. Blessed are ye, when *men* shall revile you, and persecute *you*, and shall say all manner of evil against you falsely, for my sake. Rejoice, and be exceeding glad: for great *is* your reward in heaven: for so persecuted they the prophets which were before you.

Ye are the salt of the earth: but if the salt have lost his savour, wherewith shall it be salted? It is thenceforth good for nothing, but to be cast out, and to be trodden under foot of men. Ye are the light of the world. A city that is set on an hill cannot be hid. Neither do men light a candle, and put it under a bushel, but on a candlestick: and it giveth light unto all that are in the house. Let your light so shine before men, that they may see your good works, and glorify your Father which is in heaven.

Think not that I am come to destroy the Law or the Prophets: I am not come to destroy, but to fulfil. For verily I say unto you, Till heaven and earth pass, one jot or one tittle shall in no wise pass from the law, till all be fulfilled. Whosoever therefore shall break one of these least commandments and shall teach men so, he shall be called the least in the kingdom of heaven: but whosoever shall do and teach *them*, the same shall be called great in the kingdom of heaven. For I say unto you. That except your righteousness shall exceed *the righteousness* of the scribes and Pharisees, ye shall in no case enter into the kingdom of heaven.

Ye have heard that it was said by them of old time. Thou shalt not kill; and whosoever shall kill shall be in danger of the judgment: but I say unto you. That whosoever is angry with his brother without a cause shall be in danger of the

---

* Matthew, Chap. v.

judgment: and whosoever shall say to his brother, Raca, shall be in danger of the council: but whosoever shall say, Thou fool, shall be in danger of hell fire. Therefore, if thou bring thy gift to the altar, and there rememberest that thy brother hath ought against thee, leave there thy gift before the altar, and go thy way; first be reconciled to thy brother, and then come and offer thy gift. Agree with thine adversary quickly, whilst thou art in the way with him; lest at any time the adversary deliver thee to the judge, and the judge deliver thee to the officer, and thou be cast into prison. Verily I say unto thee, Thou shalt by no means come out thence, till thou hast paid the uttermost farthing.

Ye have heard that it was said by them of old time, Thou shalt not commit adultery: but I say unto you, That whosoever looketh on a woman to lust after her, hath committed adultery with her already in his heart. And if thy right eye offend thee, pluck it out, and cast *it* from thee: for it is profitable for thee that one of thy members should perish, and not *that* thy whole body should be cast into hell. And if thy right hand offend thee, cut it off, and cast *it* from thee: for it is profitable for thee that one of thy members should perish, and not *that* thy whole body should be cast into hell. It hath been said, Whosoever shall put away his wife, let him give her a writing of divorcement: but I say unto you, That whosoever shall put away his wife; saving for the cause of fornication, causeth her to commit adultery: and whosoever shall marry her that is divorced, committeth adultery.

Ye have heard that it hath been said. Thou shalt love thy neighbour, and hate thine enemy: but I say unto you, Love your enemies, bless them that curse you, do good to them that hate you, and pray for them which despitefully use you and persecute you; that ye may be the children of your Father which is in heaven: for he maketh his sun to rise on the evil and on the good, and sendeth rain on the just and on the unjust. For if ye love them which love you, what reward have ye? do not even the publicans the same? And if ye salute your brethren only, what do ye more *than others?* do not even die publicans so? Be ye therefore perfect, even as your Father which is in heaven is perfect.

* Take heed that ye do not your alms before men, to be seen of them: otherwise ye have no reward of your Father which is in heaven. Therefore, when thou doest *thine* alms, do not sound a trumpet before thee, as the hypocrites do in the synagogues and in the streets, that they may have glory of men; Verily I say unto you, They have their reward. But when thou doest alms, let not thy left hand know what thy right hand doeth: that thine alms may be in secret: and thy Father, which seeth in secret, himself shall reward thee openly.

And when thou prayest, thou shalt not be as the hypocrites *are:* for they love to pray standing in the synagogues and in the corners of the streets, that they may be seen of men. Verily I say unto you; They have their reward. But thou, when thou prayest, enter into thy closet, and, when thou hast shut thy door, pray to thy Father which is in secret; and thy Father, which seeth in secret, shall reward thee openly. But when ye pray, use not vain repetitions, as the heathen *do:* for they think that they shall be heard for their much speaking. Be not ye therefore like unto them:

* Matthew, Chap. vi.

for your Father knoweth what things ye have need of, before ye ask him! After this manner therefore pray ye: Our Father, which art in heaven, hallowed be thy name: thy kingdom come: thy will be done in earth, as *it is* in heaven: give us this day our daily bread: and forgive us our debts, as we forgive our debtors: and lead us not into temptation, but deliver us from evil: for thine is the kingdom, and the power, and the glory, for ever. Amen. For if ye forgive men their trespasses, your heavenly Father will also forgive you: but if ye forgive not men their trespasses, neither will your Father forgive your trespasses.

Moreover, when ye fast, be not, as the hypocrites, of a sad countenance: for they disfigure their faces, that they may appear unto men to fast. Verily I say unto you, They have their reward. But thou, when thou fastest, anoint thine head, and wash thy face; that thou appear not unto men to fast, but unto thy Father who is in secret: and thy Father, who seeth in secret, shall reward thee openly.

Lay not up for yourselves treasures upon earth, where moth and rust doth corrupt, and where thieves break through and steal: but lay up for yourselves treasures in heaven, where neither moth nor rust doth corrupt, and where thieves do not break through nor steal: for where your treasure is, there will your heart be also. The light of the body is the eye: if therefore thine eye be single, thy whole body shall be full of light: but if thine eye be evil, thy whole body shall be full of darkness. If therefore the light that is in thee be darkness, how great *is* that darkness!

No man can serve two masters: for either he will hate the one, and love the other; or else he will hold to the one, and despise the other. Ye cannot serve God and Mammon. Therefore I say unto you, Take no thought for your life, what ye shall eat, or what ye shall drink; nor yet for your body, what ye shall put on. Is not the life more than meat, and the body than raiment? Behold the fowls of the air: for they sow not, neither do they reap, nor gather into barns; yet your heavenly Father feedeth them. Are ye not much better than they? Which of you by taking thought can add one cubit unto his stature? And why take ye thought for raiment? Consider the lilies of the field, how they grow; they toil not, neither do they spin: and yet I say unto you, That even Solomon in all his glory was not arrayed like one of these. Wherefore, if God so clothe the grass of the field, which to-day is and to-morrow is cast into the oven, *shall he* not much more *clothe* you, O ye of little faith? Therefore take no thought, saying, What shall we eat? or What shall we drink? or, Wherewithal shall we be clothed? (for after all these things do the Gentiles seek:) for your heavenly Father knoweth that ye have need of all these things. But seek ye first the kingdom of God, and his righteousness; and all these things shall be added unto you. Take therefore no thought for the morrow: for the morrow shall take thought for the things of itself. Sufficient unto the day *is* the evil thereof.

* Judge not, that ye be not judged. For with what judgment ye judge, ye shall be judged: and with what measure ye mete, it shall be measured to you again. And why beholdest thou the mote that is in thy brother's eye, but considerest not the

---

*   Matthew, Chap. vii.

beam that is in thine own eye? Or how wilt thou say to thy brother. Let me pull out the mote out of thine eye: and, behold, a beam *is* in thine own eye? Thou hypocrite, first cast out the beam out of thine own eye; and then shalt thou see clearly to cast out the mote out of thy brother's eye. Give not that which is hold unto the dogs, neither cast ye your pearls before swine, lest they trample them under their feet, and turn again and rend you. Ask, and it shall be given you; seek, and ye shall find; knock, and it shall be opened unto you: for every one that asketh receiveth; and he that seeketh findeth; and to him that knocketh it shall be opened. Or what man is there of you, whom if his son ask bread, will he give him a stone? Or if he ask a fish, will he give him a serpent? If ye then, being evil, know how to give good gifts unto your children, how much more shall your Father which is in heaven give good things to them that ask him? Therefore all things whatsoever ye would that men should do to you, do ye even so to them: for this is the law and the prophets.

Enter ye in at the strait gate: for wide *is* the gate and broad is the way, that leadeth to destruction, and many there be which go in thereat: because strait *is* the gate, and narrow *is* the way, which leadeth unto life; and few there be that find it. Beware of false prophets, which come to you in sheep's clothing, but inwardly they are ravening wolves. Ye shall know them by their fruits. Do men gather grapes of thorns, or figs of thistles? Even so every good tree bringeth forth good fruit; but a corrupt tree bringeth forth evil fruit. A good tree *cannot* bring forth evil fruit, neither *can* a corrupt tree bring forth good fruit. Every tree that bringeth not forth good fruit, is hewn down, and cast into the fire. Wherefore by their fruits ye shall know them. Not every one that saith unto me, Lord, Lord, shall enter into the kingdom of heaven; but he that doeth the will of my Father which is in heaven. Many will say to me in that day, Lord, Lord, have we not prophesied in thy name? and in thy name have cast out devils? and in thy name done many wonderful works? And then will I profess unto them, I never knew you: depart from me, ye that work iniquity.

Therefore whosoever heareth these sayings of mine, and doeth them, I will liken him unto a wise man, which built his house upon a rock: and the rain descended, and the floods came, and the winds blew, and beat upon that house; and it fell not: for it was founded upon a rock. And every one that heareth these sayings of mine, and doeth them not, shall be likened unto a foolish man, which built his house upon the sand: and the rain descended, and the floods came, and the winds blew, and beat upon that house; and it fell: and great was the fall of it. And it came to pass, when Jesus had ended these sayings, the people were astonished at his doctrine: For he taught them as *one* having authority, and not as the scribes.

* And it came to pass, as Jesus sat at meat in the house, behold, many publicans and sinners came and sat down with him and his disciples. And when the Pharisees saw it, they said unto his disciples. Why eateth your Master with publicans and sinners? But when Jesus heard that, he said unto them, They that be whole need not a physician; but they that are sick. But go ye and learn what that meaneth, I

---

* Matthew, Chap. ix. 10.

will have mercy, and not sacrifice: I am not come to call the righteous, but sinners to repentance. Then came to him the disciples of John, saying, Why do we and the Pharisees fast oft, but thy disciples fast not? And Jesus said unto them, Can the children of the bridechamber mourn, as long as the bridegroom is with them? but the days will come, when the bridegroom shall be taken from them, and then shall they fast. No man putteth a piece of new cloth unto an old garment; for that which is put in to fill it up taketh from the garment, and the rent is made worse. Neither do men put new wine into old bottles; else the bottles break, and the wine runneth out, and the bottles perish: but they put new wine into new bottles, and both are preserved.

* Behold, I send you forth as sheep in the midst of wolves: be ye therefore wise as serpents, and harmless as doves. But beware of men: for they will deliver you up to the councils, and they will scourge you in their synagogues; and ye shall be brought before governors and kings for my sake, for a testimony against them and the Gentiles. But when they deliver you up, take no thought how or what ye shall speak; for it shall be given you in that same hour what ye shall speak. For it is not ye that speak, but the Spirit of your Father which speaketh in you. And the brother shall deliver up the brother to death, and the father the child: and the children shall rise up against *their* parents, and cause them to be put to death. And ye shall be hated of all *men* for my name's sake; but he that endureth to the end shall be saved. But when they persecute you in this city, flee ye into another: for verily I say unto you, Ye shall not have gone over the cities of Israel till the Son of man be come. The disciple is not above *his* master, nor the servant above his lord. It is enough for the disciple that he be as his master, and the servant as his Lord. If they have called the master of the house Beelzebub, how much more *shall they call* them of his household? Fear them not therefore: for there is nothing covered that shall not be revealed; and hid, that shall not be known. What I tell you in darkness, *that* speak ye in light: and what ye hear in the ear, *that* preach ye upon the house-tops. And fear not them which kill the body, but are not able to kill the soul: but rather fear him which is able to destroy both soul and body in hell. Are not two sparrows sold for a farthing? and one of them shall not fall on the ground without your Father. But the very hairs of your head are all numbered. Fear ye not therefore; ye are of more value than many sparrows. Whosoever therefore shall confess me before men, him will I confess also before my Father which is in heaven. But whosoever shall deny me before men, him will I also deny before my Father which is in heaven. Think not that I am come to send peace on earth: I came not to send peace, but a sword. For I am came to set a man at variance against his father, and the daughter against her mother, and the daughter-in-law against her mother-in-law. And a man's foes *shall be* they of his own household. He that loveth father or mother more than me is not worthy of me: and he that loveth son or daughter more than me is not worthy of me. And he that taketh not his cross, and followeth after me, is not worthy of me. He that findeth his life shall lose it: and he that loseth

---

*   Matthew, Chap. x. 16.

his life for my sake shall find it. He that receiveth you, receiveth me; and he that receiveth me, receiveth him that sent me. He that receiveth a prophet, in the name of a prophet, shall receive a prophet's reward; and he that receiveth a righteous man, in the name of a righteous man, shall receive a righteous man's reward. And whosoever shall give to drink unto one of these little ones a cup of cold *water* only in the name of a disciple, verily I say unto you, he shall in no wise lose his reward.

* At that time Jesus answered and said, I thank thee, O Father, Lord of heaven and earth, because thou hast hid these things from the wise and prudent, and hast revealed them unto babes. Even so, Father: for so it seemed good in thy sight. All things are delivered unto me of my Father: and no man knoweth the Son but the Father; neither knoweth any man the Father, save the Son, and *he* to whomsoever the Son will reveal *him*. Come unto me, all *ye* that labour and are heavy laden, and I will give you rest. Take my yoke upon you, and learn of me, for I am meek and lowly in heart: and ye shall find rest unto your souls. For my yoke *is* easy, and my burden is light.

** At that time Jesus went on the sabbath day through the corn; and his disciples were an hungered, and began to pluck the ears of corn, and to eat. But when the Pharisees saw *it,* they said unto him, Behold, thy disciples do that which is not lawful to do upon the sabbath-day. But he said unto them, Have ye not read what David did when he was an hungered, and they that were with him; how he entered into the house of God, and did eat the shewbread, which was not lawful for him to eat, neither for them which were with him, but only for the priests? Or have ye not read in the law, how that on the sabbath-days the priests in the temple profane the sabbath, and are blameless? But I say unto you, That in this place is *one* greater than the temple. But if ye had known what *this* meaneth, I will have mercy, and not sacrifice, ye would not have condemned the guiltless. For the Son of man is Lord even of the sabbath-day.

And when he was departed thence, he went into their synagogue: and, behold, there was a man which had *his* hand withered. And they asked him, saying, Is it lawful to heal on the sabbath-days? that they might accuse him. And he said unto them, What man shall there be among you that shall have one sheep, and if it fall into a pit on the sabbath-day, will he not lay hold on it, and lift *it* out? how much then is a man better than a sheep? Wherefore it is lawful to do well on the sabbath-days. Then saith he to the man, Stretch forth thine hand. And he stretched *it* forth; and it was restored whole, like as the other.

† He that is not with me is against me; and he that gathereth not with me scattereth abroad. Wherefore I say unto you, All manner of sin and blasphemy shall be forgiven unto men: but the blasphemy *against* the *Holy* Ghost shall not be forgiven unto men. And whosoever speaketh a word against the Son of man, it shall be forgiven him: but whosoever speaketh against the Holy Ghost, it shall not be forgiven him, neither in this world, neither in the *world* to come. Either

---

*   Matthew, Chap. xi, 25.
**   Matthew, Chap. xii.
†   Matthew, Chap. xii. 30.

make the tree good, and his fruit good; or else make the tree corrupt, and his fruit corrupt: for the tree is known by *his* fruit. O generation of vipers! how can ye, being evil, speak good things? for out of the abundance of the heart the mouth speaketh. A good man, out of the good treasure of the heart, bringeth forth good things: and an evil man, out of the evil treasure, bringeth forth evil things. But I say unto you, That every idle word that men shall speak, they shall give account there of in the day of judgement. For by thy words thou shalt be justified, and by thy words thou shalt be condemned.

While be yet talked to the people, behold, *his* mother and his brethren stood without, desiring to speak with him. Then one said unto him, Behold, thy mother and brethren stand without, desiring to speak with thee. But he answered and said unto him that told him, Who is my mother? and who are my brethren? And he stretched forth his hand toward his disciples, and said, Behold my mother and my brethren! For whosoever shall do the will of my Father which is in heaven, the same is my brother, and sister, and mother.

* The same day went Jesus out of the house, and sat by the sea-side. And great multitudes were gathered together unto him, so that he went into a ship, and sat; and the whole multitude stood on the shore. And he spake many things unto them in parables, saying, Behold, a sower went forth to sow: and when he sowed, some *seeds* fell by the way side, and the fowls came and devoured them up. Some fell upon stony places, where they had not much earth: and forthwith they sprung up, because they had no deepness of earth: and when the sun was up, they were scorched; and because they had no root, they withered away. And some fell among thorns; and the thorns sprung up, and choked them. But other fell into good ground, and brought forth fruit, some an hundred-fold, some sixty-fold, some thirty-fold. Who hath ears to hear, let him hear. And the disciples came, and said unto him. Why speakest thou unto them in parables? He answered and said unto them. Because it is given unto yon to know the mysteries of the kingdom of heaven, but to them it is not given. For whosoever hath, to him shall be given, and he shall have more abundance; but whosoever hath not, from him shall be taken away even that he hath. Therefore speak I to them in parables; because they seeing, see not; and hearing, they hear not; neither do they understand. And in them is fulfilled the prophecy of Esaias, which saith, By hearing ye shall hear, and shall not understand; and seeing ye shall see, and shall not perceive: for this people's heart is waxed gross, and *their* ears are dull of hearing, and their eyes they have closed: lest at any time they should see with *their* eyes, and hear with *their* ears, and should understand with *their* heart, and should he converted, and I should heal them. But blessed *are* your eyes, for they hear. For verily I say unto you, That many prophets and righteous *men* have desired to see *those things* which ye see, and have not seen *them;* and to hear *those things* which ye hear, and have not heard *them.* Hear ye therefore the parable of the sower. When any one heareth the word of the kingdom, and understandeth *it* not, then cometh the wicked *one,* and catcheth away that which was sown in his heart. This is he which received seed by the way

---

*   Matthew, Chap. xiii.

side. But he that received the seed into stony places, the same is he that heareth the word, and anon with joy receiveth it: yet hath he not root in himself, but dureth for a while; for when tribulation or persecution ariseth because of the word, by and by he is offended. He also that received seed among the thorns is he that heareth the word; and the care of this world, and the deceitfulness of riches, choke the word, and he becometh unfruitful. But he that received seed into the good ground is he that heareth the word, and understandeth it; which also beareth fruit, and bringeth forth, some an hundred-fold, some sixty, some thirty. Another parable put he forth unto them, saying, The kingdom of heaven is likened unto a man who sowed good seed in his field: but while men slept, his enemy came and sowed tares among the wheat, and went his way. But when the blade was sprung up, and brought forth fruit, then appeared the tares also. So the servants of the householder came and said unto him. Sir, didst not thou sow good seed in thy field? from whence then hath it tares? He said unto them, An enemy hath done this. The servants said unto him, Wilt thou then that we go and gather them up? But he said. Nay; lest while ye gather up the tares, ye root up also the wheat with them. Let both grow together until the harvest: and in the time of harvest I will say to the reapers, Gather ye together first the tares, and bind them in bundles to burn them: but gather the wheat into my barn. Another parable put he forth unto them, saying, The kingdom of heaven is like to a grain of mustard-seed, which a man took and sowed in his field: which indeed is the least of all seeds; but when it is grown, it is the greatest among herbs, and becometh a tree, so that the birds of the air come and lodge in the branches thereof. Another parable spake he unto them: the kingdom of heaven is like unto leaven, which a woman took, and bid in three measures of meal, till the whole was leavened. All these things spake Jesus unto the multitude in parables; and without a parable spake he not unto them: that it might be fulfilled which was spoken by the prophet, saying, I will open my mouth in parables; I will utter things which have been kept secret from the foundation of the world. Then Jesus sent the multitude away, and went into the house: and his disciples came unto him, saying, Declare unto us the parable of the tares of the field. He answered and said unto them. He that soweth the good seed is the Son of man: the field is the world: the good seed are the children of the kingdom; but the tares are the children of the wicked *one:* the enemy that sowed them is the devil: the harvest is the end of the world; and the reapers are the angels. As therefore the tares are gathered and burned in the fire; so shall it be in the end of this world. The Son of man shall send forth, his angels, and they shall gather out of his kingdom all things that offend, and them which do iniquity; and shall cast them into a furnace of fire: there shall be wailing and gnashing of teeth. Then shall the righteous shine forth as the sun, in the kingdom of their Father. Who hath ears to hear, let him hear.

* Then came to Jesus scribes and Pharisees, which, were of Jerusalem, saying, Why do thy disciples transgress the tradition of the elders? for they wash not their hands when they eat bread. But he answered and said unto them, Why do you also transgress the commandment of God by your tradition? For God commanded,

*   Matthew, Chap. xv.

saying, Honour thy father and mother: and, He that curseth father or mother, let him die the death. But ye say, Whosoever shall say to *his* father or *his* mother. *It is* a gift, by whatsoever thou mightest be profited by me; and honour not his father or his mother, *he shall be free.* Thus have ye made the commandment of God of none effect by your tradition. *Ye* hypocrites! well did Esaias prophesy of you, saying, This people draweth nigh unto me with their mouth, and honoureth me with *their* lips; but their heart is far from me. But in vain they do worship me, teaching *for* doctrines the commandments of men. And he called the multitude, and said unto them, Hear, and understand: not that which goeth into the mouth defileth, a man; but that which cometh out of the mouth, this defileth a men. Then came his disciples, and said unto him, Knowest thou that the Pharisees were offended, after they heard this saying? But he answered and said, Every plant which my heavenly Father hath not planted, shall be rooted up. Let them alone: they be blind leaders of the blind. And if the blind lead the blind, both shall fall into the ditch. Then answered Peter and said unto him, Declare unto us this parable. And Jesus said, Are ye also yet without understanding? Do not ye yet understand, that whatsoever entereth in at the mouth goeth into the belly and is cast out into the draught? But those things which proceed out of the mouth come forth from the heart; and they defile the man. For out of the heart proceed evil thoughts, murders, adulteries, fornications, thefts, false witness blasphemies: these are *the things* which defile a man; but to eat with unwashen hands defileth not a man.

   * And when his disciples were come to the other side, they had forgotten to take bread. Then said Jesus said unto them, Take heed and beware of the leaven of the Pharisees and of the Sadducees. And they reasoned among themselves, saying. *It is* because we have taken no bread. *Which* when Jesus perceived, he said unto them, O ye of little faith; why reason ye among yourselves, because ye have brought no bread? How is it that ye do not understand that I spake *it* not to you concerning bread, that ye should be ware of the leaven of the Pharisees and of the Sadducees? Then understood they how that he bade *them* not beware of the leaven of bread, but of the doctrine of the Pharisees and of the Sadducees.

   When Jesus came into the coasts of Cesarea Philippi, he asked his disciples, saying, Whom do men say that I, the Son of man, am? And they said, Some *say that thou art* John the Baptist; some, Elias; and others, Jeremias, or one of the prophets. He saith unto them, But whom say ye that I am? And Simon Peter answered and said, Thou art Christ, the Son of the living God. And Jesus answered and said unto him. Blessed art thou, Simon Bar-jona: for flesh and blood hath not revealed *it* unto thee, but my Father who is in heaven. And I say also unto thee. That thou art Peter; and upon this rock I will build my church; and the gates of hell shall not prevail against it. And I will give unto thee the keys of the kingdom of heaven: and whatsoever thou shalt bind on earth shall be bound in heaven; and whatsoever thou shall loose on earth shall be loosed in heaven. Then charged he his disciples, that they should tell no man that he was Jesus the Christ. From that time forth

   *   Matthew, Chap. xvi. 5.

began Jesus to shew unto his disciples, how that he must go unto Jerusalem; and suffer many things of the elders and chief priests and scribes, and be killed, and be raised again the third day. Then Peter took him, and began to rebuke him, saying, Be it far from thee, Lord: this shall not be unto thee. But he turned, and said unto Peter, Get thee behind me, Satan: thou art an offence unto me: for thou savourest not the things that be of God, but those that be of men. Then said Jesus unto his disciples, If any *man* will come after me, let him deny himself, and take up his cross, and follow me. For whosoever will save his life shall lose it: and whosoever will lose his life for any sake shall find it. For what is a man profited, if he shall gain the whole world, and lose his own soul? or what shall a man give in exchange for his soul? For the Son of man shall come in the glory of his Father with his angels; and then he shall reward every man according to his works. Verily I say unto you, There be some standing here which shall not taste of death, till they see the Son of man coming in his kingdom.

* At the same time came the disciples unto Jesus, saying, Who is the greatest in the kingdom of heaven? And Jesus called a little child unto him, and set him in the midst of them, and said, Verily I say unto you, Except ye be converted, and become as little children, ye shall not enter into the kingdom of heaven. Whosoever therefore shall humble himself as this little child, the same is greatest in the kingdom of heaven. And whoso shall receive one such little child in my name, receiveth me. But whoso shall offend one of these little ones which believe in me, it were better for him that a millstone were hanged about his neck, and *that* he were drowned in the depth of the sea.

Woe unto the world because of offences! for if must needs be that offences come; but woe to that man by whom the offence cometh! Wherefore, if thy hand or thy foot offend thee, cut them off, and cast *them* from thee: it is better for thee to enter info life halt or maimed, rather than having two hands, or two feet, to be cast into everlasting fire. And if thine eye offend thee, pluck it out, and cast *it* from thee it is better for thee to enter into life with one eye, rather than having two eyes to be cast into hell-fire. Take heed that ye despise not one of these little ones; for I say unto you, That in heaven their angels do always behold the face of my Father which is in heaven. For the Son of man is come to save that which was lost. How think ye? If a man have an hundred sheep, and one of them be gone astray, doth he not leave the ninety and nine, and goeth into the mountains, and seeketh that which is gone astray? And if so be that he find it, verily I say unto you, He rejoiceth more of that *sheep*, than of the ninety and nine; which went not astray. Even so, it is not the will of your Father which is in heaven that one of these, little ones should perish. Moreover, if thy brother shall trespass against thee, go and tell him his fault between thee and him alone: if he shall hear thee, thou hast gained thy brother. But if he will not hear *thee, then* take with thee one or two more, that in the mouth of two or three witnesses every word may be established. And if he shall neglect to hear them, tell *it* unto the church; but if he neglect to hear the church, let him be unto thee as un heathen man and a publican. Verily I say unto you, Whatsoever

---

*   Matthew, Chap. xviii.

ye shall bind on earth shall be bound in heaven and whatsoever ye shall loose on earth shall be loosed in heaven. Again I say unto you, That if two of you shall agree on earth as touching any thing that they shall ask, it shall be done for them of my Father which is in heaven. For where two or three are gathered together in my name, there am I in the midst of them.

Then came Peter to him, and said, Lord how, oft shall my brother sin against me, and I forgive him? till seven times? Jesus saith unto him, I say not unto thee, Until seven times; but, Until seventy times seven. Therefore is the of kingdom of heaven likened unto a certain king, which would take account of his servants. And when he had begun to reckon, one was brought unto him which owed him ten thousand talents: but forasmuch as he had not to pay, his Lord commanded him to be sold, and his wife and children, and all that he had, and payment to be made. The servant therefore fell down, and worshipped him, saying, Lord, have patience with me, and I will pay thee all. Then the lord of that servant was moved with compassion, and loosed him, and forgave him the debt. But the same servant went out, and found one of his fellow-servants which owed him an hundred pence; and he laid hands on him, and took *him* by the throat, saying, Pay me that thou owest. And his fellow-servant fell down at his feet, and besought him, saying, Have patience with me, and I will pay thee all. And he would not; but went and cast him into prison, till he should pay the debt. So when his fallow-servants saw what was done, they were very sorry, and came and told unto their lord all that was done. Then his lord, after that he had called him, said unto him, O thou wicked servant, I forgave thee all that debt, because thou desiredst me: shouldest not thou also have had compassion on thy fellow-servant, even as I had pity on thee? And his lord was wroth, and delivered him to the tormentors, till he should pay all that was due unto him. So likewise shall my heavenly Father do also unto you, if ye from your hearts forgive not every one his brother their trespasses.

* The Pharisees also came unto him, tempting him, and saying unto him, Is it lawful for a man to put away his wife for every cause? And he answered and said unto them. Have ye not read, that he which made *them* at the beginning, made them male and female; and said, For this cause shall a man leave father and mother, and shall cleave to his wife; and they twain shall be one flesh? Wherefore they are no more twain, but one flesh. What therefore God hath joined together, let not man put asunder. They say unto him, Why did Moses then command to give a writing of divorcement, and to put her away? He saith unto them, Moses because of the hardness of your hearts, suffered you to put away your wives: but from the beginning it was not so. And I say unto you, Whosoever shall put away his wife, except *it be* for fornication, and shall marry another, committeth, adultery; and whoso marrieth her which is put away doth commit adultery. His disciples say unto him, If the case of the man be no with *his* wife, it is not good to marry, But he said unto them. All *men* cannot receive this saving, save *they* to whom it is given. For there are some eunuchs, which were so born from *their* mother's womb: and there are some eunuchs, which were made eunuchs of men and there be eunuchs,

---

*   Matthew, Chap. xix. 3.

which have made themselves eunuchs for the kingdom of heaven's sake. He that is able to receive *it*, let him receive *it*.

Then were brought unto him little children, that he should put *his* hands on them, and pray: and the disciples rebuked them. But Jesus said, Suffer little children, and forbid them not to come unto me; for of such is the kingdom of heaven. And he laid *his* hands on them, and departed thence, And, behold, one came and said unto him, Good Master, what good thing shall I do that I may have eternal life? And he said unto him, Why callest thou me good? *there is* none good but one, *that is* God: but if thou wilt enter into life, keep the commandments. He saith unto him, Which? Jesus said, Thou shalt do no murder, Thou shall not commit adultery, Thou shalt not steal, Thou shalt not bear false witness: Honour thy father and *thy* mother; and Thou shalt love thy neighbour as thyself. The young man saith unto him, All these things have I kept from my youth up: what lack I yet? Jesus, said unto him, If thou wilt be perfect, go *and* sell that thou hast, and give to the poor, and thou shalt have treasure in heaven; and come *and* follow me. But when the young man heard that saying, he went away sorrowful: for he had great possessions. Then said Jesus unto his disciples, Verily I say unto you, That a rich man shall hardly enter into the kingdom of heaven. And again I say unto yon, It is easier for a camel to go through the eye of a needle, than for a rich man to enter into the kingdom of God. When his disciples heard *it*, they were exceedingly amazed, saying, Who then can be saved? But Jesus beheld *them*, and said unto them. With men this is impossible; but with God all things are possible. Then answered Peter, and said unto him, Behold, we have forsaken all and followed thee: what shall we have therefore? And Jesus said unto them, Verily I say unto you, That ye which have followed me in the regeneration, when the Son of man shall sit in the throne of his glory, ye also shall sit upon twelve thrones, judging the twelve tribes of Israel. And every one that hath forsaken houses, or brethren, or sisters, or father, or mother, or wife, or children, or lands, for my name's sake, shall receive an hundred-fold, and shall inherit everlasting life. But many *that are* first shall be last; and the last *shall be* first.

* For the kingdom of heaven is like unto a man *that is* an householder, which went out early in the morning to hire labourers into his vineyard. And when he had agreed with the labourers for a penny a day, he sent them into his vineyard. And he went out about the third hour, and saw others standing idle in the market-place, and said unto them, Go ye also into the vineyard; and whatsoever is right, I will give you. And they went their way. Again he went out about the sixth and ninth hour, and did likewise. And about the eleventh hour he went out, and found others standing idle, and saith unto them, Why stand ye here all the day idle? They say unto him, Because no man hath hired us, He saith unto them, Go ye also into the vineyard? and whatsoever is right, *that* shall ye receive. So when even was come, the lord of the vineyard saith unto his steward. Call the labourers, and give them *their* hire, beginning from the last unto the first. And when they came that *were hired* about the eleventh hour, the received every man a penny. But when the

---

* Matthew, Chap. xx.

first came, they supposed that they should have received more; and they likewise received every man a penny. And when they had received *it*, they murmured against the good man of the house, saying, These last have wrought *but* one hour, and thou hast made them equal unto us, which have borne the burden and heat of the day. But he answered one of them, and said, Friend, I do thee no wrong: didst not thou agree with me for a penny? Take *that* thine *is* and go thy way: I will give unto this last even as unto thee. Is it not lawful for me to do what I will with mine own? Is thine eye evil because I am good? So the last shall be first, and the first last: for many be called, but few chosen.

Then came to him the mother of Zebedee's children with her sons, worshipping *him*, and desiring a certain thing of him. And he said unto her, What wilt thou? She saith unto him, Grant that these my two sons may sit, the one on they right hand, answered and said, Ye know not what ye ask. Are ye able to drink of the cup that I shall drink of and to be baptized with the baptism that I am baptized with? They say unto him, We are able, And he saith unto them, Ye shall drink indeed of my cup, and be baptized with the baptism that I am baptized with; but to sit on my right hand, and on my left, is not mine to give, but *it shall be given to them* for whom it is prepared of my Father, And when the ten heard *it*, they were moved with indignation against the two brethren. But Jesus called them *unto him*, and said, Ye know that the princes of the Gentiles exercise dominion over them, and they that are great exercise authority upon them. But it shall not be so among you; but whosoever will be great among you, let him be your minister; and whosoever will be chief among you, let him be your servant; even as the Son of man came not to be ministered unto, but to minister, and to give his life a ransom for many.

* And when he was come into the temple, the chief priests and the elders of the people came unto him as he was teaching, and said, By what authority doest thou these things? and who gave thee this authority? And Jesus answered and said unto them, I also will ask you one thing, which if ye tell me, I in lie wise will tell you by what authority I do these things. The baptism of John, whence was it? from heaven, or of men? And they reasoned with themselves, saying, If we shall say from heaven; he will say unto us, why did ye not then believe him? But if we shall say, Of men; we fear the people; for all hold John as a prophet. And they answered Jesus, and said, We cannot by what authority I do these things. But what think you? A *certain* man had two sons; and he came to the first, and said, Son, go work to-day in my vineyard. He answered and said, I will not; but afterward he repented, and went. And he came to the second, and said likewise. And he answered and said, I go, sir; and went not. Whether of them twain did the will of *his* father? They say unto him, The first. Jesus saith unto them, Verily I say unto you, That the publicans and the harlots go into the kingdom of God before you. For John came unto you in the way of righteousness, and ye believed him not; but the publicans und the harlots believed him; and ye, when ye had seen *it*, repented not afterward, that ye might believe him. Hear another parable: There was a certain householder, which planted a vineyard, and hedged it round about, and digged a winepress in it, and

---

*   Matthew, Chap. xxi. 23.

built a tower, and let it out to husbandmen, and went into a far country: and when the time of the fruit drew near, be sent his servants to the husbandmen, that they might receive the fruits of it. And the husbandmen took his servants, and beat one, and killed another, and stoned another. Again, he sent other servants more than the first: and they did unto them likewise. But last of all he sent unto them his son, saying, They will reverence my son. But when the husbandmen saw the son, they said among themselves, This is the heir; come, let us kill him, and let us seize on his inheritance. And they caught him, and cast *him* out of the vineyard, and slew *him*. When the Lord, therefore, of the vineyard cometh, what will he do unto those husbandmen? They say unto him. He will miserably destroy those wicked men, and will let out *his* vineyard unto other husbandmen, which shall render him the fruits in their seasons. Jesus saith unto them. Did ye never read in the scriptures, The stone which the builders rejected, the same is become the head of the corner: this is the Lord's doing, and it is marvellous in our eyes? Therefore say I unto you, The kingdom of God shall be taken from you, and given to a nation bringing forth the fruits thereof. And whosoever shall fall on this stone shall be broken: but on whomsoever it shall fall, it will grind him to powder.

* The kingdom of heaven is like unto a certain king, which made a marriage for his son, and sent forth his servants to call them that were bidden to the wedding: and they would not come. Again, he sent forth other servants, saying, Tell them which are bidden, Behold, I have prepared my dinner: my oxen and *my* fatlings *are* killed, and all things *are* ready: come unto the marriage. But they made light of *it,* and went their ways, one to his farm, and another to his merchandize: and the remnant took his servants, and entreated *them* spitefully, and slew *them*. But when the king heard *thereof,* he was wroth: and he. sent forth his armies, and destroyed those murderers, and burned up their city. Then saith he to his servants. The wedding is ready, but they which were bidden were not worthy. Go ye, therefore, into the highways; and as many as ye shall find, bid to the marriage. So those servants went out into the highways, and gathered together all, as many as they found, both bad and good: and the wedding: was furnished with guests. And when the king came in to see the guests, he saw there a man which had not on a wedding garment: and he saith unto him, Friend, how camest thou in hither, not having a wedding garment? And he was speechless. Then said the king to the servants, Bind him hand and foot, and take him away, and cast *him* into outer darkness; there shall be weeping and gnashing of teeth. For many are called, but few *are* chosen.

Then went the Pharisees, and took counsel how they might entangle him in *his* talk. And they sent out unto him their disciples with the Herodians, saying. Master, we know that thou art true, and teachest the way of God in truth, neither carest thou for any *man;* for thou regardest not the person of men. Tell us therefore, what thinkest thou; is it lawful to given tribute unto Caesar, or not? But Jesus perceived their wickedness, and said, Why money. And they brought unto him a penny. And he saith unto them, Whose *is* this image and superscription? They say unto him, Caesar's. Then saith he unto them, Render therefore unto Caesar the things which

---

*   Matthew, Chap. xxii. 2.

are Caesar's, and unto God the things that are God's. When they had heard *these words*, they marvelled, and left him, and went their way.

The same day came to him the Sadducees, which say that there is no resurrection, and asked him, saying, Master, Moses said, If a man die, having no children, his brother shall marry his wife, and raise up a seed unto his brother. Now there were with us seven brethren: and the first, when he had married a wife, deceased, and, having no issue, left his wife unto his brother: likewise the second also, and the third unto the seventh. And last of all the woman died also. Therefore, in the resurrection, whose wife shall she be of the seven? for they all had her. Jesus answered and said unto them, Ye do err, not knowing the scriptures, nor the power of God. For in the resurrection they neither marry, nor are given in marriage, but are as the angels of God in heaven. But as touching the resurrection of the dead, have ye not read that which was spoken unto you by God, saying, I am the God of Abraham, and the God of Issac, and the God of Jacob? God is not the God of the dead, but of the living. And when the multitude heard *this,* they were astonished at his doctrine.

But when the Pharisees had heard that he had put the Sadducees to silence, they were gathered together. Then one of them, *who was* a lawyer, asked *him a question*, tempting him, and saying, Master, which *is* the great commandment in the law? Jesus said unto him, Thou shalt love the Lord thy God with all thy heart, and with all thy soul, and with all thy mind. This is the first and great commandment. And the second is like unto it, Thou shalt love thy neighbour as thyself. On these two commandments hang all the law and the prophets.

While the Pharisees were gathered together, Jesus asked them, saying, What think ye of Christ? whose son is he? They say unto him, *The son* of David. He saith unto them, How then, doth David in spirit call him Lord: Saying, The LORD said unto my Lord, Sit thou on my right hand, till I make thine enemies thy footstool. If David then call him Lord, how is he his son? And no man was able to answer him a word; neither durst any *man,* from that day forth, ask him any more *questions.*

* Then spake Jesus to the multitude, and to his disciples, saying, The scribes and the Pharisees sit in Moses' seat: all, therefore, whatsoever they bid you observe, *that* observe, and do; but do not ye after their works; for they say, and do not. For they bind heavy burdens, and grievous to be borne, and lay *them* on men's shoulders; but they *themselves* will not move them with one of their fingers. But all their works they do for to be seen of men: they make broad their phylacteries, and enlarge the borders of their garments, and love the uppermost rooms at feasts, and the chief seats in the synagogues, and greetings in the markets, and to be called of men, Rabbi, Rabbi. But be not ye called Rabbi: for one is your Master, *even* Christ; and all ye are brethren. And call no *man* your father upon the earth; for one is your Father, who is in heaven. Neither be ye called masters: for one is your Master, *even* Christ. But he that is greatest among you shall be your servant. And whosoever shall exalt himself shall be abased; and he that shall humble himself shall be exalted. But woe unto you, scribes and Pharisees, hypocrites! for ye shut up the kingdom of heaven against men: for ye neither go in *yourselves,* neither suffer ye them that are entering

---

*   Matthew, Chap. xxiii.

to go in. Woe unto you, scribes and Pharisees, hypocrites! for ye devour widows' houses, and for a pretence make long prayer: therefore ye shall receive the greater damnation. Woe unto you, scribes and Pharisees, hypocrites! for ye compass sea and land to make one proselyte; and when he is made, ye make him twofold more the child of hell than yourselves. Woe unto you, *ye* blind guides! which say, Whosoever shall swear by the temple, it is nothing; but whosoever shall swear by the gold of the temple, he is a debtor. *Ye* fools, and blind! for whether is greater, the gold, or the temple that sanctifieth the gold? And, Whosoever shall swear by the altar, it is nothing; but whosoever sweareth by the gift that is upon it, he is guilty. *Ye* fools, and blind! for whether *is* greater, the gift, or the altar that sanctifieth the gift? Whoso, therefore, shall swear by the altar, sweareth by it, and by all things thereon. And whoso shall swear by the temple, sweareth by it, and by him that dwelleth therein. And he that shall swear by heaven, sweareth by the throne of God, and by him that sitteth thereon. Woe unto you, scribes and Pharisees, hypocrites! for ye pay tithe of mint, and anise, and cummin, and have omitted the weightier *matters* of the law, judgement, mercy, and faith: these ought ye to have done and not to leave the other undone. *Ye* blind guides! which strain at a gnat, and swallow a camel. Woe unto you, scribes and Pharisees, hypocrites! for ye make clean the outside of the cup and of the platter, but within they are full of extortion and excess. *Thou* blind Pharisee! cleanse first that *which is* within the cup and platter, that the outside of them may be clean also. Woe unto you, scribes and Pharisees, hypocrites! for ye are like unto whited sepulchres, which indeed appear beautiful outward, but are within full of dead *men's* bones and of all uncleanness. Even so ye also outwardly appear righteous unto men, but within ye are full of hypocrisy and iniquity. Woe unto you, scribes and Pharisees, hypocrites! because ye build the tombs of the prophets, and garnish the sepulchres of the righteous, and say, if we had been in the days of our fathers, we would not have been partakers with them in the blood of the prophets. Wherefore ye be witnesses unto yourselves, that ye are the children of them which killed the prophets. Fill ye up then the measure of your fathers. *Ye* serpents, *ye* generation of vipers! how can ye escape the damnation of hell? Wherefore, behold, I send unto you prophets, and wise men, and scribes; and *some* of them ye shall kill and crucify; and *some* of them shall ye scourge in your synagogues, and persecute *them* from city to city: that upon you may come all the righteous blood shed upon the earth, from the blood of righteous Abel unto the blood of Zacharias son of Barachias, whom ye slew between the temple and the altar. Verily I say unto you, All these things shall come upon this generation. O Jerusalem, Jerusalem, *thou* that killest the prophets, and stonest them which are sent unto thee, how often would I have gathered thy children together, even as a hen gathereth her chickens under *her* wings, and ye would not! Behold, your house is left unto you desolate. For I say unto you, Ye shall not see me henceforth, till ye shall say, Blessed *is* he that cometh in the name of the Lord.

* Watch therefore; for ye know not what hour your Lord doth come. But know this, that if the good man of the house had known in what watch the thief would

---

*   Matthew, Chap. xxiv. 42.

come, he would have watched, and would not have suffered his house to be broken up. Therefore be ye also ready: for in such an hour as ye think not the Son of man cometh. Who then is a faithful and wise servant, whom his lord hath made ruler over his household, to give them meat in due season? Blessed *is* that servant whom his lord, when he cometh, shall find so doing. Verily I say unto you, That he shall make him ruler over all his goods. But and if that evil servant shall say in his heart, My lord delayeth his coming; and shall begin to smite *his* fellow servants, and to eat and drink with the drunken; the lord of that servant shall come in a day when he looketh not for *him,* and in an hour that he is not aware of, and shall cut him asunder, and appoint *him* his portion with the hypocrites; there shall be weeping and gnashing of teeth.

* Then shall the kingdom of heaven be likened unto ten virgins, which took their lamps, and went forth to meet the bridegroom. And five of them were wise, and five *were* foolish. They that *were* foolish took their lamps, and took no oil with them: but the wise took oil in their vessels with their lamps. While the bridegroom tarried, they all slumbered and slept. And at midnight there was a cry made, Behold, the bridegroom cometh; go ye out to meet him. Then all those virgins arose, and trimmed their lamps. And the foolish said unto the wise, Give us of your oil; for our lamps are gone out. But the wise answered, saying, *Not so;* lest there be not enough for us and you; but go ye rather to them that sell, and buy for yourselves. And while they went to buy, the bridegroom came; and they that were ready went in with him to the marriage; and the door was shut. Afterward came also the other virgins, saying, Lord, Lord, open to us. But he answered and said, Verily I say unto you, I know you not. Watch therefore, for ye know neither the day nor the hour wherein the Son of man cometh. For *the kingdom of heaven is* as a man travelling into a far country, *who* called his own servants, and delivered unto them his goods. And unto one he gave five talents, to another two, and to another one; to every man according to his several ability; and straightway took his journey. Then he that had received the five talents went and traded with the same, and made *them* other five talents. And likewise he that *had received* two, he also gained other two. But he that had received one went and digged in the earth, and hid his lord's money. After a long time the lord of those servants cometh, and reckoneth with them. And so he that had received five talents came and brought other five talents, saying, Lord, thon deliveredst unto me five talents; behold, I have gained besides them five talents more. His lord said unto him, Well done, *thou* good and faithful servant: thou hast been faithful over a few things, I will make thee ruler over many things: enter thou into the joy of thy lord. He also that had received two talents came and said, Lord, thou deliveredst unto me two talents: behold, I have gained two other talents besides them. His lord said unto him, Well done, good and faithful servant: thou hast been faithful over a few things, I will make thee ruler over many things: enter thou into the joy of thy lord, Then he which had received the one talent came and said, Lord, I knew thee that thou art a hard man, reaping where thou hast not sown, and gathering where thou hast not

---

*   Matthew, Chap. xxv.

strawed: and I was afraid, and went and hid thy talent in the earth; lo, *there* thou hast *that is* thine. His lord answered and said unto him, *Thou* wicked and slothful servant, thou knowest that I reap where I sowed not, and gather where I have not strawed: thou oughtest therefore to have put my money to the exchangers, and *then* at my coming I should have received mine own with usury. Take therefore the talent from him, and give *it* unto him which hath ten talents. For unto every one that hath shall be given, and he shall have abundance: but from him that hath not shall be taken away even that which he hath. And cast ye the unprofitable servant into outer darkness: there shall be weeping and gnashing of teeth. When the Son of man shall come in his glory, and all the holy angels with him, then shall he sit upon the throne of his glory: and before him shall be gathered all nations; and he shall separate them one from another, as a shepherd divideth *his* sheep from the goats: and he shall set the sheep on his right hand, but the goats on the left. Then shall the King say unto them on his right hand, Come, ye blessed of my Father, inherit the kingdom prepared for you from the foundation of the world: for I was an hungred, and ye gave me meat: I was thirsty, an ye gave me drink: I was a stranger, and ye too me in: naked, and ye clothed me: I was sick, and ye visited me: I was in prison, and ye came unto me. Then shall the righteous answer him, saying, Lord, when saw we thee an hungred, and fed *thee?* or thirsty, and gave *thee* drink? When saw we thee a stranger, and took *thee* in? or naked, and clothed *thee?* Or when saw we thee sick, or in prison, and came unto thee? And the King shall answer and say unto them, Verily I say unto you, In as much as ye have done *it* unto one of the least of these my brethren, ye have done *it* unto me. Then shall he say also unto them on the left hand, Depart from me, ye cursed, into everlasting fire, prepared for the devil and his angels: for I was an hungred, and ye gave me no meat: I was thirsty, and ye gave me no drink: I was a stranger, and ye took me not in: naked, and ye clothed me not: sick, and in prison, and ye visited me not. Then shall they also answer him, saying, Lord, when saw we thee au hungred, or athirst, or a stranger, or naked, or sick, or in prison, and did not minister unto thee? Then shall he answer them, saying, Verily I say unto you, Inasmuch as ye did *it* not to one of the least of these, ye did *it* not to me. And these shall go away into everlasting punishment: but the righteous into life eternal.

* And it came to pass, that as Jesus sat at meat in his house, many publicans and sinners sat also together with Jesus and his disciples: for there were many, and they followed him. And when the scribes and Pharisees saw him eat with publicans and sinners, they said unto his disciples. How is it that he eateth and drinketh with publicans and sinners? When Jesus heard *it,* he saith unto them, They that are whole have no need of the physician, but they that are sick: I came not to call the righteous, but sinners to repentance. And the disciples of John and of the Pharisees used to fast: and they come and say unto him. Why do the disciples of John and of the Pharisees used to fast: and they come and say unto him. Why do the disciples of John and of the Pharisees fast, but thy disciples fast not? And Jesus said unto them, Can the children of the bride-chamber fast while the bridegroom is with

---

*   Mark, Chap. ii. 15.

them? as long as they have the bridegroom with them, they cannot fast. But the days will come when the bridegroom shall be taken away from them, and then shall they fast in those days. No man also seweth a piece of new cloth on an old garment: else the new piece that filled it up taketh away from the old, and the rent is made worse. And no man putteth new wine into old bottles: else the new wine doth burst the bottles, and the wine is spilled, and the bottles will be marred: but new wine must be put into new bottles.

And it came to pass, that he went through the corn-fields on the sabbath-day; and his disciples began, as they went, to pluck the ears of corn. And the Pharisees said unto him, Behold, why do they on the sabbath-day that which is not lawful? And he said unto them, Have ye never read what David did, when he had need, and was an hungred, he, and they that were with him? How he went into the house of God in the days of Abiathar the high priest, and did eat the shew-bread, which is not lawful to eat but for the priests, and gave also to them which were with him? And he said unto them, The sabbath was made for man, and not man for the sabbath: therefore the Son of man is Lord also of the sabbath.

* There came then his brethren and his mother, and, standing without, sent unto him, calling him. And the multitude sat about him; and they said unto him, Behold, thy mother and thy brethren without seek for thee. And he answered them, saying, Who is my mother, or my brethren? And he looked round about on them, and said, Behold my mother and my brethren! For whosoever shall do the will of God, the same is my brother, and my sister, and mother.

** And he taught them many things by parables, and said unto them in his doctrine, Hearken; behold, there went out a sower to sow: and it came to pass, as he sowed, some fell by the wayside, and the fowls of the air came and devoured it up. And some fell on stony ground, where it had not much earth; and immediately it sprang up, because it had no depth of earth: but when the sun was up, it was scorched; and because it had no root, it withered away. And some fell among thorns; and the thorns grew up and choked it, and it yielded no fruit. And other fell on good ground, and did yield fruit that sprang up and increased, and brought forth, some thirty, and some sixty, and some an hundred. And he said unto them, He that hath ears to hear, let him hear. And when he was alone, they that were about him with the twelve asked of him the parable. And he said unto them, Unto you it is given to know the mystery of the kingdom of God: but unto them that are without, all *these* things are done in parables: that seeing they may see, and not perceive; and hearing they may hear, and not understand; lest at any time they should be converted, and *their* sins should be forgiven them. And he said unto them, Know ye not this parable? and how then will ye know all parables? The sower soweth the word. And these are they by the way-side, where the word is sown; but when they have heard, Satan cometh immediately, and taketh away the word that was sown in their hearts. And these are they like-wise which are sown on stony ground; who, when they have heard the word, immediately receive

---

*   Mark, Chap. iii. 31.
**   Mark, Chap. iv. 2.

it with gladness; and have no root in themselves, and so endure but for a time; afterward, when affliction or persecution ariseth for the word's sake, immediately they are offended. And these are they which are sown among thorns; such as hear the word, and the cares of this world, and the deceitfulness of riches, and the lusts of other things entering in, choke the word, and it becometh unfruitful. And these are they which are sown on good ground; such as hear the word, and receive *it*, and bring forth fruit, some thirty-fold, some sixty, and some an hundred. And he said unto them, Is a candle brought to be put under a bushel, or under a bed? and not to be set on a candlestick? For there is nothing hid, which shall not be manifested; neither was any thing kept secret, but that it should come abroad. If any man have ears to hear, let him hear. And he said unto them, Take heed what ye hear; with what measure ye mete, it shall be measured to you; and unto you that hear shall more be given. For he that hath, to him shall be given; and he that hath not, from him shall be taken even that which he hath. And he said, So is the kingdom of God, as if a man should cast seed into the ground; and should sleep, and rise night and day, and the seed should spring and grow up, he knoweth not how. For the earth bringeth forth fruit of herself; first the blade, then the ear, after that the full corn in the ear. But when the fruit is brought forth, immediately he putteth in the sickle, because the harvest is come. And he said, Whereunto shall we liken the kingdom of God? or with what comparison shall we compare it? *It is* like a grain of mustard-seed, which, when it is sown in the earth, is less than all the seeds that be in the earth: but when it is sown, it groweth up, and becometh greater than all herbs, and shooteth out great branches; so that the fowls of the air may lodge under the shadow of it.

* Then the Pharisees and scribes asked him, Why walk not thy disciples according to the tradition of the Elders, but eat bread with unwashen hands? – He answered and said unto them, Well hath Esaias prophesied of you hypocrites, as it is written, This people honoureth me with *their* lips, but their heart is far from me. Howbeit, in vain do they worship me, teaching *for* doctrines the commandments of men. For laying aside the commandment of God, ye hold the tradition of men, *as* the washing of pots and cups: and many other such like things ye do. And he said unto them, Full well ye reject the commandment of God, that ye may keep your own tradition. For Moses said, Honour thy father and thy mother; and, Whoso curseth father or mother, let him die the death: but ye say, If a man shall say to his father or mother, *It is* Corban, that is to say, a gift, by whatsoever thou mightest be profited by me: *he shall be free*. And ye suffer him no more to do ought for his father or his mother; making the word of God of none effect through your tradition, which ye have delivered: and many such like things do ye. And when he had called all the people *unto him*, he said unto them, Hearken unto me every one *of you*, and understand. There is nothing from without a man, that entering into him, can defile him: but the things which come out of him, those are they that defile the man. If any man have ears to hear, let him hear. And when he was entered into the house from the people, his disciples asked him concerning the

---

*   Mark, Chap. vii. 5.

parable. And he saith unto them, Are ye so without understanding also? Do ye not perceive, that whatsoever thing from without entereth into the man, *it* cannot defile him; because it entereth not into his heart, but into the belly, and goeth out into the draught, purging all meats? And he said, That which cometh out of the man, that defileth the man. For from within, out of the heart of men, proceed evil thoughts, adulteries, fornications, murders, thefts, covetousness, wickedness, deceit, lasciviousness, an evil eye, blasphemy, pride, foolishness: all these evil things come from within, and defile the man.

* And when he had called the people *unto him*, with his disciples also, he said unto them, Whosoever will come after me, let him deny himself, and take up his cross, and follow me. For whosoever will save his life shall lose it; but whosoever shall lose his life for my sake and the gospel's, the same shall save it. For what shall it profit a man, if he shall gain the whole world, and lose his own soul? Or what shall a man give in exchange for his soul? Whosoever therefore shall be ashamed of me and of my words in this adulterous and sinful generation, of him also shall the Son of man be ashamed, when he cometh in the glory of his Father with the hold angels.

** And he came to Capernaum: and being in the house, he asked them, What was it that ye disputed among yourselves by the way? But they held their peace: for by the way they had disputed among themselves who *should be* the greatest. And he sat down, and called the twelve, and saith unto them, If any man desire to be first, *the same* shall be last of all, and servant of all. And he took a child, and set him in the midst of them: and when he had taken him into his arms, he said unto them, Whosoever shall receive one of such children in my name, receiveth me; and whosoever shall receive me, receiveth not me, but him that sent me.

And John answered him, saying, Master, we saw one casting out devils in thy name, and he followeth not us: and we forbad him, because he followeth not us. But Jesus said, Forbid him not; for there is no man which shall do miracle in my name that can lightly speak evil of me. For he that is not against us is on our part. For whosoever shall give you a cup of water to drink in my name, because ye belong to Christ, verily I say unto you, He shall not lose his reward. And whosoever shall offend one of *these* little ones that believe in me, it is better for him that a millstone were hanged about his neck, and he were cast into the sea. And if thy hand offend thee, cut it off; it is better for thee to enter into life maimed, than having two hands to go into hell, into the fire that never shall be quenched; where their worm dieth not, and the fire is not quenched. And if thy foot offend thee, cut it off; it is better for thee to enter halt into life, than having two feet to be cast into hell, into the fire that never shall be quenched; where their worm dieth not, and the fire is not quenched. And if thine eye offend thee, pluck it out; it is better for thee to enter into the kingdom of God with one eye, than having two eyes to be cast into hell fire; where their worm dieth not, and the fire is not quenched. For every one shall

---

*   Mark, Chap. viii. 34.
**   Mark, Chap. ix. 33.

be salted with fire, and every sacrifice shall be salted with salt. Salt *is* good; but if the salt have lost its saltness, wherewith will ye season it? Have salt in yourselves, and have peace one with another.

* And they brought young children to him, that he should touch them; and *his* disciples rebuked those that brought *them*. But when Jesus saw *it*, he was much displeased, and said unto them. Suffer the little children to come unto me, and forbid them not; for of such is the kingdom of God. Verily I say unto you, Whosoever shall not receive the kingdom of God as a little child, he shall not enter therein. And he took them up in his arms, put *his* hands upon them, and blessed them.

And when he was gone forth into the way, there came one running, and kneeled to him, and asked him, Good Master, what shall I do that I may inherit eternal life? And Jesus said unto him, Why callest thou me good? *there is* none good but one, *that is* God. Thou knowest the commandments. Do not commit adultery, Do not kill, Do not steal, Do not bear false witness, Defraud not, Honour thy father and mother. And he answered and said unto him, Master, all these have I observed from my youth. Then Jesus beholding him, loved him, and said unto him, One thing thou lackest: go thy way, sell whatsoever thou hast, and give to the poor, and thou shalt have treasure in heaven: and come, take up thy cross, and follow me. And he was sad at that saying, and went away grieved; for he had great possessions. And Jesus looked round about, and saith unto his disciples, How hardly shall they that have riches enter into the kingdom of God! And the disciples were astonished at his words. But Jesus answereth again, and saith unto them, Children, how hard is it for them that trust in riches to enter into the kingdom of God! It is easier for a camel to go through the eye of a needle, than for a rich man to enter into the kingdom of God. And they were astonished out of measure, saying among themselves, Who then can be saved? And Jesus looking upon them saith, With men *it is* impossible, but not with god: for with God all things are possible. Then Peter began to say unto him, Lo, we have left all, and have followed thee. And Jesus answered and said, Verily I say unto you, There is no man that hath left house, or brethren, or sisters, or father, or mother, or wife, or children, or lands, for my sake, and the gospel's, but he shall receive an hundred fold now in this time, houses, and brethren, and sisters, and mothers, and children, and lands, with persecutions; and in the world to come eternal life. But many *that are* first shall be last; and the last first.

** And James and John, the sons of Zebedee, come unto him, saying, Master, we would that thou shouldest do for us whatsoever we shall desire. And he said unto them, What would ye that I should do for you? They said unto him, Grant unto us that we may sit, one on thy right hand, and the other on thy left hand, in thy glory. But Jesus said unto them, Ye know not what ye ask. Can ye drink of the cup that I drink of? and be baptized with the baptism that I am baptized with? And they said unto him, We can. And Jesus said unto them. Ye shall indeed drink of the cup that I

---

*   Mark, Chap. x. 13.
** Mark, Chap. x. 35.

drink of; and with the baptism that I am baptized with shall ye be baptized: but to sit on my right hand and on my left hand is not mine to give; but *it shall be given to them* for whom it is prepared. And when the ten hard *it*, they began to be much displeased with James and John. But Jesus called them *to him*, and saith unto them, Ye know that they which are accounted to rule over the Gentiles exercise lordship over them; and their great ones exercise authority upon them. But so shall it not be among you: but whosoever will be great among you, shall be your minister; and whosoever of you will be the chiefest, shall be servant of all. For even the Son of man came not to be ministered unto, but to minister, and to give his life a ransom for many.

* Therefore I say unto you, What things soever ye desire when ye pray, believe that ye receive *them*, and ye shall have *them*. And when ye stand praying, forgive, if ye have ought against any; that your Father also which is in heaven may forgive you your trespasses. But if ye do not forgive, neither will your Father which is in heaven forgive your trespasses.

** And they send unto him certain of the Pharisees and of the Herodians, to catch him in *his* words. And when they were come, they say unto him, Master, we know that thou art true, and carest for no man; for thou regardest not the person of men, but teachest the way of God in truth: Is it lawful to give tribute to Caesar, or not? Shall we give, or shall we not give? But he, knowing their hypocrisy, said unto them, Why tempt ye me? bring me a penny, that I may see *it*. And they brought *it*. And he saith unto them, Whose *is* this image and superscription? And they said unto him, Caesar's. And Jesus answering said unto them, Render to Caesar the things that are Caesar's, and to God the things that are God's. And they marvelled at him. Then come unto him the Sadducees, which say there is no resurrection; and they asked him, saying, Master, Moses wrote unto us, If a man's brother die, and leave *his* wife *behind him*, and leave no children, that his brother should take his wife, and raise up seed unto his brother. Now there were seven brethren: and the first took a wife, and dying left no seed. And the second took her, and died; neither left he any seed: and the third likewise. And the seven had her, and left no seed: last of all the woman died also. In the resurrection therefore, when they shall rise, whose wife shall she be of them? for the seven had her to wife. And Jesus answering said unto them, Do ye not therefore err, because ye know not the scriptures, neither the power of God? For when they shall rise from the dead, they neither marry nor are given in marriage; but are as the angels which are in heaven. And as touching the dead, that they rise; have ye not read in the book of Moses, how in the bush God spake unto him, saying, I *am* the God of Abraham, and the God of Isaac, and the God of Jacob? He is not the God of the dead, but the God of the living: ye therefore do greatly err. And one of the scribes came, and having heard them reasoning together, and perceiving that he had answered them well, asked him, Which is the first commandment of all? And Jesus answered him, The first of all the commandments *is*, Hear, O Israel; The Lord our God is one Lord: and thou shalt love the Lord thy God with all thy heart, and with all thy soul, and

*   Mark, Chap, xi, 24.
**   Mark, Chap, xii, 13.

with all thy mind, and with all thy strength. This *is* the first commandment. And the second *is* like, *namely* this, Thou shalt love thy neighbour as thyself. There is none other commandment greater than these. And the scribe said unto him, Well, Master, thou hast said the truth: for there is one God; and there is none other but he: and to love him with all the heart, and with all the understanding, and with all the soul, and with all the strength, and to love *his* neighbour as himself, is more than all whole burnt offerings and sacrifices. And when Jesus saw that he answered discreetly, he said unto him. Thou art not far from the kingdom of God. And no man after that durst ask him *any question.*

* And Jesus sat over against the treasury, and beheld how the people cast money into the treasury and many that were rich cast in much. And there came a certain poor window, and she threw in two mites, which make a farthing. And he called *unto him* his disciples, and saith unto them, Verily I say unto you, that this poor widow hath cast more in than all they which have cast into the treasury: for all *they* did cast in of their abundance; but she of her want did cast in all that she had, *even* all her living.

** And he came to Nazareth, where he had been brought up: and, as his custom was, he went into the synagogue on the sabbath-day, and stood up for, to read. And there was delivered unto him the book of the prophet Esaias. And when he had opened the book, he found the place where it was written, The Spirit of the Lord *is* upon me, because he hath anointed me to preach the gospel to the poor; he hath sent me to heal the broken-hearted, to preach deliverance to the captives, and recovering of sight to the blind, to set at liberty them that are bruised, to preach the acceptable year of the Lord. And he closed the book, and he gave *it* again to the minister, and sat down. And the eyes of all them that were in the synagogue were fastened on him. And he began to say unto them, This day is this scripture fulfilled in your ears. And all bare him witness, and wondered at the gracious words which proceeded out of his mouth. And they said, Is not this Joseph's son? And he said unto them, Ye will surely say unto me this proverb, Physician, heal thyself: whatsoever we have heard done in Capernaum, do also here in thy country. And he said, Verily I say unto you, No prophet is accepted in his own country. But I tell you of a truth, Many widows were in Israel in the days of Elias, when the heaven was shut up three years and six months, when great famine was throughout all the land; but unto none of them was Elias sent, save unto Sarepta, *a city* of Sidon, unto a woman *that was* a widow. And many lepers were in Israel in the time of Eliseus the prophet; and none of them was cleansed, saving Naaman the Syrian.

† But their scribes and Pharisees murmured against his disciples, saying, Why do ye eat and drink with publicans and sinner? And Jesus answering, said unto them, They that are whole need not a physician; but they that are sick. I came not

---

*　　　Mark, Chap. xii. 41.
**　　Luke, Chap iv, 16.
†　　　Luke, Chap. vi. 30.

to call the righteous, but sinners to repentance. And he spake also a parable unto them: No man putteth a piece of a new garment upon an old; if otherwise, then both the new maketh a rent, and the piece that was *taken* out of the new agreeth not with the old. And no man putteth new wine into old bottles; else the new wine will burst the bottles and be spilled, and the bottles shall perish. But new wine must be put into new bottles and both are preserved. No man also having drunk old *wine* straightway desireth new: for he saith, The old is better.

* And it came to pass on the second sabbath after the first, that he went through the corn fields; and his disciples plucked the ears of corn, and did eat, rubbing *them* in *their* hands. And certain of the Pharisees said unto them, Why do ye that which is not lawful to do on the sabbath-days? And Jesus answering them said, Have ye not read so much as this, what David did, when himself was an hungered, and they which were with him; how he went into the house of God, and did take and eat the shew-bread, and gave also to them that were with him; which it is not lawful to eat, but for the priests alone? And he said unto them, That the *Son* of man is Lord also of the sabbath.

And it came to pass also on another sabbath, that he entered into the synagogue and taught; and there was a man whose right hand was withered. And the scribes and Pharisees watched him, whether he would heal on the sabbath-day, that they might find an accusation against him. But he knew their thoughts, and said to the man which had the withered hand, Rise up, and stand forth in the midst. And he arose and stood forth. Then said Jesus unto them, I will ask you one thing; Is it lawful on the sabbath-day to do good, or to do evil? to save life, or to destroy *it*?

** And he lifted up his eyes on his disciples, and said, Blessed *be ye* poor: for yours is the kingdom of God. Blessed *are ye* that hunger now: for ye shall be filled. Blessed *are ye* that weep now: for ye shall laugh. Blessed are ye when men shall hate you, and when they shall separate you *from their company,* and shall reproach *you,* and cast out your name as evil, for the Son of man's sake. Rejoice ye in that day, and leap for joy: for, behold, your reward *is* great in heaven: for in the like manner did their fathers unto the prophets. But woe unto you that are rich! for ye have received your consolation. Woe unto you that are full! for ye shall hunger. Woe unto you that laugh now! for ye shall mourn and weep. Woe unto you when all men shall speak well of you! for so did their fathers to the false prophets. But I say unto you which hear, Love your enemies, do good to them which hate you; bless them that curse you, and pray for them which despitefully use you. And unto him that smiteth thee on the *one* cheek offer also the other; and him that taketh away thy cloak forbid not *to take thy* coat also. Give to every man that asketh of thee; and of him that taketh away thy goods ask *them* not again. And as ye would that men should do to you, do ye also to them likewise. For if ye love them which love you, what thank have ye? for sinners also love those that love them. And if ye do good to them which do good to you, what thank have ye? for sinners also do even the same. And if ye lend *to them* of whom ye hope to receive, what thank have ye? for sinners

---

*   Luke, Chap. vi. 1.
**   Luke, Chap. vi. 20.

also lend to sinners, to receive as much again. But love ye your enemies, and do good, and lend, hoping for nothing again; and your reward shall be great, and ye shall be the children of the Highest: for he is kind unto the unthankful and *to* the evil. Be ye therefore merciful, as your Father also is merciful. Judge not, and ye shall not be judged: condemn not, and ye shall not be condemned: forgive, and ye shall be forgiven: give, and it shall be given unto you: good measure, pressed down, and shaken together, and running over, shall men give into your bosom. For with the same measure that ye mete withal, it shall be measured to you again. And he spake a parable unto them: Can the blind lead the blind? shall they not both fall into the ditch? The disciple is not above his master: but every one that is perfect shall be as his master. And why beholdest thou the mote that is in thy brother's eye, but perceivest not the beam that is in thine own eye? Either how canst thou say to thy brother, Brother, let me pull out the mote that is in thine eye, when they thyself beholdest not the beam that is in thine own eye? Thou hypocrite! cast out first the beam out of thine own eye, and then shalt thou see clearly to pull out the mote that is in thy brother's eye. For a good tree bringeth not forth corrupt fruit; neither doth a corrupt tree bring forth good fruit. For every tree is known by its own fruit: for of thorns men do not gather figs, nor of a bramble bush gather they grapes. A good man out of the good treasure of his heart bringeth forth that which is good; and an evil man out of the evil treasure of his heart bringeth forth that which is evil: for of the abundance of the heart his mouth speaketh. And why call ye me, Lord, Lord, and do not the things which I say? Whosoever cometh to me, and heareth my sayings, and doeth them, I will shew you to whom he is like: he is like a man which built an house, and digged deep, and laid the foundation on a rock; and when the flood arose, the stream beat vehemently upon that house, and could not shake it; for it was founded upon a rock. But he that heareth, and doeth not, is like a man that without a foundation built an house upon the earth: against which the stream did beat vehemently, and immediately it fell; and the ruin of that house was great.

* And one of the Pharisees desired him that he would eat with him. And he went into the Pharisee's house, and sat down to meat. And, behold, a woman in the city, which was a sinner, when she knew that *Jesus* sat at meat in the Pharisee's house, brought an alabaster-box of ointment, and stood at his feet behind *him* weeping, and began to wash his feet with tears, and did wipe *them* with the hairs of her head, and kissed his feet, and anointed *them* with the ointment. Now when the Pharisee which had bidden him saw *it,* he spake within himself, saying, This man, if he were a prophet, would have known who and what manner of woman *this is* that toucheth him; for she is a sinner. And Jesus answering said unto him, Simon, I have somewhat to say unto thee. And he saith, Master, say on. There was a certain creditor which had two debtors: the one owed five hundred pence, and the other fifty: and when they had nothing to pay, he frankly forgave them both. Tell me, therefore, which of them will love him most? Simon answered and said, I suppose that *he* to whom he forgave most. And he said unto him, Thou hast rightly judged. And he turned to the woman, and said unto Simon, Seest thou this

---

*   Luke, Chap. vii. 36.

woman; I entered into thine house, thou gavest me no water for my feet: but she hath washed my feet with tears, and wiped *them* with the hairs of her head. Thou gavest me no kiss: but this woman, since the time I came in, hath not ceased to kiss my feet. Mine head with oil thou didst not anoint: but this woman hath anointed my feet with ointment. Wherefore, I say unto thee, her sins, which are many, are forgiven; for she loved much: but to whom little is forgiven, *the same* loveth little. And he said unto her, Thy sins are forgiven. And they that sat at meat with him, began to say within themselves, Who is this that forgiveth sins also? And he said to the woman, Thy faith hath saved thee; go in peace.

* And when much people were gathered together, and were come to him out of every city, he spake by a parable: A sower went out to sow his seed: and as he sowed, some fell by the way-side; and it was trodden down, and the fowls of the air devoured it. And some fell upon a rock; and as soon as it was sprung up, it withered away, because it lacked moisture. And some fell among thorns; and the thorns sprang up with it and choked it. And other fell on good ground, and sprang up, and bare fruit an hundred-fold. And when he said these things, he cried, He that hath ears to hear, let him hear. And his disciples asked him, saying, What might this parable be? And he said, Unto you it is given to know the mysteries of the kingdom of God: but to others in parables; that seeing they might not see, and hearing they might not understand. Now the parable is this: The seed is the word of God. Those by the way side are they that hear; then cometh the devil, and taketh away the word out of their hearts, lest they should believe and be saved. They on the rock *are they,* which, when they hear, receive the word with joy; and these have no root, which for a while believe, and in time of temptation fall away. And that which fell among thorns are they, which when they have heard, go forth, and are choked with cares and riches and pleasures of *this* life, and bring no fruit to perfection. But that on the good ground are they, which, in an honest and good heart, having heard the word, keep *it,* and bring forth fruit with patience. No man when he hath lighted a candle, covereth it with a vessel, or putteth *it* under a bed; but setteth *it* on a candlestick, that they which enter in may see the light. For nothing is secret that shall not be made manifest; neither *any thing* hid that shall not be known and come abroad. Take heed therefore how ye hear: for whosoever hath, to him shall be given; and whosoever hath not, from him shall be taken even that which he seemeth to have.

Then came to him *his* mother and his brethren, and could not come at him for the press. And it was told him *by certain,* which said, Thy mother and thy brethren stand without, desiring to see thee. And he answered and said unto them, My mother and my brethren are these which hear the word of God, and do it.

** Then there arose a reasoning among them, which of them should be greatest. And Jesus, perceiving the thought of their heart, took a child, and set him by him, and said unto them, Whosoever shall receive this child in my name receiveth me; and whosoever shall receive me receiveth him that sent me: for he that is least

---

*   Luke, Chap. viii. 4.
**   Luke, Chap. ix. 46.

among you all, the same shall be great. And John answered and said, Master, we saw one casting out devils in thy name; and we forbad him, because he followeth not with us. And Jesus said unto him. Forbid *him* not: for he that is not against us is for us.

And it came to pass, when the time was come that he should be received up, he stedfastly set his face to go to Jerusalem. and sent messengers before his face: and they entered into a village of the Samaritans to make ready for him, and they did not receive him, because his face was as though he would go to Jerusalem, And when his disciples James and John, saw *this,* they said, Lord, wilt thou that we command fire to come down from heaven, and consume them, even as Elias did? But he turned and rebuked them, and said. Ye know not what manner of spirit ye are of. For the Son of man is not come to destroy men's lives, but to save *them.* And they went to another village.

And it came to pass, that, as they went in the way, a certain *man* said unto him, Lord, I will follow thee whithersoever thou goest. And Jesus said unto him, Foxes have holes, and birds of the air *have* nests; but the Son of man hath not where to lay *his* head. And he said unto another, Follow me. But he said, Lord, suffer me first to go and bury my father. Jesus said unto him, let the dead bury their dead: but go thou and preach the kingdom of God. And another also said, Lord, I will follow thee; but let me first go bid them farewell which are at home at my house. And Jesus said unto him, No man having put his hand to the plough, and looking back, is fit for the kingdom of God.

* After these things the Lord appointed other seventy also, and sent them two and two before his face into every city and place, whither he himself would come. Therefore said he unto them. The harvest truly *is* great, but the labourers *are* few: pray ye therefore the Lord of the harvest, that he would send forth labourers into his harvest. Go your ways: behold, I send you forth as lambs among wolves. Carry neither purse, nor scrip, nor shoes: and salute no man by the way. And into whatsoever house ye enter, first say, Peace *be* to this house. And if the Son of peace be there, your peace shall rest upon it: if not, it shall turn to you again. And in the same house remain, eating and drinking such things as they give: for the labourer is worthy of his hire: go not from house to house. And into whatsoever city ye enter, and they receive you, eat such things as are set before you: and heal the sick that are therein, and say unto them, The kingdom of God is come nigh unto you. But into whatsoever city ye enter, and they receive you not, go your ways out into the streets of the same, and say, Even the very dust of your city, which cleaveth on us, we do wipe off against you: notwithstanding, be ye sure of this, that the kingdom of God is come nigh unto you. But I say unto you, That it shall be more tolerable in that day for Sodom than for that city. Woe unto thee, Chorazin! woe unto thee, Bethsaida! for if the mighty works had been done in Tyre and Sidon which have been done in you, they had a great while ago repented, sitting in sackcloth and ashes. But it shall be more tolerable for Tyre and Sidon at the judgement than for you. And thou Capernaum, which art exalted to heaven, shalt be thrust down to

* Luke, Chap. x. 1.

hell. He that heareth you heareth me; and he that despiseth you despiseth me; and he that despiseth me despiseth him that sent me.

* And, behold, a certain lawyer stood up, and tempted him, saying, Master, what shall I do to inherit eternal life? He said unto him, What is written in the law? how readest thou? And he answering said, Thou shalt love the Lord thy God with all thy heart, and with all thy soul, and with all thy strength, and with all thy mind; and thy neighbour as thyself. And he said unto him, Thou hast answered right: this do, and thou shalt live! But he, willing to justify himself, said unto Jesus; And who is my neighbour? And Jesus answering said, A certain *man* went down from Jerusalem to Jericho, and fell among thieves, which stripped him of his raiment, and wounded *him,* and departed, leaving *him* half dead. And by chance there came down a certain priest that way: and when he saw him, he passed by on the other side. And likewise a Levite when he was at the place, came and looked *on him,* and passed by on the other side. But a certain Samaritan, as he journeyed, came where he was: and when he saw him, he had compassion *on him,* and went to *him,* and bound up his wounds, pouring in oil and wine, and set him on his own beast, and brought him to an inn, and took care of him. And on the morrow, when he departed, he took out two pence, and gave *them* to the host, and said unto him, Take care of him; and whatsoever thou spendest more, when I come again I will repay thee. Which now of these three, thinkest thou, was neighbour unto him that fell among the thieves? And he said, He that shewed mercy on him. Then said Jesus unto him, Go, and do thou likewise.

** Now it came to pass, as they went, that he entered into a certain village: and a certain woman named Martha received him into her house. And she had a sister called Mary, which also sat at Jesus' feet, and heard his word. But Martha was cumbered about much serving, and came to him, and said, Lord, dost thou not care that my sister hath left me to serve alone? bid her therefore that she help me. And Jesus answered and said unto her, Martha, Martha, thou art careful and troubled about many things: but one thing is needful: and Mary hath chosen that good part, which shall not be taken away from her.

† And it came to pass, that as he was praying in a certain place, when he ceased, one of his disciples said unto him, Lord, teach us to pray, as John also taught his disciples. And he said unto them, When ye pray, say, Our Father which art in heaven, hallowed be thy name: Thy kingdom come: Thy will be done, as in heaven, so in earth. Give us day by day our daily bread: and forgive us our sins; for we also forgive every one that is indebted to us: and lead us not into temptation; but deliver us from evil. And he said unto them, Which of you shall have a friend, and shall go unto him at midnight, and say unto him, Friend, lend me three loaves: for a friend of mine in his journey is come to me, and I have nothing to set before him. And he from within shall answer and say, Trouble me not; the door is now shut, and my children are with me in bed; I cannot rise and give thee. I say unto you,

---

* Luke, Chap. x. 25.
** Luke, Chap. x. 38.
† Luke, Chap. xi. 1.

Though he will not rise and give him because he is his friend, yet because of his importunity he will rise and give him as many as he needeth. And I say unto you, Ask, and it shall be given you; seek, and ye shall find; knock, and it shall be opened unto you. For every one that asketh receiveth; and he that seeketh findeth; and to him that knocketh it shall be opened. If a son shall ask bread of any of you that is a father, will he give him a stone? or if *he ask* a fish. will he for a fish given him a serpent? or if he shall ask an egg, will he offer him a scorpion? If ye then, being evil, know how to given good gifts unto your children, how much more shall *your* heavenly Father give the Holy Spirit to them that ask him?

* And it came to pass, as he spake these things, a certain woman of the company lifted up her voice, and said unto him, Blessed *is* the womb that bare thee, and the paps which thou hast sucked. But he said, Yea rather blessed *are* they that hear the word of God, and keep it.

** No man when he hath lighted a candle, puteth *it* in a secret place, neither under a bushel, but on a candlestick, that they which come in may see the light. The light of the body is the eye: therefore when thine eye is single, thy whole body also is full of light; but when *thine eye* is evil, thy body also *is* full of darkness. Take heed therefore that the light which is in thee be not darkness. If thy whole body therefore *be* full of light, having no part dark, the whole shall be full of light, as when the bright shining of a candle doth give thee light.

And as he spake, a certain Pharisee besought him to dine with him: and he went in, and sat down to meat. And when the Pharisee saw *it,* he marvelled that he had not first washed before dinner. And the Lord said unto him, Now do ye Pharisees make clean the outside of the cup and the platter; but your inward part is full of ravening and wickedness. *Ye* fools, did not he that made that which is without make that which is within also? But rather give alms of such things as you have; and, behold, all things are clean unto you. But woe unto you, Pharisees! for ye tithe mint and rue and all manner of herbs, and pass over judgement and the love of God: these ought ye to have done, and not to leave the other undone. Woe unto you Pharisees! for ye are as graves which appear not, and the men that walk over *them* are not aware *of them.* Then answered one of the lawyers, and said unto him, Master, thus saying, thou reproachest us also. And he said, Woe unto you also, *ye* lawyers! for ye lade men with burdens grievous to be borne, and ye yourselves touch not the burdens with one of your fingers. Woe unto you! for ye build the sepulchres of the prophets, and your fathers killed them. Truly ye bear witness that ye allow the deeds of your fathers: for they indeed killed them, and ye build their sepulchres. Therefore also said the wisdom of God, I will send them prophets and apostles, and *some* of them they shall slay and persecute; that the blood of all the prophets, which was shed from the foundation of the world, may be required of this generation; from the blood of Abel, unto the blood of Zacharias, which perished between the altar and the temple: verily I say unto you, it shall be required of this

---

*   Luke, Chap. xi. 27.
** Luke, Chap. xi. 33.

generation. Woe unto you, lawyers! for ye have taken away the key of knowledge: ye entered not in yourselves, and them that were entering in ye hindered.

* In the mean time, when there were gathered together an innumerable multitude of people, insomuch that they trode one upon another, he began to say unto his disciples first of all, Beware ye of the leaven of the Pharisees, which is hypocrisy.

For there is nothing covered that shall not be revealed; neither hid, that shall not he known. Therefore whatsoever ye have spoken in darkness shall be heard in the light; and that which ye have spoken in the ear, in closets, shall be proclaimed upon the house-tops. And I say unto you, my friends, Be not afraid of them that kill the body, and after that have no more that they can do, But I will forewarn you whom ye shall fear: fear him which, after he hath killed, hath power to cast into hell; yea, I say unto yon, Fear him. Are not five sparrows sold for two farthings? and not one of them is forgotten before God: but even the very hairs of your head are all numbered. Fear not, therefore: ye are of more value than many sparrows. Also I say unto you, Whosoever shall confess me before men, him shall the Son of man also confess before the angels of God: but he that denieth me before men, shall be denied before the angels of God. And whosoever shall speak a word against the Son of man, it shall be forgiven him: but unto him that blasphemeth against the Holy Ghost, it shall not be forgiven. And when they bring you unto the synagogues, and *unto* magistrates and powers, take ye no thought how or what thing ye shall answer, or what ye shall say: for the Holy Ghost shall teach you in the same hour what ye ought to say. And one of the company said unto him, Master, speak to my brother, that he divide the inheritance with me. And he said unto him, Man, who made me a judge or a divider over you? And he said unto them, Take heed and be ware of covetousness: for a man's life consisteth not in the abundance of the things which he possesseth. And he spake a parable unto them, saying, The ground of a certain rich man brought forth plentifully: and he thought within himself, saying, What shall I do, because I have no room where to bestow my fruits? And he said, This will I do: I will pull down my barns, and build greater; and there will I bestow all my fruits my goods. And I will say to my soul, Soul, thou hast much goods laid up for many years; take thine ease, eat, drink, *and* be merry, But God said unto him, *Thou* fool! this night thy soul shall be required of thee: then whose shall those things be which thou hast provided? So *is* he that layeth up treasure for himself, and is not rich towards God. And he said unto his disciples, Therefore I say unto you, Take no thought for your life, what ye shall eat; neither for the body, what ye shall put on. The life is more than meat, and the body *is more* than raiment. Consider the ravens: for they neither sow nor reap; which neither have storehouse nor barn; and God feedeth them. How much more are ye better than the fowls? And which of you with taking thought can add to his stature one cubit? If ye then be not able to do that thing which is least, why take ye thought for the rest? Consider the lilies how they grow; they toil not, they spin not: and yet I say unto you, That Solomon in all his glory was not arrayed like one of these. If then God so

---

*   Luke, Chap. xii. 1.

clothe the grass, which is to-day in the field, and to-morrow is cast into the oven, how much more *will he clothe* you, O ye of little faith? And seek not ye what ye shall eat, or what ye shall drink, neither be ye of doubtful mind. For all these things do the nations of the world seek after: and your Father knoweth that have need of these things. But rather seek ye the kingdom of God; and all these things shall be added unto you. Fear not, little flock; for it is your Father's good pleasure to give you the kingdom. Sell that ye have, and give alms: provide yourselves bags which wax not old, a treasure in the heavens that faileth not, where no thief approacheth, neither moth corrupteth. For where your treasure is, there will your heart be also. Let your loins be girded about, and *your* lights burning; and ye yourselves like unto men that wait for their lord, when he will return from the wedding; that when he cometh and knocketh they may open unto him immediately. Blessed *are* those servants whom the lord, when he cometh, shall find watching? verily I say unto you, That he shall gird himself, and make them to sit down to meat, and will come forth and serve them. And if he shall come in the second watch, or come in the third watch, and find *them* so, blessed are those servants. And this know, that if the good man of the house had known what hour the thief would come, he would have watched, and not have suffered his house to be broken through. Be ye therefore ready also: for the Son of man cometh at an hour when ye think not. Then Peter said unto him, Lord, speakest thou this parable unto us, or even to all? And the Lord said, Who then is that faithful and wise steward, whom *his* lord shall make ruler over his household, to give *them their* portion of meat in due season? Blessed *is* that servant, whom his lord, when he cometh, shall find so doing. Of a truth I say unto you, That he will make him ruler over all that he hath. But and if that servant say in his heart, My lord delayeth his coming; and shall begin to beat the men-servants and maidens, and to eat and drink, and to be drunken; the lord of that servant will come in a day when he looketh not for *him,* and at an hour when he is not aware, and will cut him in sunder, and will appoint him his portion with the unbelievers. And that servant, which knew his lord's will, and prepared not *himself,* neither did according to his will, shall be beaten with many *stripes.* But he that knew not, and did commit things worthy of stripes, shall be beaten with few *stripes.* For unto whomsoever much is given, of him shall be much required: and to whom men have committed much, of him they will ask the more. I am come to send fire on the earth; and what will I, if it be already kindled? But I have a baptism to be baptized with; and how am I straitened till it be accomplished! Suppose ye that I am come to give peace on earth? I tell you, Nay; but rather division: for from henceforth there shall be five in one house divided, three against two, and two against three. The father shall be divided against the son, and the son against the father; the mother against the daughter, and the daughter against the mother; the mother-in-law against her daughter-in-law, and the daughter-in-law against her mother-in-law. And he said also to the people, When ye see a cloud rise out of the west, straightway ye say, There cometh a shower; and so it is. And when *ye see* the south wind blow, ye say, There will be heat: and it cometh to pass. *Ye hypocrites!* ye can discern the face of the sky and of the earth; but how is it that ye do not discern this time? Yea, and why even of yourselves judge ye not what is right? When thou goest with thine adversary to the magistrate, *as thou art* in the way, give diligence that thou mayest be delivered from him; lest he hale thee to the judge, and the judge deliver thee to the officer, and the officer cast thee into prison. I tell thee, thou shalt not depart thence, till thou hast paid the very last mite.

* There were present at that season some that told him of the Galileans, whose blood Pilate had mingled with their sacrifices. And Jesus answering said unto them, Suppose ye that these Galileans were sinners above all the Galileans, because they suffered such things? I tell you, Nay: but except ye repent, ye shall all likewise perish. Or those eighteen, upon whom the tower in Siloam fell, and slew them think ye that they were sinners above all men that dwelt in Jerusalem? I tell you, Nay: but except ye repent, ye shall all likewise perish. He spake also this parable: A certain *man* had a fig-tree planted in his vineyard; and he came and sought fruit thereon, and found none. Then said he unto the dresser of his vineyard, Behold, these three years I come seeking fruit on this fig-tree, and find none; cut it down; why cumbereth it the ground. And he answering said unto him, Lord, let it alone this year also, till I shall dig about it, and dung *it*: and if it bear fruit, *well*: and if not *then* after that thou shalt cut it down.

** And the ruler of the synagogue answered with indignation because that Jesus had healed on the sabbath-day, and said unto the people, There are six days in which men ought to work: in them therefore come and be healed, and not on the sabbath-day. The Lord then answered him, and said, *Thou* hypocrite! doth not each one of you on the sabbath loose his ox or *his* ass from the stall, and lead *him* away to watering? And ought not this woman, being a daughter of Abraham, whom Satan hath bound, lo these eighteen years, to be loosed from this bond on the sabbath-day? And when he had said these things, all his adversaries were ashamed: and all the people rejoiced for all the glorious things that were done by him.

Then said he, Unto what is the kingdom of God like? and whereunto shall I resemble it? It is like a grain of mustard seed, which a man took, and cast into his garden: and it grew, and waxed a great tree; and the fowls of the air lodged in the branches of it. And again he said, Whereunto shall I liken the kingdom of God? It is like leaven, which a woman took and hid in three measures of meal, till the whole was leavened.

Then said one unto him, Lord, are there few that be saved? And he said unto them, Strive to enter in at the strait gate: for many, I say unto you, will seek to enter in, and shall not be able. When once the master of the house is risen up, and hath shut to the door, and ye begin to stand without, and to knock at the door, saying, Lord, Lord, open unto us; and he shall answer and say unto you, I know you not whence ye are; Then shall ye begin to say, We have eaten and drunk in thy presence, and thou hast taught in our streets. But he shall say, I tell you, I know you not whence ye are; depart from me, all *ye* workers of iniquity. There shall be

---

*   Luke, Chap. xiii. 1.
** Luke xiii. 14.

weeping and gnashing of teeth, when ye shall see Abraham, and Isaac, and Jacob, and all the prophets, in the kingdom of God, and you *yourselves* thrust out. And they shall come from the east, and *from* the west, and from the north, and *from* the south, and shall sit down in the kingdom of God. And, behold, there are last which shall be first, and there are first which shall be last.

The same day there came certain of the Pharisees, saying unto him. Get thee out, and depart hence: for Herod will kill thee. And he said unto them, Go ye, and tell that fox, Behold, I cast out devils, and I do cures to-day and to-morrow, and the third *day* I shall be perfected. Nevertheless I must walk to-day, and to-morrow, and the *day* following: for it cannot be that a prophet perish out of Jerusalem. O Jerusalem, Jerusalem, which killest the prophets, and stonest them that are sent unto thee; how often would I have gathered thy children together, as a hen *doth gather* her brood under *her* wings, and ye would not! Behold, your house is left unto you desolate: and verily I say unto you, Ye shall not see me, until *the time* come when ye shall say, Blessed *is* he that cometh in the name of the Lord.

* And it came to pass, as he went into the house of one of the chief Pharisees to eat bread on the sabbath-day that they watched him. And, behold, there was a certain man before him which had the dropsy. And Jesus answering, spake unto the lawyers and Pharisees, saying, is it lawful to heal on the sabbath-day? And they held their peace, And he took *him,* and healed him, and let him go; and answered them, saying, Which of you shall have an ass or an ox fallen into a pit, and will not straightway pull him out on the sabbath-day? And they could not answer him again to these things, And he put forth a parable to those which were bidden, when he marked how they chose out the chief rooms; saying unto them, When thou art bidden of any *man* to a wedding, sit not down in the highest room; lest a more honorable man than thou be bidden of him; and he that bade thee and him come and say to thee, Give this man place; and thou begin with shame to take the lowest room. But when thou art bidden, go and sit down in the lowest room; that when he that bade thee cometh, he may say unto thee, Friend, go up higher; then shalt thou have worship in the presence of them that sit at meat with thee. For whosoever exalteth himself shall be abased; and he that humbleth himself shall be exalted. Then said he also to him that bade him, When thou makest a dinner or a supper, call not thy friends, nor thy brethren, neither thy kinsman, nor *thy* rich neighbours; lest they also bid thee again, and a recompence be made thee. But when thou makest a feast, call the poor, the maimed, the lame, the blind: and thou shalt be blessed; for they cannot recompense thee; for thou shalt be recompensed at the resurrection of the just. And when one of them that sat at meat with him heard these things, he said unto him, Blessed *is* he that shall eat bread in the kingdom of God. Then said he unto him, A certain man made a great supper, and bade many: and sent his servant at supper time to say to them that were bidden, Come; for all things are now ready. and they all with one *consent* began to make excuse. The first said unto him, I have bought a piece of ground and I must needs

---

*   Luke, Chap. xiv. 1.

go and see it: I pray thee have me excused. And another said, I have bought five yoke of oxen, and I go to prove them: I pray thee have me excused. And another said, I have married a wife, and therefore I cannot come. So that servant came, and shewed his lord these things. Then the master of the house, being angry, said to his servant, Go out quickly into the streets and lanes of the city, and bring in hither the poor, and the maimed and the halt, and the blind. And the servant said, Lord, it is done as thou hast commanded, and yet there is room. And the lord said unto the servant, Go out into the highways and hedges, and compel *them* to come in, that my house may be filled. For I say unto you, That none of those men which were bidden shall taste of my supper.

And there went great multitudes with him: and he turned and said unto them, If any *man* come to me, and hate not his father, and mother, and wife, and children, and brethren, and sisters, yea, and his own life also, he cannot be my disciple. And whosoever doth not bear his cross, and come after me, cannot be my disciple. For which of you intending to build a tower, sitteth not done first and counteth the cost, whether he have *sufficient* to finish *it?* Lest haply, after he hath laid the foundation, and is not able to finish *it,* all that behold *it* begin to mock him, Saying, This man began to build, and was not able to finish. Or what king, going to make war against another king, sitteth not down first, and consulteth whether he be able with ten thousand to meet him that cometh against him with twenty thousand? Or else, while the other is yet a great way off, he sendeth an ambassage, and desireth conditions of peace. So likewise, whosoever he be of you that forsaketh not all that he hath, he cannot be my disciple. Salt *is* good; but if the salt have lost its savour, wherewith shall it be seasoned? It is neither fit for the land, nor yet for the dunghill; *but* men cast it out. He that hath ears to hear, let him hear.

* Then drew near unto him all the publicans and sinners, for to hear him. And the Pharisees and scribes murmured, saying, This man receiveth sinners, and eateth with them. And he spake this parable unto them, saying, What man of you, having an hundred sheep, if he lose one of them, doth not leave the ninety and nine in the wilderness, and go after that which is lost, until he find it? And when he hath found *it,* he layeth *it* on his shoulders, rejoicing. And when he cometh home, he calleth together *his* friends and neighbours, saying unto them, Rejoice with me; for I have found my sheep which was lost. I say unto you, that likewise joy shall be in heaven over one sinner that repenteth, more than over ninety and nine just persons which need no repentance. Either what woman having ten pieces of silver, if she lose one piece, doth not light a candle, and sweep the house, and seek diligently till she find *it?* And when she hath found *it,* she calleth *her* friends and *her* neighbours together, saying, Rejoice with me; for I have found the piece which I had lost. Likewise, I say unto you, There is joy in the presence of the angels of God over one sinner that repenteth. And he said, A certain man had two sons: and the younger of them said to *his* father, Father, give me the portion of goods that falleth *to me.* And he divided unto them *his* living. And not many days after the younger son gathered all together, and took his journey into a far country,

---

*   Luke, Chap. xv. 1.

and there wasted his substance with riotous living. And when he had spent all, there arose a mighty famine in that land; and he began to be in want. And he went and joined himself to a citizen of that country; and he sent him into his fields to feed swine. And he would fain have filled his belly with the husks that the swine did eat: and no man gave unto him. And when he came to himself, he said, How many hired servants of my father's have bread enough and to spare, and I perish with hunger! I will arise and go to my father, and will say unto him, Father, I have sinned against heaven, and before thee, and am no more worthy to be called thy son: make me as one of thy hired servants. And he arose, and came to his father. But when he was yet a great way off, his father saw him, and had compassion, and ran, and fell on his neck, and kissed him. And the son said unto him, Father, I have sinned against heaven, and in thy sight, and am no more worthy to be called thy son. But the father said to his servants, Bring forth the best robe, and put *it* on him; and put a ring on his hand, and shoes on *his* feet: and ring hither there fatted calf, and kill *it*; and let us eat and be merry: for this my son was dead, and is alive again; he was lost, and is found. And they began to be merry. Now his elder son was in the field: and as he came and drew nigh to the house, he heard music and dancing; and he called one of the servants, and asked what these things meant. And he said unto him, Thy brother is come; and thy father hath killed the fatted calf, because he hath received him safe and sound. And he was angry, and would not go in: therefore came his father out, and entreated him. And he answering said to *his* father, Lo, these many years do I serve thee, neither transgressed I at any time thy commandment: and yet thou never gavest me a kid, that I might make merry with my friends: but as soon as this thy son was come, which hath devoured thy living with harlots, thou hast killed for him the fatted calf. And he said unto him, Son, thou art ever with me, and all that I have is thine. It was meet that we should make merry and be glad: for this thy brother was dead, and is alive again; and was lost, and is found.

    * And he said also unto his disciples, There was a certain rich man which had a steward; and the same was accused unto him that he had wasted his goods. And he called him, and said unto him, How is it that I hear this of thee? give an account of thy stewardship, for thou mayest be no longer steward. Then the steward said within himself, What shall I do, for my lord taketh away from me the stewardship? I cannot dig; to beg I am ashamed. I am resolved what to do, that, when I am put out of the stewardship, they may receive me into their houses. So he called every one of his lord's debtors *unto him,* and said unto the first, How much owest thou unto my lord? And he said, An hundred measures of oil. And he said unto him, Take thy bill, and sit down quickly, and write fifty. Then said he to another, And how much owest thou? And he said, An hundred measures of wheat. And he said unto him, Take they bill, and write fourscore. And the lord commended the unjust steward, because he had done wisely: for the children of this world are in their generation wiser than the children of light. And I say unto you, Make to yourselves

---

    *   Luke, Chap. xvi. 1.

friends of the mammon of unrighteousness; that, when ye fail, they may receive you unto everlasting habitations, He that is faithful in that which is least is faithful also in much: and he that is unjust in the least is unjust also in much. If therefore ye have not been faithful in the unrighteous mammon, who will commit to your trust the true *riches?* And if ye have not been faithful in that which is another man's, who shall give you that which is your own? No servant can serve two masters: for either he will hate the one, and love the other; or else he will hold to the one, and despise the other. Ye cannot serve God and mammon. And the Pharisees also, who were covetous, heard all these things: and they derided him. And he said unto them, Ye are they which justify yourselves before men; but God knoweth your hearts; for that which is highly esteemed amongst men is abomination in the sight of God. The law and the prophets *were* until John: since that time the kingdom of God is preached, and every man presseth into it. And it is easier for heaven and earth to pass, than one tittle of the law to fail. Whosoever putteth away his wife, and marrieth another, committeth adultery: and whosoever marrieth her that is put away from *her* husband, committeth adultery. There was a certain rich man, which was clothed in purple and fine linen, and fared sumptuously every day: and there was a certain beggar named Lazarus, which was laid at his gate, full of sores, and desiring to be fed with the crumbs which fell from the rich man's table: moreover, the dogs came and licked his sores. And it came to pass that the beggar died, and was carried by the angels into Abraham's bosom: the rich man also died, and was buried; and in hell he lifted up his eyes, being in torments, and seeth Abraham afar off, and Lazarus in his bosom: and he cried and said, Father Abraham, have mercy on me, and send Lazarus, that he may dip the tip of his finger in water, and cool my tongue; for I am tormented in this flame. But Abraham said, Son, remember that thou in thy lifetime receivedst thy good things, and likewise Lazarus evil things: but now he is comforted and thou art tormented. And besides all this, between us and you there is a great gulf fixed: so that they which would pass from hence to you cannot; neither can they pass to us that *would come* from thence. Then he said, I pray thee therefore, father, that thou wouldest send him to my father's house; for I have five brethren: that he may testify unto them, lest they also come into this place of torment. Abraham saith unto him, They have Moses and the prophets; let them hear them. And he said, Nay, father Abraham: but if one went unto them from the dead, they will repent. And he said unto him, If they hear not Moses and the prophets, neither will they be persuaded though one rose form the dead.

* Then said he unto the disciples, It is impossible but that offences will come: but woe *unto him* through whom they come! It were better for him that a millstone were hanged about his neck, and he cast into the sea, than that he should offend one of these little ones. Take heed to yourselves: if thy brother trespass against thee, rebuke him; and if he repent, forgive him. And if he trespass against thee seven times in a day, and seven times in a day turn again to thee, saying, I repent; thou shalt forgive him. And the apostles said unto the Lord, Increase our faith. And the Lord said, If ye had faith as a grain of mustard-seed, ye might say unto this

---

*   Luke, Chap. xvii. 1.

sycamine tree, Be thou plucked up by the root, and be thou planted in the sea: and it should obey you. But which of you, having a servant plowing, or feeding cattle, will say unto him by and by, when he is come from the field, Go and sit down to meat? and will not rather say unto him, Make ready wherewith I may sup, and gird thyself, and serve me, till I have eaten and drunken; and afterward thou shall eat and drink? Doth he thank that servant because he did the things that were commanded him? I trow not. So likewise ye, when ye shall have done all those things which are commanded you, say, We are unprofitable servants; we have done that which was our duty to do.

* And he spake a parable unto them *to this end,* that men ought always *to* pray, and not to faint: saying, There was in a city a judge, which feared not God, neither regarded man: and there was a widow in that city; and she came unto him, saying, Avenge me of mine adversary. And he would not for a while: but afterward he said within himself. Though I fear not God, nor regard man; yet, because this widow troubleth me, I will avenge her, lest by her continual coming she weary me. And the Lord said, Hear what the unjust judge saith. And shall not God avenge his own elect, which cry day and night unto him, though he bear long with them? I tell you that he will avenge them speedily. Nevertheless, when the Son of man cometh, shall he find faith on the earth?

And he spake this parable unto certain which trusted in themselves that they were righteous, and despised others: two men went up into the temple to pray; the one a Pharisee, and the other a publican. The Pharisee stood and prayed thus with himself: God, I thank thee that I am not as other men *are,* extortioners, unjust, adulterers, or even as this publican: I fast twice in the week, I give tithes of all that I possess. And the publican, standing afar off, would not lift up so much as *his* eyes unto heaven, but smote upon his breast, saying, God be merciful to me a sinner. I tell you, This man went down to his house justified *rather* than the other: for every one that exalteth himself shall be abased; and he that humbleth himself shall be exalted.

And they brought unto him also infants, that he would touch them: but when *his* disciples saw *it,* they rebuked them. But Jesus called them *unto him,* and said, Suffer little children to come unto me, and forbid them not: for of such is the kingdom of God. Verily I say unto you, Whosoever shall not receive the kingdom of God as a little child, shall in no wise enter therein.

And a certain ruler asked him, saying, Good Master, what shall I do to inherit eternal life? And Jesus said unto him, Why callest thou me good? none *is* good, save one, *that is,* God, Thou knowest the commandments, Do not commit adultery, Do not kill, Do not steal, Do not bear false witness, Honour thy father and thy mother. And he said, All these have I kept from my youth up. Now when Jesus heard these things, he said unto him, Yet lackest thou one thing: sell all that thou hast, and distribute unto the poor, and thou shalt have treasure in heaven: and come, follow me. And when he heard this, he was very sorrowful: for he was very rich. And when Jesus saw that he was very sorrowful, he said, How hardly shall

---

*   Luke, Chap. xviii. 1.

they that have riches enter into the kingdom of God! For it is easier for a camel to go through a needle's eye, than for a rich man to enter into the kingdom of God. And they that heard *it* said, Who then can be saved? And he said, The things which are impossible with men are possible with God. Then Peter said, Lo, we have left all, and followed thee. And he said unto them, Verily I say unto you, There is no man that hath left house, or parents, or brethren, or wife, or children, for the kingdom of God's sake, who shall not receive manifold more in this present time, and in the world to come life everlasting.

* He said therefore, A certain nobleman went into a far country to receive for himself a kingdom, and to return. And he called his ten servants, and delivered them ten pounds, and said unto them, Occupy till I come. But his citizens hated him, and sent a message after him, saying, We will not have this *man* to reign over us. And it came to pass, that when he was returned, having received the kingdom, then he commanded these servants to be called unto him, to whom he had given the money, that he might know how much every man had gained by trading. Then came the first, saying, Lord, thy pound hath gained ten pounds. And he said unto him, Well, thou good servant: because thou hast been faithful in a very little, have thou authority over ten cities. And the second came, saying, Lord, thy pound hath gained five pounds. And he said likewise to him, Be thou also over five cities. And another came, saying, Lord, behold, *here is* thy pound, which I have kept laid up in a napkin: for I feared thee, because thou art an austere man: thou takest up that thou layedst not down, and reapest that thou didst not sow. And he saith unto him, Out of thine own mouth will I judge thee, *thou* wicked servant. Thou knewest that I was an austere man, taking up that I laid not down, and reaping that I did not sow: wherefore then gavest not thou my money into the bank, that at my coming I might have required mine own with usury? And he said unto them that stood by, Take from him the pound, and give *it* to him that hath ten pounds. (And they said unto him Lord, he hath ten pounds.) For I say unto you, that unto every one which hath shall be given; and from him that hath not, even that he hath shall be taken away from him. But those mine enemies, which would not that I should reign over them, bring hither, and slay *them* before me.

** And the chief priests and the scribes the same hour sought to lay hands on him; and they feared the people: for they perceived that he had spoken this parable against them. And they watched *him,* and sent forth spies, which should feign themselves just men, that they might take hold of his words, that so they might deliver him unto the power and authority of the governor. And they asked him, saying, Master, we know that thou sayest and teachest rightly, neither acceptest thou the person *of any,* but teachest the way of God truly: is it lawful for us to give tribute unto Caesar, or no? But he perceived their craftiness, and said unto them, Why tempt ye me? Shew me a penny. Whose image and superscription hath it? They answered and said, Caesar's. And he said unto them, Render therefore unto Caesar the things which be Caesar's and unto God the things which be God's.

*   Luke, Chap. xix. 12.
**   Luke, Chap. xx. 19.

And they could not take hold of his words before the people: and they marvelled at his answer, and held their peace. Then came to *him* certain of the Sadducees, which deny that there is any resurrection; and they asked him, saying, Master, Moses wrote unto us, If any man's brother die, having a wife, and he die without children, that his brother should take his wife, and raise up seed unto his brother. There were therefore seven brethren: and the first took a wife, and died without children. And the second took her to wife, and he died childless. And the third took her; and in like manner the seven also: and they left no children, and died. Last of all the woman died also. Therefore in the resurrection whose wife of them is she? for seven had her to wife. And Jesus answering said unto them, The children of this world marry, and are given in marriage: but they which shall be accounted worthy to obtain that world, and the resurrection from the dead, neither marry, nor are given in marriage: neither can they die any more: for they are equal unto the angels; and are the children of God, being the children of the resurrection. Now that the dead are raised, even Moses shewed at the bush, when he calleth the Lord the God of Abraham, and the God of Isaac, and the God of Jacob. For he is not a God of the dead, but of the living; for all live unto him. Then certain of the scribes answering said, Master, thou hast well said.

* And he looked up, and saw the rich men casting their gifts into the treasury. And he saw also a certain poor widow casting in thither two mites. And he said, Of a truth I say unto you, That this poor widow hath cast in more than they all: for all these have of their abundance cast in unto the offerings of God: but she of her penury hath cast in all the living that she had.

** There was a man of the Pharisees, named Nicodemus, a ruler of the Jews: the same came to Jesus by night, and said unto him, Rabbi, we know that thou art a teacher come from God; for no man can do these miracles that thou doest, except God be with him. Jesus answered and said unto him, Verily, verily, I say unto thee, Except a man be born again, he cannot see the kingdom of God. Nicodemus saith unto him, How can a man be born when he is old? can he enter the second time into his mother's womb, and be born? Jesus answered, Verily, verily, I say unto thee. Except a man be born of water and *of* the Spirit, he cannot enter into the kingdom of God. That which is born of the flesh is flesh; and that which is born of the Spirit is spirit. Marvel not that I said unto thee, Ye must be born again. The wind bloweth where it listeth, and thou hearest the sound thereof, but canst not tell whence it cometh, and whither it goeth: so is every one that is born of the Spirit. Nicodemus answered and said unto him, How can these things be? Jesus answered and said unto him, Art thou a master of Israel, and knowest not these things? Verily, verily, I say unto thee, We speak that we do know, and testify that we have seen; and ye receive not our witness. If I have told you earthly things, and ye believe not, how shall ye believe if I tell you *of* heavenly things? And no man hath ascended up to heaven, but he that came down from heaven, *even* the Son of man, which is in heaven. And as Moses lifted up the serpent in the

---

* Luke, Chap. xxi. 1.
** John, Chap. iii. 1.

wilderness, even so must the Son of man be lifted up; that whosoever believeth in him should not perish, but have eternal life. For God so loved the world, that he gave his only-begotten Son, that whosoever believeth in him should not perish, but have everlasting life. For God sent not his Son into the world to condemn the world; but that the world through him might be saved. He that believeth on him is not condemned: but he that believeth not is condemned already, because he hath not believed in the name of the only begotten Son of God. And this is the condemnation, that light is come into the world, and men loved darkness rather than light, because their deeds were evil. For every one that doeth evil hateth the light, neither cometh to the light, lest his deeds should be reproved: but he that doeth truth cometh to the light, that his deeds may be made manifest that they are wrought in God.

* But the hour cometh, and now is, when the true worshippers shall worship the Father in spirit and in truth: for the Father seeketh such to worship him. God *is* a Spirit: and they that worship him must worship *him* in spirit and in truth.

** Labour not for the meat which perisheth, but for that meat which endureth unto everlasting life, which the Son of man shall give unto you: for him hath God the Father sealed.

† And the scribes and Pharisees brought unto him a woman taken in adultery; and when they had set her in the midst, they say unto him, Master, this woman was taken in adultery, in the very act. Now Moses in the law commanded us, that such should be stoned: but what sayest thou? This they said tempting him, that they might have to accuse him. But Jesus stooped down, and with *his* finger wrote on the ground, *as though he heard them not.* So when they continued asking him, he lifted up himself, and said unto them, He that is without sin among you, let him first cast a stone at her. And again he stooped down, and wrote on the ground. And they which heard *it,* being convicted by *their own* conscience, went out one by one, beginning at the eldest *even* unto the last: and Jesus was left alone, and the woman standing in the midst. When Jesus had lifted up himself, and saw none but the woman, he said unto her, Woman, where are those thine accusers? hath no man condemned thee? She said, No man, Lord. And Jesus said unto her, Neither do I condemn thee: go, and sin no more.

‡ And Jesus said, For judgement I am come into this world; that they which see not might see, and that they which see might be made blind. And *some* of the Pharisees which were with him heard these words, and said unto him, Are we blind also? Jesus said unto them, If ye were blind, ye should have no sin: but now ye say, We see; therefore your sin remaineth.

¶ I am the true vine, and my Father is the husbandman. Every branch in me that beareth not fruit he taketh away: and every *branch* that beareth fruit he purgeth

---

* John, Chap. iv. 23.
** John, Chap. vi. 27.
† John, Chap. viii. 3.
‡ John, Chap. xi. 30.
¶ John, Chap. xv. 1.

it, that it may bring forth more fruit. Now ye are clean through the word which I have spoken unto you. Abide in me, and I in you. As the branch cannot bear fruit of itself, except it abide in the vine; no more can ye, except ye abide in me. I am the vine, ye *are* the branches: he that abideth in me, and I in him, the same bringeth forth much fruit: for without me ye can do nothing. If a man abide not in me, he is cast forth as a branch, and is withered; and men gather them, and cast *them* into the fire, and they are burned. If ye abide in me, and my words abide in you, ye shall ask what ye will, and it shall be done unto you. Herein is my Father glorified, that ye bear much fruit; so shall ye be my disciples. As the Father hath loved me, so have I loved you: continue ye in my love. If ye keep my commandments, ye shall abide in my love; even as I have kept my Father's commandments, and abide in his love. These things have I spoken unto you, that my joy might remain in you, and *that* your joy might be full. This is my commandment, That ye love one another, as I have loved you. Greater love hath no man than this, that a man lay down his life for his friends. Ye are my friends, if ye do whatsoever I command you. Henceforth I call you not servants; for the servant knoweth not what his lord doeth: but I have called you friends; for all things that I have heard of my Father I have made known unto you. Ye have not chosen me, but I have chosen you, and ordained you, that ye should go and bring forth fruit, and *that* your fruit should remain; that whatsoever ye shall ask of the Father in my name, he may give it you. These things I command you, that ye love one another.

BIBLIOGRAPHY

'An Account of the Life and Writings of Rammohun Roy, a Learned Brahmin, and of the New Sect in India, of which he is the founder'. *The Monthly Repository* 15, no. 169 (1820): 1–7.

Adams, Dickinson W., ed. *Jefferson's Extracts from the Gospels: 'The Philosophy of Jesus' and 'The Life and Morals of Jesus'*. Princeton, NJ: Princeton University Press, 1983.

Appasamy, A.J. *Christianity as Bhakti Marga: A Study of the Johannine Doctrine of Love.* Madras: Christian Literature Society, 1928.

Appasamy, A.J. *What is Moksha: A study in the Johannine Doctrine of Life.* Madras: Christian Literature Society, 1951.

Asirvatham, Eddy. *Christianity in the Indian Crucible.* Calcutta: YMCA Publishing House, 1955.

Baago, Kaj. 'Ram Mohun Roy's Christology: An Early Attempt at Demythologization'. *Bangalore Theological Forum* (1967): 1, 30–42.

Banerjea, K.M. *The Arian Witness: Or the Testimony of Arian Scriptures in Corroboration of Biblical History and the Rudiments of Christian Doctrine, Including Dissertations on the Original and Early Adventures of Indo-Arians.* Calcutta: Thacker, Spink & Co, 1875.

Belsham, Thomas. 'Introduction'. In *The New Testament in an Improved Version, Upon the Basis of Archbishop Newcome's New Translation; with a Corrected Text, and Notes Critical and Explanatory*, iii–xxx. Boston, MA: Society for Promoting Christian Knowledge and Practice of virtue by the Distribution of Books, 1809.

Bose, Ram Chandra. *Brahmoism; or. History of Reformed Hinduism from Its Origins in 1830 Under Rajah Mohun Roy to the Present Time.* New York: Funk and Wagnalls, 1884.

Boyd, Julian P., ed. *The Papers of Thomas Jefferson*, vol. 1, *1760–1776*. Princeton, NJ: Princeton University Press, 1950.

Boyd, Julian P., ed. *The Papers of Thomas Jefferson*, vol. 12, *7 August 1787 to 31 March 1788*. Princeton, NJ: Princeton University Press, 1955.

Bultmann, Rudolf. *Existence and Faith: Shorter Writings of Rudolf Bultmann.* Selected, trans. and intro. Schubert M. Ogden. London: Collins, 1964.

Bultmann, Rudolf. 'New Testament and Mythology: Mythological Elements in the Message of the New Testament and the Problem of Its Re-Interpretation'. In *Kerygma and Myth: A Theological Debate*, ed. Hans Werner Bartsch, trans. Reginald H. Fuller, 1–16. New York: Harper and Row, [1951] 1962.

Bultmann, Rudolf. *Theology of the New Testament*, vol. 1. London: SCM Press, 1952.

Carpenter, Mary. *The Last Days in England of the Raja Rammohun Roy.* London: Trübner and Co, 1866.

Collected Works of Mahatma Gandhi, vol. 23, *6 April 1921–21 July 1921*. Available online: https://www.gandhiashramsevagram.org/gandhi-literature/mahatma-gandhi-collected-works-volume-23.pdf (accessed 20 June 2019).

Chinard, Gilbert, ed. *The Literary Bible of Thomas Jefferson: His Commonplace Book of Philosophers and Poets.* Baltimore: John Hopkins Press, 1928.

Christopher, Duraisingh and Cecil Hargreaves, *India's Search for Reality and the Relevance of the Gospel of John*. Delhi: SPCK, 1975.

Collet, Sophia Dobson. *The Life and Letters of Raja Rammohun Roy*, eds. Dilip Kumar Biswas and Prabhat Chandra Ganguli. Calcutta: Sadharan Brahmo Samaj, 1900.

Das, S.K. 'Rammohun: His Religious Thought'. In *Rammohun Roy: A Bi-Centenary Tribute*, ed. Ray Niharranjan, 71–91. New Dehli: National Book Trust, 1974.

A Defence of Some Important Scripture Doctrines. Calcutta: Baptist Missionary Press, 1822.

'Eusebius - The Two Theodoti: Historia Ecclesiastica, 5.28'. *Early Church Texts*. Available online: https://earlychurchtexts.com/public/eusebius_theodotus_monarchianism.htm (accessed 10 February 2019).

'Free Press and Unitarianism in India'. *The Monthly Repository* 17, no. 203 (1822): 584.

Ghazi, Abidullah Al-Ansari. *Raja Rammohun Roy: An Encounter with Islam and Christianity and the articulation of Hindu self-consciousness*. Bloomington, IN: Xlibris Corporation, 2010.

Goel, Sita Ram. *Jesus Christ: An Artifice for Aggression*. New Delhi: Voice of India, 1994.

Hatcher, Brian A. *Bourgeois Hinduism, or Faith of the Modern Vedantists: Rare Discourses from Early Colonial Bengal*. New York: Oxford University Press, 2008.

Haus, Cari. *The Reverse Jefferson Bible: What the President left out*, Clear Words.org, 2009.

Hoby, James. *Memoir of William Yates, D.D., of Calcutta*. London: Houlston & Stoneman, 1847.

Jefferson, Thomas. *The Jefferson Bible: The Life and Morals of Jesus of Nazareth*. Boston, MA: Beacon Press, 1989.

Joseph, Betty. *Reading the East India Company, 1720–1840: Colonial Currencies of Gender*. Chicago: Chicago University Press, 2004.

Joshi V.C., ed. *Rammohun Roy and the Process of Modernization in India*. Delhi: Vikas Publishing House, 1975.

Le Bas, Charles Webb. *The Life of the Right Reverend Thomas Fanshaw Middleton Late Lord Bishop of Calcutta in Two Volumes*, vol. 2. London: C.J.G & F. Rivington, 1831.

Lazarus-Yafeh, Hava. *Intertwined Worlds: Medieval Islam and Bible Criticism*. Princeton, NY: Princeton University Press, 1992.

Lillingston, Frank. *The Brahmo Samaj & Arya Samaj in Their Bearing Upon Christianity: A Study in Indian Theism*. London: Macmillan and Co., Limited, 1901.

Lin, Yii-Jan. *The Erotic Life of Manuscripts: New Testament Textual Criticism and the Biological Sciences*. New York: Oxford University Press, 2016.

Luz, Ulrich. *Matthew 1–7 A Commentary*. Edinburgh: T & T Clark, 1990.

Moore, Adrienne. *Rammohun Roy and America*. Calcutta: Satis Chandra Chakravti, 1942.

Majumdar, Jatindra Kumar, ed. *Raja Rammohun Roy and Progressive Movements in India: A Selection from Records (1775–1845)*. Calcutta: Art Press, 1941.

Marshman, John Clark. *The Life and Times of Carey, Marshman, and Ward Embracing the History of the Serampore Mission*, vol. 2. London: Longman, Brown, Green, Longmans, Roberts, & Green, 1859.

Marshman, John Clark. *The Story of Cary, Marshman and Ward: The Serampore Missionaries*. London: Alexander Strahan and Co, 1864.

Marshman, Joshua. *A Defence of the Deity and Atonement of Jesus Christ, in Reply to Ram-Mohun Roy of Calcutta*. London: Kingsbury, Parbury, and Allen, 1822.

McArthur, Harvey K. *The Quest Through the Centuries: The Search for the Historical Jesus*. Philadelphia, PA: Fortress Press, 1966.

Mineka, Francis E. *The Dissidence of Dissent: The Monthly Repository, 1806–1838*. Chapel Hill: University of North Carolina Press, 1944.

Müller, Max F. *Biographical Essays*. London: Longmans, Green, & Co, 1884.
Müller, Max F. *A History Ancient Sanskrit Literature as so far it illustrates the Primitive Religion of the Brahmans*, 2nd rev. edn. London: Williams and Norgate, 1860.
Monier-Williams, Monier. 'Indian Theistic Reformers'. *Journal of the Royal Asiatic Society of Great Britain and Ireland New Series* 13, no. 1 (1881): 1–41.
Murdoch, J., complier. *The Brahmo Samaj and Other Modern Eclectic Systems of Religion in India: Religious Reform Part IV*. Madras: Christian Literature Society, 1893.
The New Testament in an Improved Version, Upon the Basis of Archbishop Newcome's New Translation; with a Corrected Text, and Notes Critical and Explanatory. Boston, MA: Thomas B. Wait and Company, 1809.
Panikkar, K.M. *Asia and Western Dominance: A Survey of the Vasco Da Gama Epoch of Asian History 1498-1945*. London: George Allen and Unwin Ltd, 1959.
Radhakrishnan, S. *Eastern Religions and Western Thought*. Oxford: Clarendon Press, 1939.
'Review: Hindoo Unitarianism'. *Monthly Repository* 14, no. 165 (1819): 561–569.
Roy, Rammohun. *Translation of Several Principal Books, Passages, and Texts of the Veds, Some Controversial Works on Brahmanical Theology*. London: Parbury, Allen, &Co, 1832.
Roy, Rammohun. *The Correspondence of Raja Rammohun Roy*, vol. 1, *1809–1831*, ed. Dilip Kumar Biswas. Calcutta: Sarawat Library, 1960.
Roy, Rammohun. *The English Works of Raja Rammohun Roy*, ed. Jogendra Chunder Ghose. New Delhi: Cosmo Print, 1906.
Roy, Rammohun. *Selected Works of Raja Rammohun Roy*. Ahmedabad: Publications Division Ministry of Information and Broadcasting, Government of India, 1958.
Said, Edward W. *On Late Style*. London: Bloomsbury, 2006.
Said, Edward W. *Orientalism*. London: Penguin Books, 1978.
Sen, Amiya, P. *Rammohun Roy: A Critical Biography*. New Delhi: Viking, 2012.
Sen, Keshub Chunder. *Keshub Chunder Sen's Lectures in India*. London: Cassell and Company, 1901.
Schweitzer, Albert. *The Quest of the Historical Jesus: A Critical Study of its progress from Reimarus to Wrede*. London: A.C. Black, 1910.
Schweitzer, Albert. *The Quest of the Historical Jesus: The First Complete Edition Edited by John Bowden*. London: SCM Press, 2000.
Spindler, M.R. 'Indian Studies of the Gospel of John: Puzzling Contextualization'. *Exchange* 9, no. 27 (1980): 1–55.
Sugirtharajah, R.S. *Asian Biblical Hermeneutics and Postcolonialism*. Sheffield: Sheffield Academic Press, 1988.
Sugirtharajah, R.S. *The Bible and Empire: Postcolonial Explorations*. Cambridge: Cambridge University Press, 2005.
Swami Vivekananda. *The Complete Works of Swami Vivekananda. Mayavati Memorial Edition*, vol. 4. Almora: Advaita Ashrama, 1923.
'Thomas Jefferson', *Faith of Our Fathers*. Available online: http://www.faithofourfathers.net/jefferson.html (accessed on 10 February 2019).
Us Salam, Ziya. 'Now, Vedic Science'. *Frontline*, 23 November 2018. Available online: https://www.frontline.in/the-nation/article25437649.ece?homepage=true (accessed 13 November 2018).

GENERAL INDEX

advaita Vedanta 84, 92
Aspland, Robert 21

Baago, Kaj 31
Banerjea, K.M. 87
Belsham, Thomas 40
Bibles
   Authorized Version (King James Version) 9, 13, 27, 40, 41
   Bengali Bible 42
   Geneva Bible 13
   Improved Version 2, 40–41
   Jefferson's Bible 69, 78
   Unitarian Bible 2, 41
Brahmanical Magazine 43
British and Foreign Bible Society 40
Bultmann, Rudolf 5, 31, 32

Carey, William 1
Carr, Peter 71, 73
Chakkarai, Vengal 91
Chenchiah, Pandipeddi 91
The Christian Register 5

Defence of Some Important Scripture Doctrines, A 24
Demythologization 3, 27, 31
Diatessaron 39

East India Company 46, 85, 94
Essays and Reviews 31
Eusebius of Caesarea 69

Gandhi, M.K. 55, 82, 87
Gospel Harmonies 2, 13, 39, 40

History of Ancient Sanskrit Literature, A 53

Institutes of Ecclesiastical History Ancient and Modern 48

Jesus (see also Jefferson and Roy)
   death and burial 18
   and Ram 45
   resurrection 18
Jesus Seminar 41
Jefferson, Thomas
   on Bible 72–73, 75
   on Christian tenets 72
   hermeneutical practice 71
   on Jesus 75–78
   on John 74
   Last Supper 74
   motives 70–71
   on Paul 74
   search for the historical Jesus 77–78
   his sources 72
   virgin birth 75

Kumarappa, J.C 91

Lachmann, Karl 31
Lazarus-Yafeh, Hava 27
Lessing, Gotthold 30
Lin, Yii-Jan 30
Life and Morals of Jesus of Nazareth, the 2, 69
Lillingston, Frank 21

Marshman, John 21
Marshman, Joshua 1, 2, 16, 21, 22, 23, 24, 46, 47, 48, 51, 64, 65, 72, 91, 95
Mazoomdar, P.C. 66
McArthur, Harvey K 39
Middleton, Thomas 21, 35, 58
Mill, W.H. 42
Mimamsa methods 28
missionaries
   Anglicans 21, 24, 33, 35, 70
   Baptists 16, 24, 59, 69
Mleccha 59
Modi, Narendra 5, 83, 93

Mohammed, prophet 19, 61
Monthly Repository 21, 79, 86
Moore, Adrienne 5
Mosheim, Johann 48
Müller, Max F 53, 66, 81, 85, 90, 94

Obama, Barack Hussein, 93
Owen, Robert Dale 82

Pakiamuttu, Sarojini 91
Precepts of Jesus, The 2, 3, 5, 6, 9, 10, 11, 12
  general observations 13
    political context 9
    religious context 9
Proposed Version of Theological Terms 42

Radhakrishnan, S 79
Ramabai, Pandita 91
Reimarus, H.S. 30, 66
Renan, Ernest 66
Roy, Rammohun
  on atonement 29, 46-48, 76-77,
  on Bible 72-73, 75
  biblicism 30
  on colonialism 90
  on conversion 57-58, 91-92
  exegetical practices 29
  Father and Son relationship 65-66
  on Golden Rule 27, 54-56, 85
  Gospel harmonies 39-40
  on Holy Spirit 49-50
  Improved Version 40-41
  on Jesus 61-62, 75-78
  Jesus as an Asiatic 76, 77, 85, 87, 88, 90
  Jesus and divine status 63-64
  Jesus as the wisdom of God 90
  on John 31, 33, 74, 75
  Late Style 86-87
  Lord's prayer 15, 40
  on miracles 19, 85
  on monotheism 36, 43, 53-54
  on morality of Jesus 54
  on Mughals 94-95
  on Paul 74
  and the Qur'an 61, 73

resurrection 18
his sources 72, 86
search for the historical Jesus 77-78
translations 41-44
on Trinity 48-49, 86
understanding of miracles 18-19
Vedas 36-37
virgin birth 19, 75

Said, Edward 86-87
Semler, Johann Salomo 30
Sen, Keshub Chunder 66, 87
Sermon the Plain 15
Sermon on the Mount 13, 55, 62
Smith, Margret Bayard 72
source criticism 40
Sutherland, James 89
Strauss, D.F. 66
Synoptic Problem 13
Swaraj, Sushma 93

Thapar, Romila 85
Tatian 39
Thomas, M.M. 91
Trinity, the 10, 18, 41, 72
Tytler, R. 46, 66, 85
Tuhfat ul Muwahidin 61, 86

Unitarianism 21, 72
Unitarians 2, 21, 31, 40, 86,

Vivekananda, Swami 87
Vedas (see also Roy)
  as good as the Bible 36
  Hindu religion depicted in 43
  true Bible of India 35
  'stigmatize the Veda' 36
  Translations of 42-44

Ward William 1
Ware, Henry 58
Westcott, B.F. 33
Western Orientalists 3, 43, 85, 95
Wilson, H.H. 42
Wycliffe, John 41

SCRIPTURAL REFERENCES

Biblical texts

Reference	Page	Reference	Page
Genesis	23, 27, 42	3.17	16
17.8	42	5. 33-43	13
27	42	5.39	13
		10	13
Deuteronomy		11	14
6.5	54	11.22	16
		12	14
Leviticus		13. 44-58	14
19.18	55	14	14
		15	14
Judges		18	14
2	23	19	14
		20	14
Isaiah		21	14
9.6	42	22	14
60:2-6	17	23	16
		24.42	15
Hosea	30	27	73
11.1	17	28.18-20	17
		28.19	18
Obadiah	63		
		Mark	40
Nehemiah	63	1.10-11	18
		3	15
Zechariah		4	15
9.9	17	5.32-39	15
12.10	47	8.27-33	14
		10. 47	16
Job		13.33	64
36.26	36		
		Luke	40, 41
Psalms		3.21-22	18
145.3	36	6.3	16
		7.22	18
Proverbs		9.18-22	14
6.6	56	10.28	48
		11	15
Matthew	30, 40, 41	12	16
1.1	16	17.20-21	17
3.16	18	24.46-49	17

John		Jude	41
1.32	18		
3.1-21	16	Book of Revelation	23, 41
4.23	16		
6.27	16	**Hindu texts**	
8.3-11	16	Brahma-Sutra	35
9.39	16		
14.16-17	18	Ishopanishad	27
15.3	47	Kenopanishad	
15.1-17	16	1.3	36
17.8	64	Mahabharata	
20.21	17	5.1517	27
Colossians		Upanishads	35, 85, 93
1.15	63		
		Vishnu-Purana	35
Hebrews	41		
		Islamic texts	
James	41	Qur'an	37, 61, 73, 82
		4.36	55
2 Peter	41		
		Zoroastrian texts	
2 John	41	Zend Avesta	37
3 John	41		

www.ingramcontent.com/pod-product-compliance
Lightning Source LLC
Chambersburg PA
CBHW052050300426
44117CB00012B/2064